D1543310

Dining
on the
France

Dining
on the
France

Henri Le Huédé

preface by Craig Claiborne
introduction by Joseph Wechsberg

The Vendome Press
New York   Paris   Lausanne

*To my valiant team
on the great liner S.S. France,
who brought the greatness of French cuisine
to the whole world
on all seas and in all winds.*

Henri Le Huédé

Illustrations courtesy of Dover Publications

General Editor: Alexis Gregory
Recipes translated from the French by Dale McAdoo
   and adapted by Helen Feingold
Designed by Marlene Rothkin Vine
Copyedited by Carole Berglie

Distributed in the United States of America
by The Viking Press, 625 Madison Avenue, New York 10022

Library of Congress Cataloging in Publication Data
Le Huédé, Henri
   Dining on the France
   Includes index
   1. Cookery, French.   2. France (Steamship)
I. Title.
TX719.L424   641.5   81–7579
                           AACR2

ISBN: 0—86565—013—6
Printed and bound in the United States of America
by Book Press, New York

Preface

In all my recollections of dining around the world, there are few that can rival the memory of my voyages on the late, lamented S.S. *France*, where Henri Le Huédé was chef. In an account that appeared in the *New York Times* in early January 1969, I stated quite flatly that the first-class dining room on that vessel was, to my mind, the greatest restaurant in the world. I had found that each menu on the boat—for breakfast, lunch, or dinner—was a masterpiece of variety, a veritable cornucopia of things to "amuse, beguile and conquer the palate."

For hors d'oeuvre I dined on caviar almost every night; but that was commonplace. If I wished, there was fresh *foie gras* baked *en croute*, or more earthly things such as an elegant ballotine of duckling, pâté of veal, cold *langouste* with freshly made mayonnaise, or a fancifully marbled, delicately seasoned terrine of chicken.

And among the courses that followed, I particularly recall a rich cream of *petits pois* Lamballe and a double consommé, a medallion of brill with champagne sauce followed by roast saddle of lamb or stuffed squab with truffle sauce. Or, for that matter, a rack of hare, venison stew, or a chartreuse of pheasant, the menu changing from day to day and night to night. The pastries were marvels and so were the ices, sherbets, custards, and spun-sugar fantasies.

After one or two nights out, I asked for an appointment with the chef. In my enthusiasm, this was like requesting an audience with the Pope. I was enchanted when our meeting was fixed, and was ushered into a small cabin, one deck below the kitchen. It was large enough to accommodate only a sleeping bunk, desk, and record player. Beneath the desk were the chef's favorite albums; works of Beethoven, Mozart, and Chopin. On the starboard wall hung a poster of Napoleon Bonaparte who, I discovered, was a particular hero of Le Huédé. Tucked under one corner of the poster was a small bunch of dried yellow flowers which he had picked on a visit to the island of St. Helena, Napoleon's last place of exile.

Le Huédé, the Merlin and master of the *France's* cuisine, stood only 5 foot 4 inches tall; I learned that he was a Breton, born in the ancient, small town of Batz near St. Lazare where the *France* was built.

I asked if he had any regrets about his work and he told me that his chief and sole lament was that in all the world there were but a limited number of foods to deal with.

"We try never to prepare the same dish twice on one crossing or cruise. And we don't," he added, "unless someone specifically requests it. And we use only the finest ingredients."

Pierre Franey and I were witness to this a while later when the *France* was anchored at Le Havre and was about to make an Atlantic crossing. We joined Le Huédé on the dock while cranes were already loading the kitchen's precious cargo into the hold. The chef, dressed in immaculate white apron and trousers and his *toque blanche*, was passing fastidious judgment on the produce. One by one, trucks arrived to disgorge crates of shellfish, fruits, vegetables, meat, and poultry, along with Styrofoam containers of all varieties of fresh fish. We watched the chef as he carefully inspected whole baby lambs, grain-fed chickens from Bresse, and sides of veal and beef. He would examine the produce piece by piece, joint by joint, poking, smelling, and peering at it with a surgeonlike intentness. Then came more trucks with oranges and apples and pears, green beans, and spinach.

He took special delight in his shellfish and fish. The lobsters clawed the air and he smiled with complacency. He looked each fish straight in the eye and opened the gills to determine their redness and therefore the degree of freshness. There was Dover sole, magnificent turbot, whiting, green pollock, red mullet, mackerel and eels, much of which would go into some of the finest bouillabaisse I have ever tasted; indeed it was on a par with the best to be found in Marseilles or its environs.

A great deal of the produce had to be sampled before it was taken aboard. This included caviar, *foie gras*, various hams, and choice cheese. The process, known as a *dégustation*, took place with great solemnity in a company dining room located on the dock. On a large, oval table, set with china, silver, and wine glasses, the foods were tasted and tabulated and the findings enclosed in a large black book for future references. The *dégustation* occupied more than two hours and lasted until afternoon. The hams were from Parma and York, from Bayonne and the Ardennes. Cheeses included Roquefort, Camembert, Port Salut, Pont-l'Évêque, Duc de Bourgogne, and a Valençay.

The chef told us that the boat carried the finest wines from Bordeaux and Burgundy, the best-quality beef from Charolais, the sweetest butter from Normandy, and tender veal from the Charente region. The sole came from the English Channel, turbot and lobster from Brittany, and so on. In New York they took on beef, fresh vegetables, and fruits. "We know that Americans prefer their own beef and we give it to them."

I once expressed astonishment at the highly maneuverable, productive nature of the kitchen where each day the kitchen's skillets turned out crêpes by the thousands while the ovens baked more than 2,000 *petits pains*, the small, crisp rolls served at each place setting. "How can you," I asked "produce such splendor on such a vast scale?" The gentleman smiled and shrugged. And in his typical, modest fashion answered, "It is only the work of the cuisinier."

Alas, the boat was removed from service some years ago. It was truly the last of the great, never-to-be-matched luxury liners, and its loss caused sadness and sorrow around the world, particularly from devoted ship buffs, many of whom had never even set foot aboard the flagship of the French Line.

This publication is perhaps the last "living" remnant of a great ship and its astonishing culinary achievement. Although I have had no involvement in the preparation of this book of Henri Le Huédé's recipes, I am pleased to write this short preface as a tribute to a great chef whose talents are ineradicable in my memory and who—I am proud to say—has remained a good friend.

Craig Claiborne
East Hampton, May 8, 1981

Contents

	Preface	5
	Introduction	9
1	Menus	21
2	Sauces	31
3	Soups	53
4	Eggs	73
5	Poultry	85
6	Fish	111
7	Shellfish	137
8	Meats, Pâtés, and Terrines	151
9	Vegetables	187
10	Potatoes, Rice, and Pasta	207
11	Salads	217
12	Doughs and Desserts	225
	Postscript	242
	Index	243

Introduction

By common consent, eating was always the second most important physical activity aboard a French Line ship, perhaps the only important one for some people. Food was the leading topic of conversation, and experienced travelers studied the enormous, beautifully printed menu with great attention, looking for half-hidden opportunities the way true stock market experts study the quotations. On the S.S. *France* the menu was the thing. The tradition went back to the great days of the *Île-de-France*, the *Normandie*, the *Liberté*. The incredible *carte* was closer to Carême and Escoffier, who offered their connoisseurs an *embarrass de richesses*, than to the more sensible menu of what is now known as *la nouvelle cuisine Française*, the last phase so far in the evolution of gastronomy that has been a steady development from riches to rags. In my own time I saw how Fernand Point "simplified" the cooking of Escoffier—*simple* in this context similar to a "simple" evening dress made by the House of Dior. Point had discovered that we are unable to eat the way people ate a hundred years ago. He understood that man's appetite has declined while his taste has become more refined.

Our eyes are greedier than our stomach. Point's finest dishes had an exquisite texture. They looked deceptively simple though they were the result of complex work and supreme technique. Compared to the extravaganzas of Carême, now revered as the founder of *la grande cuisine*, and even to the lavish gastronomic symphonies of Escoffier, respected as the great reformer, a meal created by Fernand Point for his beloved Restaurant de la Pyramide, at Vienne (Isère), was a subtle work of art, where the natural flavors were enhanced and nothing was camouflaged. And a generation later, the stars of *la nouvelle cuisine* such as the brilliant Michel Guérard, continue the quest for simplicity, searching for *la nature des choses* which means inventing, trying out and testing new techniques.

The French Line's gastronomic tradition was always closer to the Rabelaisian concept of overabundance than to the leaner style of the modern cooks that seem to have started the renaissance of French gastronomy which has been overdue for social reasons and reasons of health. Had the *France* been in service today, the cuisine might have been lighter, more elegant even. Unfortunately the great liner stopped running just as many serious epicures, especially in France, were getting convinced that a completely new dimension of *la grande cuisine* was needed. The cuisine on the *France* was frankly opulent, in the classical style, and occasionally overpowering. It was conceived on the once-in-a-lifetime principle. For many people a crossing or a cruise remained a unique experience, the fulfillment of a dream. The gastronomic excitement should match that uniqueness. It was taken for granted that most people had never eaten so well before and might never eat so well again, so why not enjoy it and make the most of the few glorious days? It was frankly designed for those who love fine cooking—the more the better.

No one ever wrote a pamphlet on "How to Enjoy French Line Cuisine" that might have been placed in your stateroom as you came aboard. It would have tried to help you find your way through the miraculous landscape of the menu where it was often difficult to see the epicurean forest for the trees. Reading the menu, many people would greedily salivate. Soon emotion would sweep away reason. On the *France* the first-class passenger was confronted by an *embarrass de richesses* as early as breakfast. The menu offered sixteen different egg dishes and several omelets, kippers, grilled ham, a small steak, several kinds of coffee—French, American, decaffeinated, Nescafé, espresso—and freshly made croissants, brioches, and, best of all, the delicious *petits pains,* that transported you miraculously into the nirvana of living-like-a-god-in-France. Five thousand of these were freshly baked, three times a day, and the incision on top of each was made with a razor, by hand. You put a little *beurre d'Isigny,* the delicately flavored butter from Normandy, on a piece of *petit pain* and closed your eyes, enjoying the true taste: you were in *la belle France* no matter where you happened to be.

Perhaps the greatest attraction of shipboard gastronomy is the *mystique* that it's all for free. You have, of course, paid for it but that was a long time ago, and you no longer think of it. The absence of prices on a menu has an exhilarating effect even on millionaires who can afford the most expensive food as a matter of daily routine. Such a millionaire, who also happened to be French and a genuine connoisseur, once explained to me that even he wouldn't think of ordering the sort of déjeuner—refined and complex and probably quite rich—that he composed for himself on the *France,* if he went to a three-star restaurant in France.

"They wouldn't like it," he said. "In the really good places they want you to be happy when you get up from the table. They want you to feel fine the next day. Because they want you to come back. Aboard a luxury liner, there is a different philosophy. Let's be merry for tommorow.... Well, you know. They will suggest wonderful things. You are tempted. On land you would regretfully decline, thinking of your appointment in the afternoon, or of the place you have to be at night, that is two hundred kilometers away on the dangerous *autoroute.* Here you have no appointment. You don't have to go elsewhere. All you have to do is to order the sort of lunch that will enable you later to order a fine dinner. Also, there is the wonderful knowledge that you may order practically *any*thing you want, and they'll do it for you. You don't *have* to do it, it's sufficient to know that you *can* do it."

Reading and understanding the first-class menu of the *France* demanded considerable gastronomic knowledge. For many passengers it remained an occult science which they never learned. Going there was half the fun, the Cunard people used to say. The French might have added that ordering was more than half the fun, provided you knew how. I remember the bewildered look in the eyes of many people as the waiter handed them the menu of their first lunch or dinner. Nine different hors d'oeuvre. Caviar, saumon fumé, sturgeon, *foie gras*, and something called *Terrine de Volaille Lucullus*. A clear consommé and at least two other soups. Two egg dishes and omelets. At least two fish dishes. A tempting *spécialité régionale*. Always a roast, always some sort of poultry. Game in season. And, naturally, the last resort of the confused diner, at least two *grillades* that often showed you the complexities of the language and confused the poor passenger even more. The American sirloin steak would have the form of what the French call a *contrefilet double*. The American chateaubriand, made for at least two persons and weighing three hundred grams, was what the French call a double tournedo, or, more exactly, *coeur de filet*. But since the waiters had studied both the American and the French terminology, steak enthusiasts would get exactly the steak they wanted, and it would be prepared exactly the way they wanted it, from *saignant* to well done (God forbid). Still, there are fine nuances in American steak terminology, among rare, medium-rare, and medium, while the French, who accepted the blessings of steaks from the Americans, ask for their steak *à point* which means just a little pinkish inside.

The confusion would be confounded by the elegant fact that the *France* had French steak (from Charolles), American steak, and often there was also English beef. Though the choice might please even sophisticated steak-eaters, there were passengers who complained that the *France* didn't have steak from Tuscany "though Italian steak is the best." Had passengers known what the polite, well-educated waiters and *maîtres d'hôtel* thought of *that*, they might have kept their mouth shut. Everybody was relieved when Steak au Poivre was on the menu. That, at least, was something they all knew.

To further confuse the passengers, there was often an Italian pasta dish on the menu (the French claim that Americans love pasta almost as much as Italians, and they might be right) and there was also a rich *buffet froid*, a dozen fine things including four different hams (*Île-de-France*, Morvan, Progue, and Virginia), cold roast beef, French *boeuf à la mode* (a great treat), chicken, duck, and tongue. At least three salads. The *plateau des fromoges*. Half a dozen desserts, ice creams, fruit salads, and fresh fruit.

On the *France*, as in every good restaurant, the right order would make the difference between a good restaurant meal and a gastronomic experience. Seasoned travelers would try not to be overwhelmed by the tempting, terrific menu which, admittedly, was not easy. They would select carefully, aware that tomorrow would be another day, with two great meals. One of the sad moments in a man's eating life was to look at the menu knowing damn well that what one really ought to have was a glass of Evian. Sailing from Le Havre or Southampton, the wise voyager would order fresh sole and fresh turbot that hadn't seen yet the inside of the cold chamber, preferably grilled or poached. Later on, they would offer you the sole with a fancy sauce or *turbot au Champagne*. Very fine, but nothing like a fresh, grilled turbot. Other things, such as oysters, clams, or wild strawberries, would also be served within two days. Even a great cook cannot improve the fine, fresh taste that Nature gives to things. It was also important to go easy on sauces though the French call them the glory of French cuisine. The sauces on the *France* were often beautiful but not always very light. You would also be careful about starch; who travels on the *France* to eat potatoes?

Personally, it took me quite a few years before I really knew what I wanted. I would decide on the main dish first and then work back and forth, trying to establish a harmonious balance. Caviar, with half a lemon, be sure to put a few drops of lemon juice into the mild, mellow Wodka Wyborowa, Poland's contribution to great capitalistic dining. Very warm toast and butter with the caviar, only exceptionally a baked Idaho. Next, a grilled fresh fish that leaves you still moderately hungry for your main dish, one of M. Le Huédé's great creations such a Filet de Boeuf Bressane (page 154). Not a "light" dish but a very good one: the beef marinated in Madeira, white wine, and aromates for twelve hours, quickly roasted, served with a dreamy sauce made with fresh mushrooms, truffles, olives, and pistachio nuts. Quenelles de Volaille and Pommes Noisette accompanied the dish. Afterwards perhaps just a tiny slice of Brie, if the Brie was right. With the right wines, you'd dined and wined like a king, and tomorrow you might be able to eat again.

Henri Le Huédé, the *chef des cuisines* aboard the *France*, was pleased when people said his restaurant belonged to the great gastronomic temples of France, but he felt that the *France* should not be compared with them. Madame Point's magnificent Pyramide in Vienne rarely serves more than sixty people, and the most prominent disciples of the School of Point—Paul Bocuse, the Troisgros Brothers, Alain Chapel—serve not many more. At the Tour d'Argent in Paris they might serve one hundred and fifty but Claude Terrail admits that may be a strain. Contrarily, the kitchens of the *France* might serve two thousand passengers on an Atlantic crossing, three times a day, as well as eleven hundred crew members. On cruises when the *France* became all first class, in an attempt to establish the semblance of democracy, M. Le Huédé was asked to provide gastronomic miracles in the Chambord and Versailles dining rooms, for fourteen hundred people. The very size of the enterprise was out of proportion, compared to the terrestrial temples of gastronomy, and so was the organization and the entire philosophy.

"We had well-known French chefs here," Le Huédé once told me. "They had been successful in great restaurants in France but were completely lost on the *France*, unable to cope with the problems of maritime gastronomy." Every good kitchen is a masterpiece of organization and teamwork, but the kitchens of the *France* were organized almost like an automobile factory. Various things were done at various stations, and at some point everything was put together. But the food never tasted as though it had come off an assembly line. "The problem is not only size," said M. Le Huédé. "But inspite of size every dish should give the passenger the feeling that it was made especially for him. I dread the cooking in some luxury hotels where everything seems to have the same taste after the third or fourth day. It is said that good hotels in France rarely have outstanding restaurants. Perhaps the combination is too demanding. On the *France*, a great moving luxury hotel, we proved that it can be done."

M. Le Huédé achieved the impossible with the help of 180 cooks and helpers in his kitchens, and with a network of buyers, administrators, bakers, butchers, confectioners, and other experts who were not strictly in the kitchens. Practically every cook was a specialist. There were *sous-chefs*, hors d'oeuvre experts, *potagiers, poissoniers, grilladiers* (grill cooks), *sauciers*, vegetable cooks, *pâtissiers*. There were also *tournants* (who were shifted around where they might be needed), buffet froid artists (providing magnificent buffets on the decks at noon and midnight, especially on cruises), special night cooks, breakfast cooks, additional cooks for the crew. And there were the *plongeurs* (dishwashers) whom M. Le Huédé much respected, deservedly so, for doing a good job.

These workers helped Le Huédé to produce quality in spite of quantity, and quite often great cooking. They had found solutions for problems that don't exist in great restaurants on land. How can you turn out three thousand lamb chops in less than an hour? On the *France* steak eventually became one of the most popular dishes. Everybody loved steak. The original three charcoal grills had been expanded to seven, and they were talking of a further expansion. The grill cooks, working with the concentration and accuracy of the mechanics in the box of a racing driver where they manage to change four tires in nine seconds, were able to prepare up to eighty steaks at the same time. When Steak au Poivre was on the menu, eight hundred orders might come in within forty minutes, causing a slight traffic jam at the grill station. Some people would have to wait, but people who wouldn't mind a delay in New York or London or Paris, sometimes get very impatient aboard ship. Since each order was a special one, M. Le Huédé invented a code system, using the arrangement of watercress and Pommes Frites in such a way, that the waiters would be able to distinguish among medium, *à point*, and medium rare, so that everybody would get his or her steak exactly as ordered.

To complicate matters, M. Le Huédé had multinational supplies, and finicky customers knew it amd would ask for French *homard* but not Maine lobster, or vice versa. There was French duck from Nantes and Long Island duckling from the States. No restaurant on both sides of the ocean offered you such choice, not to mention again the various kinds of steak. The French passengers were more enterprising eaters. They would at least try everything once and when they liked something that wasn't French, they would order it again: they were not chauvinistic so far as their food was concerned. They admitted that a baked American potato, from Idaho or Maine, was unique. They were also much more difficult than the American customers, much more demanding.

The French justly love calf's liver, kidneys, and sweetbreads, all of which many Americans dislike. The French like to have their big meal at lunchtime; for them *déjeuner* is what matters. The Americans like their important meal at dinnertime, possibly after three cocktails, which dulled their palate and demanded more seasoning. No matter how much salt and pepper the cooks have put into a dish, some Americans will put in more salt and pepper even *before* they have tasted it. The very thought made the *sauciers* unhappy.

M. Le Huédé had problems which the late Fernand Point or today Michel Guérard never dreamed about. Le Huédé couldn't send out to the market for more oysters or partridges when he hadn't enough. A sudden storm might wreck his carefully made plans. In fact, his greatest problem was not the complicated special orders of postgraduate gourmets. Rather, it involved trying to guess how many people would order a certain dish on the menu. His first command was, *"Il faut surtout honorer le menu,"* the menu must be honored. It would be bad if he found himself stuck with hundreds of artichokes and other highly perishable things. But it would be worse if he put them on the menu and had not enough of them. Once something was printed there, there was no excuse for running out of it. In a great French restaurant, latecomers accept the fact that something may be sold out. Not in the first-class dining room of the *France*, however.

To make life even more difficult for himself, M. Le Huédé once in a while tried what no other maritime chef had done before. On one crossing when I was aboard he put Cailles Souvaroff, a complicated *grande-cuisine* quail dish, on the menu. "Escoffier would have done it, for thirty or forty people," he said. "I took a chance. We served almost five hundred. But I don't think we'll do it again. It turned out well but it was a *tour de force*. Too risky."

Other achievements, considered small miracles by serious epicures, were almost routine to Le Huédé and his experienced fellow-artists. I remember Boeuf Bourguignonne, that day the "regional dish" on the menu, and thus not made especially for me, that tasted almost more Burgundian than the best I'd ever had in Burgundy. Delicately flavored, melting in my mouth, and so well made that it wasn't "rich" at all. The Blanquette de Veau à l'Ancienne (page 169), an old-fashioned veal fricassée, the sort of dish that Le Huédé might order for his own lunch because it reminded him of home, tasted as though it had been made at home; but we were a long way from home, and the dish came from a kitchen where they were at the same time doing other things, for thousands of people. These were the *real* miracles, not the extravagant creations for jaded connoisseurs. Most regional or provincial specialties—Bouillabaisse (p. 70), Quiche Lorraine (p. 84), Cassoulet, Choucroute, and many others—gave the impression of having been made in a special corner of France, not in the middle of the ocean.

They made what had long been a popular Transat specialty, Boeuf à la Ficelle (p. 162), a large piece of beef cooked in the steam and fragrance of a Pot-au-Feu in a large, clay sealed vessel and served at the table the moment it is ready. M. Le Huédé and his staff respected you for ordering complicated creations if they were convinced that you knew what you wanted. When M. Le Huédé asked me what I would like, I suggested that he prepare what *he* considered the gastronomic specialties of the *France*. He nodded as though this was what he'd expected.

"We'll let you try several things. They are all classic but we've developed them and consider them almost our own recipes."

I remember the Turbot Saumonée à la Presidente (p. 118), filets of *turbotin* and scallops of salmon marinated in Muscadet, finished with a *mousse de poisson* (preferably whiting, the chef said), and served with two sauces; a pink *velouté de crevettes* and a *sauce vin blanc*. M. Le Huédé's own favorite super specialty was called Gourmandines de Veau au Gratin (p. 167), a dish I'd never tasted before (and don't expect to ever taste again). Very thin veal scallops, quickly sautéed, stuffed with minced mushrooms, rolled in thin crêpes, covered with a Sauce Mornay *crèmeuse*, sprinkled with grated Gruyère, and finished under the salamander. In the kitchens of the *France*, it took the clockwork operation of four *sous-chefs* (who, naturally, were not available for anything else though they might be needed elsewhere). One made the crêpes, very light and thin. The second had already prepared the minced-mushroom stuffing. The third sautéed the veal scallops, "very fast, possibly forty seconds on each side so they won't get dry," said M. Le Huédé. And the fourth put it all together and added the sauce, a contribution from a *saucier*. All this in the middle of the service, mind you, while four hundred other first-class passengers were waiting for *their* orders. M. Le Huédé said that the *commis* would have to wait in the kitchen while the *gourmandines* were being finished. All things considered, I was convinced that the *France* was, by terrestrial standards, a very great restaurant. And M. Le Huédé's subtle and refined creation was truly and honestly *grande cuisine*.

M. Le Huédé, who came from the vicinity of Saint-Nazaire where the *France* had been built, is a short, quiet, soft-spoken man. Compared to some of his French Line predecessors, he is almost unassuming. He is also very competent, a craftsman, and, sometimes, an artist. He saw everything and said little. Some senior members of his staff told me they had never heard him raise his voice, "even when something went wrong," and in the kitchens of the *France* things *did* go wrong occasionally. The men said that Le Huédé kept his cool even in critical moments, and there *were* critical moments almost every day. He had worked for the Transat since 1937, on the *De Grasse*, the *Île-de-France*, and the *Liberté*, doing everything except the *buffet froid*, which didn't interest him.

"*Je suis cuisinier*," he explained. "I never learned to design. I tell my staff what I want and they make beautiful decorations. I even started a school aboard ship. I admit that the presentation is an important element of *la grande cuisine* but what really matters is the flavor. One must never sacrifice the taste of a dish to its appearance."

M. Le Huédé called the cooking aboard the *France* "*classique*." Occasionally, a little *fantaisie* might be added, but basically he followed the school of the great *maîtres*. He had no use for what he called "experiments" and he disliked the "pyrotechnical" cuisine. There was nothing he could do about the Crêpes Suzette, which have been a dining room institution for generations and enhanced the ego of captains, and possibly got them special tips. Many *maîtres de rang* (captains), who were former waiters, loved to prepare flaming dishes in the dining room, from Steak Diane to Cherries Jubilée, possibly because they knew that the hardworking cooks get no glory. A not-so-hardworking captain, who makes an impressive show of Crêpes Suzette, gets much admiration from the passengers. M. Le Huédé knew this very well and couldn't change it, but at least he made sure that the crêpes were fresh.

He refused to imitate a so-called *spécialité de maison* that a passenger had discovered in an obscure Provençal bistro and, possibly under the influence of wine and *amour*, considered the greatest dish this side of heaven.

"We cannot re-create such a dish," Le Huédé said. "The passenger won't be happy and we won't be happy, so what's the use?" He was right. Without the very special garnish of personal emotion and the inimitable Provençal mood, the "great" dish might turn out commonplace and uninteresting.

"But we love difficult passengers who understand fine food. A while ago, a man asked us for Quenelles de Sole. *Tiens*, I said to myself, this one really knows what he wants. Quenelles are usually made of pike mousseline. It's much more difficult to make them of sole, which has less body, but Quenelles de Sole are of course much finer. Well, we made them, and the passenger was happy. He came to thank me for the genuine Quenelles de Sole and he sent a bottle of Champagne to my men, and *they* were happy."

Twice a day Le Huédé took the freight elevator down to the eighteen cold chambers of the *France*, kept at different temperatures, from minus five to forty-eight degrees Fahrenheit, scientifically established, where all supplies were stored. He needed no printed statistics. He had a visual impression of what there was which helped him to plan the various menus for the next day.

Once he asked me to accompany him. Housewives everywhere would have loved the cleanliness and the arrangement of Le Huédé's super pantry. In the coldest chamber, for fish, there was turbot from the Channel, Dover sole, and many of the Mediterranean fish varieties that were needed to make a reasonable copy of a Bouillabaisse Marseillaise. In the vegetable chamber I saw cleaned salad leaves that were kept in large baskets, covered with white cloths. They would be taken to the kitchen just prior to the service, resulting in salads that are always crisp and fresh, the sort of well-made salad you rarely get in a good American restaurant.

There were special chambers for butter and cream, for cheese (difficult to store because some cheeses demand lower temperatures than others), for *charcuterie* (also difficult, for the same reason), and for the boxes of caviar, from Iran or Russia, which presented no problem when you stored them "right next to the door," where the air current was, at a temperature of around zero Centigrade, thirty-two Fahrenheit.

Half an hour before each meal M. Huédé was at his command post, a small table in the middle of his kitchen empire, from which he could see everybody and everything. Like a good general or a good conductor he was always mentally prepared for the worst. In front of him was a list of the day's special orders. At his left was the push-button speaking box on which he announced the incoming orders to the various stations.

When I joined him there one evening, half an hour before the beginning of the service, the kitchens were quiet and businesslike, but it was the quiet before the storm. In a good kitchen the *mise en place*—the many detailed preparations from splitting thin string beans to cleaning crayfish tails for the Gratin de Queues d'Écrevisses—is done in the early morning. In a truly well-organized kitchen one sees very little food standing around shortly before the service, but it's all there, in the refrigerators, ready to be used. Only the large pots with the fonds, the smaller pots with the sauces, and *plats cuisinés* are visible. The *sous-chefs* and cooks and their helpers were waiting at their posts, like good soldiers or actors listening for their call; I felt the healthy tension that fills a theater or a concert hall prior to the performance. The *France* kitchen ensemble had often reminded me of a great symphony orchestra. Every player was an accomplished virtuoso who knew exactly what to do, and all of them perfectly integrated, each listening to all the others, the triumph of teamwork. Such an orchestra often has a showman conductor but the orchestra of the *France* had Henri Le Huédé, who displayed no star allure yet had his men pretty well under control.

Shortly before the service he said he was going to make a *tour des fourneaux* and suggested I come along. There would still be time to correct anything that had gone wrong. We began the inspection at the hors d'oeuvre counter. The caviar boxes were arranged in containers with crushed ice. On large trays in the cold chamber I saw hundreds of small brioches filled with *foie gras*. M. Le Huédé expected to serve "at least seven to eight hundred" that night. How did he know? He shrugged. He knew.

At the soup station, he filled a *tastevin*, the shallow silver saucer used by winetasters, with Bisque de Homard and tested it, with great concentration.

"Almost perfect, well perfumed, well seasoned, very light," he said to the *potagier*, and asked him to add just a tiny bit of cream. Next, he commented on the bright color of the consommé and the complete lack of fat in it. "Maybe you ought to put in a little more salt," he said. Both tasted it again, thoughtfully looking at each other. Then the *potagier* nodded. Yes, the *chef* was right. A little salt might give it that imperceptible uplift.

At the salamander Tomates Farcies stood on large trays, ready to be given the final touch. "The principle," said Le Huédé, "is to have everything prepared but very little actually ready to be served. The *tomates* will be finished only when the orders come in. That is, of course, the law in all good kitchens. But we may have to serve a thousand of them, and each will have the fresh taste that's absolutely necessary—and that isn't easy. Here, take a bite of the Potato Croquettes. Good, aren't they? They were fried just a moment ago. There you are. We must always be ready without really having anything ready."

At the vegetable station M. Le Huédé tasted the freshly prepared spinach, the asparagus, the delicious mashed potatoes, the noodles. At the fish station he tried the sauce for the turbot, explaining to me that the fish cook was making his own sauces. He commended the *poissonier*, a small man who seemed happy and a little embarrassed. I tasted the Sauce Champagne and thought the praise was well deserved. Le Huédé critically surveyed the garnish for the Lobster à l'Américaine (p. 140) and then he stopped briefly at a special station for the Onion Soup (p. 67) ("very important, many people ask for it") before he turned to the grill station. The charcoal broilers were ready for spits with *rognons de veau*, and the grill cooks were ready for large steak orders. Nearby was the *rôtisserie*, and the *chef* inspected the Roast Lamb Apollinaire, prepared in servings for two, three, or more. Later, after the orders came in, the roast crown of lamb would be attractively garnished.

M. Le Huédé stopped briefly at the dishwashers' station, behind the kitchens, and greeted the men. "The *plongeurs* have a tough, important job," he said to me, in a louder voice than usual, to be sure that everybody could hear him. "It's not a pleasant job, and I always come through to give them a little encouragement."

The dishwashers seemed pleased and two of them gave the chef a thankful smile. There was none of the gloomy, almost revolutionary mood that often surrounds a dishwashers' station. M. Le Huédé had shrewdly realized that this station was the crucial test of his popularity around the kitchens.

Farther away, we stepped into the butchers' department. Men with white aprons stood around sides of beef and legs of veal. Some were cutting steaks. At full capacity the *France* needed over two thousand pounds of meat daily. If more steak orders than expected would come in, the butchers would quickly cut additional portions and send them to the grill station.

One butcher worked on a side of American beef. The meat, from a fattened animal, was handsomely marbled. It would be easy to eat and also less flavorful than steaks from Charolles that were prepared nearby. The meat had a thin yellowish crust, it looked tougher, and when Le Huédé pressed his thumb in, one didn't see the imprint as clearly as in the American meat. Inevitably, comparisons were made. They were as pointless as arguments among opera lovers over the respective virtues of Verdi versus Wagner. Both can be wonderful.

One of the butchers asked me what I like best.

I said personally I believed that the delicious taste of a French sirloin was hard to beat. If I *had* to make that dreadful choice between composers, I might prefer Verdi to Wagner, and what was wrong with Bizet? Everybody smiled but I expect all good Wagnerians and American sirloin lovers to disagree with me, violently.

At this point, M. Le Huédé, the perfect diplomat, said that narrow-minded chauvinism must not exist in a well-run kitchen. "I always buy the best supplies available at a certain moment in France, in England, or in America," he said. "The decision is based only on quality. Usually I order everything two weeks in advance, which gives the suppliers a chance to fill large orders. If supplies in different countries are almost alike, I buy what is less expensive at the moment. I always buy certain things in New York: the finest sea bass and red snapper, Maine lobster, clams, shrimps and crab meat, Virginia ham, and the large, mealy potatoes. Naturally."

"And American meat," a butcher said, somewhat truculently, I noticed.

"*Décidemment*," said M. Le Huédé.

M. Le Huédé's inspection ended logically where dinner would end, at the *pâtisserie* department. There were trays with tempting delicacies—Baba au Rhum, Tarte de Pomme, Éclairs, Friandises. Two *Pâtissiers* were working on a *pièce montée*, a beautiful and edible sculptural masterpiece, for the gala the next night, and one man was masterfully pulling a colored sugar band that had a silky sheen. (Some of the greatest French chefs, from Carême to Guérard, began as *pâtissiers*.) The artists on the *France* worked with deep concentration. I asked one of them why they spent long hours on these *pièces* that were so beautifully made that many passengers believed they were made of plastic.

"It's a tradition," he said. "They made them exactly like that sixty years ago."

Tradition also made the service at the first-class Chambord dining room on the *France* the best in the world—even according to people who were not always completely happy with the cuisine. (There were such people; some of them considered the style too opulent.) Perhaps to remind us that perfection *per se* does not exist, the architects made the Chambord dining room too cool and functional, and the lights too bright and cold to flatter women over thirty. Some people remembered nostalgically the beautiful dining rooms of the *Ile-de-France*, the *Normandie*, the *Liberté*. (They didn't think that everything on the *France* was made of metals and plastics that cannot burn.)

But the service in the imperfect dining room was always impeccable, often perfect. The *maître d'hôtel principal* had his assistant *maîtres*, and they, in turn had several *maîtres de rang* (captains) working under them. Each captain was in charge of several tables, took the orders, and surveyed the teams of waiters. On some crossings and cruises our captain was Pierre Naffrechoux. He and his brother Guy, also a captain, were the sons of Olivier Naffrechoux, retired but remembered as "Monseigneur," the greatest *maître d'hôtel* in Transat memory. Naffrechoux had educated generations of waiters, captains, and maîtres; he was said to be highly pleased with his sons, and no wonder. They loved their *métier*; they tried to make each meal a memorable experience. Pierre was considerate and enthusiastic. He would go into the kitchen and tell us what looked especially good. He would so temptingly describe a special dish he might order for the next day, that you couldn't turn him down.

The waiters worked in groups of two. The *commis* would bring the dishes from the kitchen, and the *garçon* would serve them. The *commis* didn't mind making extra trips to the kitchen, often waiting near the range for a tricky dish that had to be served immediately. He too loved to bring us top secret bits of culinary intelligence: "today the Civet de Lièvre looks *épatant*," and he was always right. And the *garçon* would serve in style and elegance. Even the late Henri Soulé, the unforgotten master of impeccable service, would have liked it. You might not see your *garçon* but he always saw you. To be sure, there were moments, especially on sold-out cruises, when four hundred people arrived almost at the same time for dinner, and captains and waiters were under some pressure. But if you were patient and came a little later, you were rewarded by the kind of service that has become very rare on land.

They didn't work so hard because they thought of the tips. They worked hard because they cared. Once Jean-Jacques, our *garçon* (waiters were not supposed to tell you their family names), artfully scooped a thin slice of Terrine de Foie Gras with a spoon and placed it, like a nicely turned leaf of a rose, on my plate. It looked lovely and was delicious. Another *garçon* (his name was Albert) would wander all over the dining room trying to find a piece of Brie that was just right. When there was none, he would suggest another good cheese.

The *sommeliers*, too, knew their business, though some of them took a cynical view of certain passengers who traveled first-class on the *France*, and asked only for ice water. There were five *sommeliers* in the dining rooms, well informed and honest about their wines. (They were not responsible for the small wine glasses on the *France* that no one liked. These were for the complimentary table wines. Special wines were always served in the proper glasses.) The best *sommeliers* didn't try to sell the more expensive wines. One of them, Paul Blanchard, once suggested a less expensive "but better kept" wine than the one with the greater name I had wanted to order.

The wine list was well composed and clearly presented. Selecting the wines was less complicated than ordering from the menu. The wine card offered three dozen red Bordeaux wines, among them the four Médoc *premiers crus* (Mouton-Rothschild had not yet quite made it), and some fine Saint-Emilion and Pomerol growths at low prices by American standards. There were fine Burgundy wines, other French wines, and there were even German and Italian wines, though one would think that people going on a French boat would find a wine they like among the large choice of French wines, white or red, dry or sweet.

Keeping fine wines aboard ship was always a problem, the *chef sommelier*, M. Brazzi, once explained to me. The ship's motion and the somewhat high temperatures in the cellar, about sixty-five degrees Fahrenheit, might make a delicate Margaux seasick, might even madeirize the sweet Sauternes.

"Some wines acquire a bitter aftertaste following a few crossings but recover when we put them back in our cellars at Le Havre," said M. Brazzi. "We take only what we think we need even at the risk of running out of some wines."

On American cruises Champagne was the most popular wine, especially the *fantaisie* bottles put out by Moët et Chandon (Dom Pérignon), Mumm (Cordon Rouge), Veuve Laurent-Perrier, Mercier (Réserve de l'Empereur), Piper-Heidsieck (Florens-Louis). Late in 1972, they had sixty-seven different Champagnes, running from $9 for a Lepitre Crémant Blanc de Blancs to $13 for a Dom Pérignon. All wines were stored in a slightly reclining position, not horizontally as on land, otherwise the bottles might rattle. The *France* was a steady, stable ship but it was a ship, after all, and is still in existence cruising throughout the world as the S.S. *Norway*.

When the *France* was taken out of service, many people in France were concerned because so many would lose their jobs. But much more was lost: a proud tradition, created in decades of Transat service, lovingly nurtured and handed over from one generation to the next.

In the pages to follow, the delights of the *France*'s master chef, Henri Le Huédé, come to life once more in a form that will enrich many a kitchen and bring back fond memories to those fortunate enough to have shared one of the great gastronomic experiences of our time.

Joseph Wechsberg
Vienna, May 1981

MENU

1

1

Les Oeufs frits Ali-Bab
Le Turbot poché, sauce mousseline
Le Carré d'agneau des Causses rôti sarladaise
Les Haricots verts sautés frais, au beurre noisette
La Salade Lakmé
Le Parfait Rothschild

2

(English menu)
Barley broth, Miss Belsey
Les Delices de sole de Douvres étuvés au whisky
Grouse écossaise rôti avec bread sauce
Pilaw de riz sauvage
Plum Pudding

3

Le Velouté de petits pois Fontanges
Le Medaillon de barbue nordique sauté Perinette
Le Suprême de pintadeau fermier doré Belle Otéro
Les Asperges de Malmaison tièdes, sauce sanguine
La Tarte aux mirabelles

4

La Soupe à l'oignon gratinée au Traminer
La Darne de saumon grillée sauce béarnaise
La Ballotine de dindonneau truffée et braisée,
aux marrons de l'Ardèche
La Tomate du val de Loire farçie provençale
La Salade Mercedès
Le Sorbet aux fraises

5

(American menu)
La Crème de maïs Washington
Le Homard de l'Atlantique grillé à la Léonard
Le Filet de boeuf de Kansas rôti à la façon de Virginie
Chocolate Ice cream

6

Les Oeufs en cocotte Bridaine
Le Coquille St.-Jacques au gratin "France"
Le Caneton braisé au Chambertin
Les nouilles fraîches
La Salade châtelaine
La Tarte aux framboises

7

Le Consommé de volaille Boieldieu
Les Filets de sole de la Manche étuvés Coquelin
La Longe de veau de l'Allier braisée vallée de Bray
Le Mont Blanc aux marrons

8

Le Consommé double Belle Gabrielle
La Langouste de tropiques étuvée Newburg
Le Coquelet de Metairie grillé languedocienne
La Courgette frite à l'anglaise
Le Soufflé Harlequin

9

Le Velouté de laitue Choisy
Les Goujonettes de sole frites sauce Gribiche
La Poularde de louragois farci, rôti périgourdine
Le Coeur de céleri braisé bolognese
La Salade chiffonade
l'Omlette aux fruits

10

l'Omlette brayaude
Le Saumon de gare braisé Castel de Nérac
Le Tournedos de Charolais sauté Rossini
La Jardinière de primeurs étuvée au beurre fin
Le Riz à l'impératrice

11

(Brazilian menu)
Le Consommé de caret aux herbes
Le Valapa de poissons de Bahia
Le Churrarco en brochette Paulista
Le Pudding à la noix de coco

12

Le Velouté de champignons Agnès Sorel
Le Medaillon de turbot boulonnaise braisé bonne hôtesse
La Côte de veau de l'Allier sauté Prince Orloff
Les Concombres étuvés à la crème
l'Omlette à la norvégienne

13

Les Oeufs mollets aubergistes
Les Délices de sole étuvés Castiglione
Le Contrefilet auvergnat rôti Armenonville
Les Choux de Bruxelles rissolés polonaise
Le Mille feuilles

14

Le Consommé de volaille chancelière
Le Saumon de Gave braisé "France"
Le Tournedos de Charolais grillé Henri IV
L'Aubergine frite nîmoise
La Tarte à l'orange

15

Le Thourin roumanille
La Coupe de fruits de mer sauce chilienne
Le Caneton nantais rôti Dame Catherine
Les Petits Pois du val de Loire paysanne
Le Sorbet à l'orange

16

Le velouté d'asperges comtesse
La Sole de la Manche frite Saint-Honorat
Le Carré d'agneau des Causses rôti bazadaise
Les Cèpes à la bordelaise
La Salade Figaro
La Tarte aux poires

17

Le Gazpacho
Le Medaillon de saumon quebecois farci, sauté Gastéra
Le Gigot de pré-salé rôti savoyarde
La Crème renversée au caramel

CARTE du JOUR

18

La Bouillabaisse du Vieux Port
La Sauce rouille
Les Cailles farcies de la Suisse, normandes
La Glace au café

19

Le Melon au porto
Les Cuisses de grenouilles sautées arlésiennes
Le Caneton ruoennais rôti aux beignets augerons
Les Coeurs de laitue braisés à l'écarlate
La Salade caprice
La Mousse au chocolat

20

La Terrine de lièvre à la Diane
Le Turban de coquilles St.-Jacques "France"
Le Riz pilaw
Le Tournedos de Charolais grillé bergerette
Le Soufflé sucré

21

La Branche de céleri garnie au bleu d'Auvergne
Les Quenelles de brochet de Loire "France"
Le Pigonneau de nid en compôte St.-Germain
La Salade madécasse
Le Gâteau St.-Honoré

22

Les Oeufs pochés Belle Otéro
Le Petit Homard aux douze aromates
Le Kebâb d'agneau grillé persane
l'Orge perlé
La Salade des Augustins
La Tarte aux pommes

23

Le Velouté de lentilles Premier Consul
La Brandade de morue bénédictine
Le Couscous marocain
Le Gâteau au miel portugais

24

Le Velouté d'artichauts danois
Le Loup de Calanque grillé aux herbes de Lavandou
Le Contre-Filet limousin grillé au beurre d'échalottes
La Tomate farcie navarraise
La Salade archiduc
La Mousse au mocha

25

Les Oeufs en cocotte chanoinesse
Les Crêpes de fruits de mer au gratin "France"
Le Caneton de Long Island rôti à l'ananas frais
La Salade Gadski
Le Soufflé glace à la vanille

26

La Terrine de poularde angevine
La Langouste fraîche de Bonne Espérance rôtie aux épices
l'Escalope de veau laitier sauté Verdunoise
Le Coeur de laitue à la Russe
Le Flan aux cerises

27

Les Oeufs au gratin Antonin Carême
Le Medaillon de turbot lorientais sauté Périnette
Les Sûpremes de pintadeau doré "France"
La Salade beaucaire
La Tarte aux abricots

28

La Crème de volaille Germiny à l'oseille
Le Cardinal des mers au gratin Thermidor
Le Jarret de veau laitier à l'italienne (ossobucco)
La Salade Gadski
La Cassata à la Néapolitaine

29

Le Soufflé au parmesan
Le Turbot gravelinois poché, sauce moutarde
Les Gourmandines de veau laitier au gratin "France"
La Salade turquoise
La Tarte aux abricots

30

Les Oeufs farcis Nissardes
Le Petit Homard de l'Atlantique à la nage
Le Pigeonneau Biset grillé crapaudine
La Salade Santiago
La Bavaroise au café

31

La Coupe de camarons, sauce mousquetaire
Les Délices de sole étuvés Castiglione
La Blanquette de veau à l'ancienne
Le Riz pilaw
La Salade Béatrice
Le Soufflé aux framboises

32

Les Oeufs brouillés Offenbach
La Petite Langouste rose du Cap au gratin dunkerquois
Les Paupiettes de jambon d'York dorées Viroflay
La Tarte aux pêches

33

(Easter menu)
Le Consommé des gladiateurs
Le Turbot poché sauce Gavarnie
L'Agnelet Pascal rôti St.-Laud
Les Oeufs à la neige

34

Le Pâté de foies de lapin en crépinettes
La Lotte de mer sautée girondine
Le Salmis de perdreaux à la solognote
La Salade de pissenlits aux rillons
Le Soufflé praline

35

Le Soufflé aux épinards
La Rouelle de thonine au four à l'algérienne
Le Caneton nantais braisé aux navets nouveaux
La Salade cauchoise
La Glace au chocolat liègeoise

36

Le Caviar d'Astrakhan aux blinis Gretschnevoi
Les Truites de torrent étuvées "France"
Les Brochettes de foies de volaille grillées
La Charlotte à la russe

37

Les Croquignolles savoyardes
Les Crabes farcies à l'antillaise
Le Filet de Charolais rôti à la Boston
La Glace aux amandes et fruits

Note: The recipes for the dishes listed in the menus
can be found through the index,
beginning on page 243.

Sauces

2

SAUCES

Sauces are still the glory of French cuisine, despite the attacks by proponents of *la nouvelle cuisine*. On the *France*, we had batteries of *sauciers*, who prepared these delightful accompaniments which dressed up the most simple dishes and lent their wonderful names to our elaborate menus. In this section, I have listed many of my favorites. Some appear in other recipes in this book, others are there to use as you like. I would like to suggest the following guide to their use.

Beef, boiled: Sauce Gribiche, Raifort, Verte.
Beef, grilled: Sauce Arlésienne, Béarnaise, Bordelaise, Bercy II,
        Chateaubriand, Choron, Diable, Foyot, Irlandaise, Lavallière,
        Maître de Chai, Polonaise, Réforme, Régence.
Beef, roast: Sauce Chasseur, au Madère, au Porto.
Chicken, poached: Sauce au Currie, Caruso, Périgueux, Raifort, Suprême.
Chicken (and other fowl), grilled: Sauce Diable, Gribiche, Réforme, Tomate,
        Yorkshire.
Chicken (and other fowl), roast: Sauce Diable, Gribiche, Réforme, Yorkshire.
Fish, cold: Sauce Aïoli, Albigeoise, Andalouse, Biarotte, Brignolaise,
        Cambridge, Cingalaise, Gribiche, Magali, Mayonnaise,
        Mont Bry, Mousquetaire, Occitane, Rémoulade, Russe, Tango,
        Tartare, Tolosa, Verte, Vert-Pré, Vincent.
Fish, grilled: Sauce Aurore, Béarnaise, Bercy I, Nantua, Normande, Tartare,
        Vin Blanc.
Fish, poached: Sauce au Currie, Gavarnie, Messine, Mornay, Mousseline,
        Moutarde, Nantua, Normande, Vin Blanc.
Game, furred: Sauce Chevreuil, Poivrade I and II.
Meats, cold. Sauce Andalouse, Cingalaise, Gênoise, Grimod, Magali,
        Mayonnaise, Mont Bry, Périgueux, Suédoise, Tango, Tolosa, la
        Varenne, Vincent.
Pasta: Sauce Bolognese, Caruso, Genovese, Hussarde, Italienne, Livournaise,
        Tomate, Tascane, Tyrolienne, Venitienne, Zingara.
Pork, grilled: Sauce Diable, Piquante, Robert, Charcutière.
Tongue: Sauce Piquante, Robert.
Veal, roast: Sauce Allemande, Chasseur, au Madère, Paulette, Périgueux, au
        Porto.
Vegetables, hot: Sauce Zingara, Hollandaise, Mousseline; for asparagus
        particularly, Maltaise and Mikado.
Vegetables, cold and salads: Sauce Andalouse, Antiboise, Brignolaise,
        Chantilly, Cingalaise, Gênoise, Gribiche, Grimod, Magali,
        Mont Bry, Mousquetaire, Occitane, Ravigote, Rémoulade, Russe,
        Tango, Tolosa, Verte, Vert-Pré, Vinaigrette, Vincent.

BASES FOR BROWN
AND WHITE SAUCES

Glace de Viande
(Meat Glaze)

**2 quarts Brown Veal Stock or
Chicken Consommé**

Boil stock, straining and skimming several times, until liquid is dark brown (veal) or golden brown (chicken) and has thickened to the point where it covers the back of a spoon. Strain through cheesecloth and place in a jar. Use when needed.

If kept refrigerated, this glaze will last for a long time without spoiling. **Makes about 1 cup**.

Sauce Demi-Glace
(Half-Glace)

Once French cooks used Sauce Espagnole as a base for their demi-glace. This sauce has disappeared from modern kitchens, so today it is replaced by Brown Veal Stock, lightly thickened with arrowroot and greatly reduced.

**2 quarts Brown Veal Stock
¼ cup arrowroot**

Whisk together stock and arrowroot in a saucepan, then bring to a boil. Reduce heat and simmer, stirring occasionally, until reduced to half. Refrigerate or freeze until needed. **Makes 4 cups**.

Sauce Velouté Ordinaire
(Ordinary Velouté)

**¼ cup (4 tablespoons) butter   5 cups White Veal and Poultry
⅓ cup flour   Stock, heated to almost boiling**

Melt the butter in the top of a double boiler over simmering water. Add the flour and mix well with a whisk. Cook gently without browning for about 5 minutes.

Add stock, stirring with a whisk. Bring to a boil, reduce heat, and simmer, covered, for about 1 hour. Skim as needed.

Strain liquid into a bowl, then refrigerate or freeze. **Makes 4 cups**.

Variations

Fish Velouté

Prepare according to above recipe, substituting Fish Stock for White Veal and Poultry Stock.

Veal Velouté

Prepare according to above recipe, substituting Brown Veal Stock for White Veal and Poultry Stock.

Sauce Béchamel

½ cup (8 tablespoons) butter
½ cup flour
1 quart milk, heated to almost boiling

Salt and white pepper
Freshly grated nutmeg
1 medium onion, studded with 4 whole cloves

Melt butter in a saucepan and add flour. Cook without browning for about 5 minutes. Add hot milk, stirring vigorously with a whisk. Season with salt and pepper, generous pinch of nutmeg, and put in onion. Bring to a boil and simmer gently for about 30 minutes, or until thick.

Strain through a fine sieve, discard solids, and reserve sauce for use in recipes as directed. **Makes 3 cups**.

Court Bouillon
(Court Bouillon)

3 quarts water
½ teaspoon salt
1 leek (green part only), chopped
1 bay leaf

1 sprig fresh thyme
Few sprigs of fresh parsley
1 tablespoon vinegar or 2 slices lemon

In a large pot, bring water to a boil and add salt, leek, bay leaf, thyme, parsley, vinegar, or lemon. Simmer gently for about 15 minutes, then use it to poach fish. It is not necessary to strain before using. **Makes 3 quarts**.

Glace de Poisson
(Fish Glaze)

1 quart Fish Stock

Boil the stock, uncovered, in a saucepan until reduced to 1 cup liquid. Strain and reserve for recipes as indicated. **Makes 1 cup**.

Essence de Poisson
(Fish Extract)

1 quart Fish Stock, strained
2 pounds fish bones and heads
2 large onions, minced

½ cup chopped fresh mushrooms
1 cup dry white wine

Mix stock, bones, onions, mushrooms, and wine in a large pot. Bring to a boil, reduce heat, and simmer, covered, for about 45 minutes. Strain through a sieve into another saucepan, then boil until reduced by half. Refrigerate or freeze until needed. **Makes about 2 cups**.

BUTTERS AND CREAMS

Beurre Manié

Mix equal amounts of flour and softened butter into a smooth, thick paste. Cover and refrigerate.

1½ tablespoons added to 1 cup liquid makes a thin sauce.

2½ tablespoons added to 1 cup liquid makes a medium-thick sauce.

Crème Fraîche

1 cup heavy cream

1 teaspoon buttermilk

Combine cream and buttermilk in a saucepan and heat to lukewarm. Let stand at room temperature until thickened, from 6 to 36 hours depending on the temperature of the room. Will keep refrigerated up to 1 week. **Makes 1 cup**.

Clarified Butter

Heat butter until melted; let stand 20 minutes. Remove foamy crust, then spoon liquid into a jar and refrigerate. Discard milky residue.

Beurre de Fines Herbes
(Herbed Butter)

1 shallot, minced
1 clove garlic, minced

2 teaspoons chopped fresh parsley
1½ cups butter

Sauté the shallot, garlic, and parsley in 1 tablespoon butter. Cool, then soften the remaining butter and beat in the vegetables. Shape the mixture with wet hands into a roll 1½ inches in diameter. Roll in wet parchment paper and chill until hard.

When ready to use, cut into 6 slices. **Makes 6 servings**.

BROWN SAUCES

Sauce Arlésienne

1 medium eggplant, peeled and
  diced
1 zucchini, diced
¼ cup olive oil

Salt
2 large tomatoes, peeled,
  seeded, and diced
1 quart Sauce Demi-Glace

Sauté eggplant and zucchini in oil, cooking until perfectly brown. Salt lightly, and drain after cooking to remove excess oil. Set aside.

In a large saucepan, bring tomatoes to a boil, then simmer until all the juice has evaporated. Add the Demi-Glace and vegetables and mix well with a wooden spatula. Simmer 15 minutes, then serve with grilled beef. **Makes 6 cups**.

Sauce Bolognese

¼ cup butter
1 large onion, chopped
1 stalk celery, chopped
1 carrot, chopped
4 ounces prosciutto, minced
2 tablespoons olive oil

1 pound ground round beef
4 ounces ground boneless pork
1 cup dry white wine
1½ cups Classic Beef Consommé
2 tablespoons tomato paste
Salt and pepper

Heat butter in a large saucepan and sauté onion, celery, carrot, and prosciutto for 5 minutes. Add oil and ground meats, and stir until meats are brown and crumbly. Add wine and simmer until wine has evaporated. Drain excess fat and add consommé and tomato paste. Simmer, covered, for 30 minutes, stirring occasionally. Season to taste with salt and pepper. Serve with pasta. **Makes 4 cups**.

Sauce Bordelaise

½ cup plus 1 teaspoon butter
3 shallots, finely chopped
1 cup red Bordeaux wine

1 quart Sauce Demi-Glace
1 tablespoon chopped fresh parsley

Heat 1 teaspoon butter in a large saucepan and sauté shallots. Add wine, reduce to 1 tablespoon, then add Demi-Glace. Bring to a boil, reduce heat, and simmer gently until reduced to 2 cups.

Remove pan from heat and, using a whisk, blend in remaining butter, cut into small pieces. Sprinkle parsley over sauce just before serving dish. This sauce is particularly good with grilled beef. **Makes 2½ cups**.

Sauce Caruso

12 ounces chicken livers, diced
1 tablespoon olive oil
1¼ cups Brown Veal Stock

1 teaspoon arrowroot
1 tablespoon catsup

Sauté the livers in oil, then set aside.

Thicken the stock with the arrowroot and then stir in the catsup and the livers. Simmer until hot. This sauce is very good with pasta, omelets, and poached chicken. **Makes 2 cups.**

Sauce Chasseur

10 large, fresh mushrooms, washed and trimmed
3 tablespoons butter
Salt

2 large shallots, minced
¾ cup dry white wine
3 cups Sauce Demi-Glace
1 tablespoon chopped fresh parsley

Sauté mushrooms in 2 tablespoons butter, browning lightly. Add salt and set aside.

Sauté shallots in remaining butter, then add mushrooms and wine. Boil for 10 minutes, then add Demi-Glace. Simmer 30 minutes, skimming carefully. Just before serving the sauce, add parsley. This sauce is good with roast beef and roast veal. **Makes 3½ cups.**

Varation

Sauce Lavallière

This is a Sauce Chasseur to which ¼ cup finely chopped truffles and 2 teaspoons chopped fresh tarragon have been added. It is good with grilled beef.

Sauce Chateaubriand

2 shallots, finely chopped
½ teaspoon chopped fresh tarragon
½ teaspoon fresh thyme leaves
1 cup dry white wine

1 cup butter, cut into small pieces
1 tablespoon-Glace de Viande
Salt
1 tablespoon chopped fresh parsley

Place herbs in a saucepan with the wine and boil until reduced to ¼ cup. Beat the sauce with a whisk while slowly blending in the butter and the Glace de Viande.

Strain sauce through a fine sieve, season lightly with salt, and sprinkle parsley on top just before serving. This sauce is good with grilled beef. **Makes 1⅓ cups.**

Sauce Chevreuil

3 medium shallots, minced
1 cup red wine vinegar
½ teaspoon crushed white
   peppercorns
1 sprig fresh tarragon

1 quart Sauce Demi-Glace (prepared
   with stock from game bones
   instead of veal)
1 teaspoon Glace de Viande

Combine shallots and vinegar with peppercorns in a saucepan. Add tarragon and bring to a boil. Reduce the heat and simmer until liquid has evaporated.

     Add Demi-Glace to the sauce and simmer 20 minutes. Stir in Glace de Viande. Degrease the sauce carefully, then strain through a fine sieve. This sauce is good with game. **Makes 3½ cups**.

Sauce Diable

3 medium shallots, finely
   chopped
2 tablespoons butter
¾ cup dry white wine
3 teaspoons red wine vinegar

Pinch of freshly ground white
   pepper
1 quart Sauce Demi-Glace
1 teaspoon tomato paste

Sauté shallots in butter until wilted, then add wine, vinegar, and pepper. Boil until reduced to three-fourths the quantity, then add Demi-Glace and tomato paste. Bring to a boil, reduce heat, and simmer, uncovered, for about 30 minutes.

     Strain sauce through a fine sieve into a bowl and reserve for recipe. This sauce is good with grilled or roasted fowl. **Makes about 3 cups**.

Sauce Genovese

6 fresh mushrooms, trimmed and
   diced
1 teaspoon butter
Salt
1 quart crème fraîche or heavy
   cream

½ cup chopped boiled ham
½ cup chopped cooked chicken
Pinch of grated nutmeg

Sauté mushrooms in butter without browning; salt lightly.

     Boil the crème fraîche until reduced by half, then add the mushrooms, ham, and chicken. Simmer 10 minutes and season to taste with salt and nutmeg. Serve with pasta. **Makes about 4 cups**.

Sauce Hussarde

3 shallots, finely chopped
¼ cup (4 tablespoons) butter
1 cup Muscadet wine (or other
   dry white wine)
3 cups Sauce Demi-Glace
1 teaspoon tomato paste

Bouquet garni (lettuce leaves,
   thyme, parsley)
1 cup diced Bayonne or smoked ham
1 tablespoon grated horseradish
2 teaspoons chopped fresh parsley

Sauté the shallots in a saucepan with the butter for 5 minutes. Add the wine, the Demi-Glace, the tomato paste, and the bouquet garni. Bring to a boil, reduce the heat, and simmer for about 20 minutes. Strain the sauce into a bowl and add ham and horseradish. Just before serving, add parsley. Serve with pasta. **Makes 3½ cups**.

Sauce Italienne

3 medium shallots, finely chopped	½ cup dry white wine
10 fresh mushrooms, finely chopped	4 large tomatoes, peeled, seeded, and diced
2 tablespoons plus 1 teaspoon butter	Salt
1 quart Sauce Demi-Glace	3 slices boiled ham, minced
	3 slices smoked tongue, minced

Sauté shallots and mushrooms in 2 tablespoons butter until soft. Add Demi-Glace and wine, bring to a boil, and reduce by simmering over low heat for 20 minutes. Skim carefully.

Cook tomatoes in remaining butter and add a pinch of salt. Add ham and tongue to tomatoes and stir well. Add tomato mixture to sauce and reheat. This sauce is good with pasta and various kinds of meat and fowl. **Makes 6 cups**.

Sauce Livournaise

4 ounces boneless lean pork, diced	Salt
4 ounces boneless veal, diced	1 teaspoon tomato paste
2 tablespoons butter	2 cups Brown Veal Stock
½ cup minced celery	1 teaspoon arrowroot
1 tomato, peeled, seeded, and chopped	

Sauté the pork and veal in butter until browned, then add the celery and tomato. Cook for 5 minutes, then season with salt. Add the tomato paste and the stock mixed with the arrowroot. Stir until thickened and season to taste. Use with pasta. **Makes 3 cups**.

Sauce Maître de Chai

2 shallots, finely chopped	Salt and pepper
1 cup plus 1 tablespoon butter	1 tablespoon finely chopped fresh parsley
1 cup dry red wine	

Sauté the shallots in 1 tablespoon butter, then add the wine and boil until reduced to ¼ cup. Using a whisk, blend in 1 cup butter, adding it in small pieces. Season lightly with salt and pepper and stir in the parsley just before serving. This sauce is good with grilled beef. **Makes 1¼ cups**.

Sauce Périgueux

1 quart Sauce Demi-Glace

⅓ cup minced truffles (reserve juice from can)

Place Demi-Glace into a saucepan and add 6 tablespoons of the canning juice from the truffles. Simmer for about 15 minutes, then stir in the truffles. This sauce is good with cold meats, poached chicken, veal, and roast fowl. **Makes 4 cups**.

Sauce Piquante

2 medium shallots, chopped
½ cup dry white wine
⅔ cup vinegar
½ teaspoon crushed white peppercorns

1 quart Sauce Demi-Glace
5 medium-sweet pickles, minced or cut into julienne
1 tablespoon chopped fresh parsley

In a saucepan, combine the shallots, wine, vinegar, and peppercorns. Boil until reduced to 1 tablespoon.

Add Demi-Glace to saucepan and simmer for 15 minutes. Strain sauce through a fine sieve, then mix in the pickles and parsley. This sauce is good with grilled pork and braised beef tongue. **Makes 4½ cups.**

Sauce Poivrade I

3 tablespoons olive oil
1 onion, chopped
1 carrot, peeled and chopped
1 clove garlic, chopped
1 cup diced raw lamb

1 cup cider vinegar
1 cup Sauce Demi-Glace
1 teaspoon crushed white peppercorns

Heat oil in a skillet, then add onion, carrot, garlic, and lamb. Brown lightly, then add vinegar and Demi-Glace, along with peppercorns. Bring to a boil and simmer for 1 hour, skimming as needed. Strain sauce through a sieve and serve with venison. Also used with beef. **Makes 2 cups.**

Sauce Poivrade II

1 medium onion, finely chopped
1 carrot, finely chopped
1 stalk celery, chopped
2 tablespoons oil

1 cup red wine vinegar
1 teaspoon crushed white peppercorns
1 quart Sauce Demi-Glace

Sauté onion, carrot, and celery in oil. Add vinegar and peppercorns and bring to a boil. Lower the heat and simmer until reduced by half.

Add Demi-Glace to sauce, bring back to a boil, and simmer over low heat for 20 minutes, skimming as needed. Strain sauce through a sieve and serve with game. **Makes 4 cups.**

Sauce au Porto

1 quart Sauce Demi-Glace   ½ cup Port wine

Combine Demi-Glace with wine and bring to a boil. Lower heat and simmer for 30 minutes, then strain through a fine sieve. This sauce is good with roasts of beef or veal. **Makes 3½ cups**.

Sauce Régence

2 carrots, chopped   1 quart Sauce Demi-Glace
1 stalk celery, chopped   2 tablespoons chopped truffles
2 tablespoons butter

Sauté carrots and celery in butter for 5 minutes. Add Demi-Glace and bring to a boil. Reduce heat and simmer for about 20 minutes. Strain sauce through a fine sieve and stir in truffles. This sauce is good with grilled beef. **Makes 3½ cups**.

Sauce Robert

3 tablespoons red wine vinegar   1 quart Sauce Demi-Glace
½ teaspoon crushed peppercorns   2 tablespoons Dijon-style mustard
1 cup dry white wine

Combine vinegar and peppercorns with wine in a saucepan. Boil until reduced by one-quarter.

Mix mustard into Demi-Glace and add to reduced wine mixture. Bring to a boil, reduce heat, and simmer 20 minutes. Strain sauce through a fine sieve, then serve with grilled pork and braised beef tongue. **Makes 4 cups.**

Varation

Sauce Charcutière

This is simply a Sauce Robert to which 6 medium-sweet pickles (cut into julienne strips) have been added. It is good with grilled or roast pork.

Sauce Tomate

3 tablespoons butter   1½ cups Brown Veal Stock
1 carrot, peeled and chopped   2 cloves garlic, chopped
1 onion, chopped   2 sprigs fresh thyme
¼ cup flour   1 bay leaf
3 cups chopped, peeled, and   2 tablespoons sugar
  seeded tomatoes   Salt and pepper

Heat the butter in a large saucepan and sauté the carrot and onion for 5 minutes. Sprinkle with flour and add the tomatoes, stock, garlic, herbs, and sugar. Cover and simmer, stirring occasionally, for 1 hour. Season to taste with salt and pepper, and remove herbs before serving. **Makes 2 cups**.

Varation

Sauce au Madère

Follow the recipe for Sauce au Porto, substituting aged Madeira wine for the Port. It is good with roast beef and roast veal.

Sauce Réforme

1 large truffle	4 large fresh mushrooms
3 medium-sweet pickles	Whites of 2 hard-cooked eggs
2 slices cooked smoked beef tongue	1 quart Sauce Poivrade II

Cut truffle, pickles, tongue, mushrooms, and egg whites into thin julienne.
Bring sauce to a boil and add julienne ingredients; simmer 15 minutes. This sauce is good with grilled beef and fowl. **Makes 4 cups.**

Sauce Toscane

2 green-and-red sweet peppers, diced	½ cup cooked chicken
1 tablespoon butter	1½ cups Brown Veal Stock
Salt	1 teaspoon arrowroot

Sauté the peppers in the butter for 5 minutes, then season with salt. Add the chicken, stock, and arrowroot. Mix to blend well, and simmer until thickened. Serve with pasta. **Makes 2½ cups.**

Sauce Tyrolienne

2 cups clarified Brown Veal Stock	8 ounces beef filet tip, finely diced
1 teaspoon arrowroot	2 tablespoons butter
1 teaspoon tomato paste	Salt
½ cup dry white wine	2 large tomatoes, peeled, seeded, and chopped

Thicken hot stock with arrowroot. Dilute tomato paste with wine.
Sauté beef in a skillet in 1 tablespoon butter until brown. Cook the tomato pulp in remaining butter until thick.
Add the beef, tomatoes, and tomato paste mixture to the stock and simmer 10 minutes. Season with salt and then serve with pasta. **Makes 3½ cups.**

Sauce Yorkshire

½ cup Port wine	1 orange, peel grated and juice reserved
1 tablespoon currant jelly	Pinch of cayenne
Pinch of ground cinnamon	
1 quart Sauce Demi-Glace, heated to boiling	

Combine in a saucepan the wine, jelly, and cinnamon. Add the Demi-Glace, orange peel, and orange juice, along with cayenne. Simmer 30 minutes, then serve with grilled fowl.

Note: When this sauce is served cold, it is generally referred to as a Cumberland Sauce. **Makes 3 cups**.

Sauce Zingara

1 quart Sauce Demi-Glace
½ cup julienne strips of boiled ham
½ cup julienne strips of smoked tongue

6 fresh mushrooms, cut into julienne strips
½ cup Madeira wine
Salt

Bring Demi-Glace to a boil and simmer 15 minutes. Add meat and mushrooms, along with wine. Simmer an additional 15 minutes, then season with salt. This sauce is good for pasta or braised vegetables. **Makes 5 cups**.

WHITE SAUCES

Sauce Américaine

1 2-pound lobster
1 carrot, chopped
1 onion, chopped
1 clove garlic, chopped
¼ cup (4 tablespoons) butter
1 sprig fresh thyme, chopped
1 sprig fresh parsley, chopped

½ cup olive oil
2 shallots, minced
½ cup dry white wine
2 cups Sauce Tomate
¼ cup Fish Stock
Salt
Freshly ground white pepper

Cut lobster into 8 pieces; remove tomalley and set aside.

Sauté carrot, onion, and garlic in butter for 5 to 6 minutes. Add herbs and set aside.

Heat oil in a pot and cook lobster until done. Remove pieces and add to vegetables. Add shallots and wine along with tomato sauce and stock. Simmer 20 to 25 minutes.

Stir reserved tomalley into lobster mixture and cook until thickened. Season to taste. Used mostly with shellfish. **Makes 3 cups**.

Sauce Aurore

1 cup Fish Velouté
⅓ cup chopped tomato pulp

Pinch of cayenne

Mix velouté with tomato and season with cayenne. Used with fish. **Makes 1½ cups**.

Sauce Béarnaise

3 medium shallots, chopped
5 fresh tarragon leaves, chopped
⅔ cup red wine vinegar
6 crushed white peppercorns
3 egg yolks
1¼ cups clarified butter
Salt

1 tablespoon finely chopped fresh
parsley
1 tablespoon finely chopped
fresh tarragon
Pinch of cayenne (optional)
Juice of 1 lemon

Place shallots and tarragon leaves in the top of a double boiler with vinegar and peppercorns. Over boiling water, reduce mixture to 2 tablespoons, then remove from heat and add yolks. Either in a double boiler or over low heat, whisk the sauce until the yolks thicken and become creamy. Continue whisking while you blend in the butter. (A good Béarnaise sauce should have the consistency of mayonnaise.) Salt and mix in parsley and tarragon along with cayenne and lemon juice. This sauce goes well with grilled meats and fish. **Makes 1½ cups**.

Variations

Sauce Choron

This is Sauce Béarnaise mixed with ½ teaspoon tomato paste or tomato sauce. It is good with grilled beef.

Sauce Foyot

This is Sauce Béarnaise to which has been added 1 teaspoon Glace de Viande. It should have a deep beige color and is good with grilled beef.

Sauce Paloise

This is Sauce Béarnaise prepared without tarragon but with 5 or 6 fresh mint leaves finely chopped. It is good with grilled beef.

Sauce Bercy I

2 shallots, finely chopped
1 cup plus 1 tablespoon butter

1 cup dry white wine
1 teaspoon Glace de Poisson

Sauté shallots briefly in 1 tablespoon butter without browning. Add wine and reduce to about ¼ cup.

Adding in small pieces, gradually whisk in the remaining butter blending well. Add the Glace de Poisson and serve with fish. **Makes 1¼ cups**.

Sauce Bercy II

2 shallots, finely chopped
1 cup plus 1 tablespoon butter
1 cup dry white wine

8 ounces beef marrow, poached
and cut into cubes
1 tablespoon chopped fresh parsley
Salt

Proceed as for Sauce Bercy I, adding the butter to the sauce, then the marrow. Just before serving, add parsley and adjust seasoning. Good with grilled meat. **Makes 1¼ cups**.

Sauce Crème à l'Anglaise

6 tablespoons butter
8 tablespoons flour
3½ cups White Veal and Poultry
  stock

6 tablespoons liquid from cooking
  mushrooms
1 cup créme fraîche or heavy cream

Blend together the butter and flour, then cook the roux without allowing to brown. Gradually blend in the stock and mushroom liquid, stirring well until smooth. Add the créme fraîche and blend well. **Makes about 5 cups.**

Sauce au Currie

1 onion, diced
1 carrot, peeled and diced
½ cup sifted flour
1 tablespoon curry powder
2 quarts White Veal and
  Poultry Stock

2 apples, peeled and quartered
3 bananas, minced
½ teaspoon salt
½ cup crème fraîche or heavy
  cream

Place onion and carrot in a saucepan and add flour and curry powder. Cook this roux, then add stock, apples, and bananas. Season with salt, bring to a boil, and simmer, uncovered, for 1 hour.

Press sauce through a fine sieve, then stir in crème fraîche. This sauce is good with egg dishes, chicken, fish, and shellfish. **Makes 6 cups.**

Sauce Hollandaise

2 tablespoons white wine vinegar
1 teaspoon crushed white peppercorns
3 egg yolks

2 tablespoons water
1 cup clarified butter
Salt

Place vinegar and peppercorns in a saucepan and boil until reduced to 1 tablespoon. Remove from the heat and whisk in the egg yolks and water. When the yolks are well blended and lightly whitened, replace over low heat and slowly blend in the butter. Season with salt, then strain through a sieve. Serve at once, with vegetables or poached fish. **Makes 1⅓ cups.**

Variations

Sauce Riche

Prepare Hollandaise, then add 2 tablespoons finely diced truffles and 1 small (4 ounces) poached and diced lobster tail. This sauce is good with poached fish.

Sauce Irlandaise

This is Sauce Hollandaise to which 2 teaspoons of finely chopped fresh mint leaves have been added. It is served with grilled meats.

Sauce Maltaise

This is Sauce Hollandaise in which, instead of the vinegar and peppercorns, 1 teaspoon of grated orange rind and ⅓ cup of Curaçao are substituted. It is usually served with asparagus.

Sauce Mikado

This is Sauce Hollandaise in which, instead of the vinegar and peppercorns, the grated rind and juice of 2 tangerines are substituted. It is usually served with asparagus.

Sauce Mousseuse

Prepare Hollandaise, then blend in 3 stiffly beaten egg whites. This sauce is good with poached vegetables and fish.

Sauce Moutarde

Prepare Hollandaise, then add 1 tablespoon Dijon-style mustard. This is good with poached fish.

Sauce Mornay

3 cups Sauce Béchamel	6 egg yolks, lightly beaten
4 ounces grated Gruyère cheese	½ cup (8 tablespoons) butter

Add cheese to the Béchamel and then blend in the yolks. Slowly add the butter, whisking in well. Serve with egg dishes, fish, and gratinéed fowl. **Makes 4 cups**.

Sauce Mousseline

1⅓ cups Sauce Hollandaise	½ cup whipped crème fraîche or heavy cream

Blend ingredients and serve with asparagus or poached fish. **Makes 2 cups**.

Variations

Sauce Gavarnie

To the Sauce Mousseline, add ½ cup minced cooked lobster (use lobster tail meat). It is good with poached fish.

Sauce Messine

To the Sauce Mousseline, add 1 tablespoon of chopped fresh parsley. This is good with poached fish.

Sauce Nantua

12 crayfish shells, crushed
3 tablespoons water
3 tablespoons butter

2 cups Sauce Béchamel
½ cup crème fraîche or heavy
  cream

Place the shells in a saucepan and add water and butter. Simmer 15 minutes, then strain and reserve liquid. Allow the cooking liquid to harden by chilling it.
    Heat the Béchamel and add the hardened butter and the crème fraîche. This is good for seafood dishes. **Makes 2½ cups.**

Sauce Normande

2 cups Fish Velouté
⅓ cup strained juices from
  mussels and oysters

⅓ cup crème fraîche or heavy
  cream

Stir the strained juices into the velouté and add the crème fraîche. Simmer until thickened, then serve with broiled or poached fish. **Makes 2½ cups**.

Sauce Raifort

2 cups crème fraîche or heavy
  cream
Pinch of grated nutmeg

2 tablespoons freshly grated
  horseradish
Salt

Bring the crème fraîche to a boil and reduce to 1½ cups. Add nutmeg and horseradish, and season with salt. This sauce is good for boiled beef or boiled fowl. **Makes 1½ cups.**

Sauce Suprême

2 cups Chicken Consommé
3 fresh mushrooms, chopped
1 cup Veal Velouté

1 cup crème fraîche or heavy
  cream
Salt
Pinch of cayenne

Mix the consommé with the mushrooms in a saucepan and simmer until reduced by half. Add the velouté and simmer again until reduced to 1 cup. Stir in the crème fraîche and season to taste with salt and cayenne. Used mostly with chicken. **Makes 2 cups**.

Variations

Sauce Allemande

To the Sauce Suprême, add 2 egg yolks, ¼ cup cream, and 2 tablespoons crème fraîche and stir constantly over low heat until the sauce thickens; do not allow to boil. This is a rich sauce that is good with delicate foods such as roast chicken or veal.

Sauce Paulette

To the Sauce Suprême, add the ingredients for Sauce Allemande and then also add 8 fresh mushrooms that have been chopped and sautéed in 2 tablespoons of butter for 5 minutes.

Sauce Vénitienne

2 cups White Veal and Poultry Stock
1 teaspoon arrowroot dissolved in 1 tablespoon water
½ cup diced cooked chicken

1 truffle, chopped
½ cup chopped boiled ham
6 fresh mushrooms, diced
1 tablespoon butter
Salt

Heat, then thicken the stock with the arrowroot mixture, then add the chicken, truffle, and ham. Keep warm.

Sauté the mushrooms in butter for 5 minutes, then add to the sauce. Season to taste with salt. Serve with pasta. **Makes 3 cups**.

Sauce Vin Blanc

2 shallots, minced
2 tablespoons butter
1 cup dry white wine

3 egg yolks
2 cups Sauce Velouté Ordinaire

Sauté the shallots in butter for 5 minutes. Add wine and simmer until reduced to ¼ cup.

Beat the yolks into the velouté and then stir this mixture into the shallot mixture. Stir constantly over low heat until the sauce thickens; do not allow to boil. **Makes 2½ cups**.

MAYONNAISES AND OTHER COLD SAUCES

Sauce Aïoli

1 potato, cooked and peeled
12 cloves garlic
3 egg yolks
1 teaspoon salt

Pinch of cayenne
2 cups olive oil
Juice of 1 lemon

Grind potato and garlic in a mortar or process in a food processor. Add the yolks, salt, and cayenne. While stirring with the pestle or a wooden spoon, beat in olive oil, pouring it into bowl in a thin stream. Beat in lemon juice and serve with fish. **Makes about 3 cups**.

Variation

Sauce Audoise

Prepare Aïoli, then stir in 2 tablespoons of capers. Fold in 2 chopped shallots, 3 chopped medium-sweet pickles, 3 chopped sprigs of fresh parsley, and 5 chopped sprigs of fresh chervil.

Sauce Chilienne

3 egg yolks	1 tablespoon curry powder
1 teaspoon Dijon-style mustard	1 tablespoon cooked long-grain
1 tablespoon vinegar	rice
2 cups peanut oil	Pinch of cayenne
½ cup crème fraîche or heavy	Salt
cream, whipped	

In a blender, beat the yolks, mustard, and vinegar until smooth. While blender is whirling, gradually add oil, drop by drop, until mixture is thick. Fold in the crème fraîche, curry powder, and rice and season to taste with cayenne and salt. **Makes about 3 cups.**

Sauce Mayonnaise

3 egg yolks	1 teaspoon Dijon-style mustard
½ teaspoon salt	1 tablespoon vinegar
Pinch of cayenne	2½ cups vegetable oil

Put yolks in a bowl. Add salt, cayenne, mustard, and vinegar. Whisk these ingredients together vigorously, then slowly add oil, pouring it very slowly in a fine stream. Mayonnaise should be very smooth and firm; if too thick, thin with vinegar or cream.

Note: Mayonnaise can be made quite successfully in either a blender or food processor if, again, the oil is added in a slow, steady stream. **Makes 3 cups**.

Variations

Sauce Albigeoise

To the mayonnaise, stir in 2 chopped hard-cooked eggs, 1 tablespoon capers, 2 chopped medium-sweet pickles, 1 chopped pimiento, and 2 finely chopped anchovy filets. Do not season with salt since anchovies are already heavily salted.

Sauce Andalouse

Prepare ½ cup of thick Sauce Tomate and strain through a sieve. Add to mayonnaise, together with ½ cup of finely chopped red-and-green sweet pepper.

Sauce Antiboise

To the mayonnaise, fold in ½ cup of whipped crème fraîche, ¼ cup of minced pimientos, and 5 chopped anchovy filets. (Do not season with salt since the anchovy filets are already salted.)

Sauce Biarrotte

To the mayonnaise, add 3 chopped anchovy filets, the finely diced pulp of a ripe tomato, and several finely chopped tarragon leaves. (Do not season with salt since the anchovy filets are already salted.)

Sauce Brignolaise

Prepare ½ cup of thick Sauce Tomate, strain through a sieve and add to mayonnaise.

Sauce Cambridge

To the mayonnaise add 1 teaspoon *each* finely chopped parsley, tarragon, and chervil, together with 3 chopped anchovy filets. Stir in the juice of ½ lemon. (Do not season with salt since the anchovy filets are already salted.)

Sauce Chantilly

To the mayonnaise add ½ cup crème fraîche and the juice of ½ lemon.

Sauce Cingalaise

To the mayonnaise add 2 tablespoons cooked long-grain rice and 2 pinches of curry powder.

Sauce Gênoise

Blanch ¼ cup each pistachio nuts and almonds; peel and finely chop. Add to mayonnaise, together with the juice of ½ lemon.

Sauce Grimod

To the mayonnaise, add 2 tablespoons finely chopped truffles and 2 teaspoons Madeira wine.

Sauce La Varenne

Finely chop 1 shallot and 1 tablespoon truffles. Sauté 3 chopped fresh mushrooms with 2 tablespoons butter. Season with salt and the juice of ½ lemon. Add all ingredients to mayonnaise.

Sauce Magali

To the mayonnaise, add ½ cup minced tomato pulp, 2 chopped hard-cooked eggs, and a pinch each of finely chopped parsley, chives, and tarragon.

Sauce Mont Bry

Cook 1 carrot and ¼ stalk celery until softened; chop fine. Chop 1 tablespoon truffles. Mix carrot, celery, truffles, and ½ teaspoon curry powder into mayonnaise.

Sauce Mousquetaire

Finely chop 2 shallots and add to ½ cup dry white wine. Bring to a boil and simmer until the wine has evaporated. Add 1 tablespoon finely chopped chives and season with a pinch of cayenne. Add to mayonnaise.

Saucy Occitane

Sauté 3 diced large mushrooms in 1 tablespoon oil. Cool. Add to the Sauce Verte (variation of mayonnaise) together with 1 pimiento cut into small cubes.

Sauce Rémoulade I

Finely chop 1 tablespoon capers, 2 dill gherkins, 2 sprigs parsley, a few tarragon leaves, and 2 sprigs chervil. Add to mayonnaise strongly flavored with 1 tablespoon Dijon-style mustard, then add 1 teaspoon anchovy paste. (Do not season with salt since the anchovy paste is already salted.) See p. 52 for Sauce Remoulade II.

Sauce Russe

Add 2 tablespoons black caviar and 1 tablespoon minced onion to mayonnaise.

Sauce Suédoise

Add 2 tablespoons thick apple butter and 1 tablespoon horseradish to mayonnaise.

Sauce Tango

Press ¼ cup pimientos through a sieve, add the juice of 1 lemon, and add both to mayonnaise.

Sauce Tolosa

Add 1 finely chopped clove garlic and the diced pulp of 1 large, ripe tomato to mayonnaise.

Sauce Verte

Whirl ½ cup cooked spinach and 1 tablespoon each chopped fresh parsley and chives in a food processor. Add to mayonnaise.

Sauce Vert-Pré

To the mayonnaise, add ¼ bunch finely chopped watercress.

Sauce Vincent

Mix 2 teaspoons each chopped fresh parsley, chives, watercress, raw spinach, and sorrel into the mayonnaise.

Sauce Ravigote

⅓ cup red wine vinegar
½ teaspoon salt
¼ teaspoon freshly ground black
 pepper
1 cup peanut oil

1 medium onion, chopped
2 tablespoons capers
½ teaspoon fresh tarragon, chopped
2 sprigs fresh parsley, chopped
3 sprigs fresh chervil, chopped

Whisk together the vinegar, salt, and pepper. Add the oil in a thin stream, whisking constantly. The sauce should be smooth and thick.

Mix onion, capers, tarragon, parsley, and chervil into the sauce with a wooden spatula. **Makes 1½ cups**.

Sauce Rémoulade II

⅓ cup vinegar
1 teaspoon Dijon-style mustard
 Salt and freshly ground pepper
1 cup olive or peanut oil

2 hard-cooked eggs, minced
1 tablespoon capers
2 large dill pickles, chopped
1 tablespoon chopped fresh parsley

Mixing with a whisk, combine the vinegar, mustard, salt, and pepper. Continue whisking and pour in a thin stream of oil. The sauce should be smooth. Add the eggs, capers, and pickles to the sauce, together with the parsley and stir.

Note: See also recipe given as variation of Mayonnaise. **Makes 1½ cups**.

Sauce Tartare

3 egg yolks from hard-cooked
 eggs
2 shallots, finely chopped
½ teaspoon salt
 Pinch of cayenne

1 teaspoon Dijon-style mustard
1 tablespoon vinegar
2½ cups vegetable oil
1 teaspoon minced fresh chives

Put yolks in a bowl and add shallots, salt, cayenne, mustard, and vinegar. Whisk these ingredients together vigorously, then slowly add oil, pouring it very slowly in a fine stream. As the sauce thickens, add chives. **Makes 3 cups**.

Variation

Sauce Gribiche

Prepare Sauce Tartare, then stir in 1 tablespoon finely chopped capers, 3 chopped sprigs of fresh parsley, and the chopped whites of 3 hard-cooked eggs.

Sauce Vinaigrette

2 tablespoons vinegar
1 teaspoon salt
¼ teaspoon freshly ground white
 pepper

1 teaspoon Dijon-style mustard
6 tablespoons peanut oil

Mix the vinegar, salt, pepper, and mustard in a bowl with a whisk. Continue whisking, adding oil in a thin stream; the sauce should be smooth and thick. Let stand at room temperature. Beat again before using. **Makes ½ cup**.

Soups

3

Nowadays, people pay less attention to soups than they do to other courses. That's a big mistake, because it's with the soup course that the meal really gets underway. Soup is to dinner what hors d'oeuvre are to lunch, and both must be prepared with great care. In a restaurant, the preparation and flavor of the hors d'oeuvre must make a good impression on the diner; otherwise the other courses, no matter how fine they may be, will suffer. The same applies to the soup course.

   Note: The recipes for the classic consommés—both beef and chicken—yield 3 quarts each. Considering the amount of time required for preparation, it's best to make a large amount and store it in the refrigerator or freezer until needed.

STOCKS AND CONSOMMÉS

Classic Beef Consommé

3 beef knuckle or marrow bones
1 shin of beef
3 tablespoons coarse (kosher) salt
3 carrots, sliced
6 leeks (green part only), chopped

1 large onion, stuck with 4 whole cloves
1 stalk celery, chopped
5 quarts water

In a heavy-bottomed stock pot, combine all the ingredients and bring to a boil. Simmer, uncovered, for 3 hours, skimming foam as it rises to the surface. Strain through a fine sieve; discard the solids. Cool, chill, and then remove fat. Refrigerate not longer than 1 week, or freeze for several months. **Makes 3 quarts**.

Clear Double Beef Consommé

Classic Beef Consommé
1 pound beef scraps
3 carrots, chopped
3 leeks (green part only), chopped

2 stalks celery, chopped
4 egg whites
½ cup water

In a heavy-bottomed stock pot, combine the consommé with the beef scraps, carrots, leeks, and celery. Beat the egg whites with the water and add to the consommé. Bring to a boil, then lower the heat and simmer, uncovered, 1 hour, skimming foam as it rises to the surface. Strain through several thicknesses of cheesecloth; discard the solids. **Makes 3 quarts**.

Chicken Consommé

Prepare Classic Beef Consommé, using 1 6-pound chicken and 3 pounds of chicken bones, necks, backs, wings, feet, and gizzards instead of the beef bones and shin of beef. **Makes 3 quarts.**

Clear Double Chicken Consommé

Prepare as for Clear Double Beef Consommé, using Chicken Consommé instead of Classic Beef Consommé and chicken trimmings instead of beef.
Makes 3 quarts.

White Veal and Poultry Stock

2½ pounds gelatinous veal bones,
    including joints
  6 chicken necks, or other fowl
12 chicken feet, or other fowl
  2 cups chopped carrots
  2 large onions, chopped

Bouquet garni (bay leaf,
    celery leaves, thyme, marjoram)
2 stalks celery, chopped
2 leeks (green part only), chopped
1 teaspoon salt
5 quarts water

Soak the veal bones for several hours in cold water. Put the bones in a heavy-bottomed stock pot together with the chicken necks and feet. Add carrots, onions, bouquet garni, celery, leeks, and salt. Add water, bring to a boil, and reduce heat and simmer, covered, for 3 hours, skimming foam as needed. Strain the stock through cheesecloth into a bowl or other container. Refrigerate or freeze until needed. **Makes 3 quarts**.

Brown Veal Stock

4½ pounds veal bones, preferably
    joints
    Oil
  5 quarts water
  2 carrots, chopped
  1 pound onions, chopped

2 stalks celery, chopped
    Bouquet garni (bay leaf, celery
    leaves, parsley, thyme, tarragon)
3 ripe tomatoes, diced
2 teaspoons salt

Preheat oven to 450 degrees. Cut the bones into pieces and place on a baking sheet. Pour a little oil over them. Place bones in hot oven until nicely browned; turn occasionally until all sides are browned. Transfer bones to a heavy-bottomed stock pot. Add water, carrots, onions, celery, bouquet garni, and tomatoes. Season with salt. Bring to a boil, reduce heat, and simmer, covered, for 7 hours, skimming foam as needed. Cool and chill. Remove layer of hardened fat. Heat and strain stock through cheesecloth into a bowl.

      Note: The flavor of the stock can be intensified by adding necks and legs of chicken or other fowl. Brown these parts along with the veal bones, then proceed with recipe. **Makes 2 quarts.**

Fish Stock

1 tablespoon butter	2 cups dry white wine
1 large onion, chopped	½ teaspoon salt
½ cup diced carrot	Bouquet garni (celery leaves,
½ cup chopped mushrooms	bay leaf, piece of lemon rind,
4 pounds fish heads and bones	few sprigs fresh dill)
8 cups water	6 whole peppercorns

In a large saucepan or heavy-bottomed stock pot, heat the butter and sauté the onion, carrot, and mushrooms for 5 minutes. Add the fish heads and bones, water, wine, salt, and bouquet garni. Bring to a boil, then lower the heat and simmer, uncovered, 40 to 45 minutes. Add the peppercorns the last 10 minutes of cooking. Strain through cheesecloth; discard the solids. **Makes 2 quarts**.

CONSOMMÉS WITH GARNISHES

Barley Broth Miss Belsey

6 cups Classic Beef Consommé or Chicken Consommé	4 tomatoes, peeled, seeded, and chopped
2 tablespoons fine barley, cooked 15 minutes in water and drained	Salt
	Chopped fresh parsley and chervil
2 tart apples, peeled, cored, and diced	

In a large saucepan, combine the consommé, cooked barley, apples, and tomatoes. Simmer, uncovered, 30 minutes. Season to taste with salt. Sprinkle with parsley and chervil and serve.

Consommé de Caret aux Herbes
(Turtle Consommé with Herbs)

It is impossible to find sea turtle in the market. The true turtle consommé (caret) is made with the legs, head, and flesh adhering to the shell. The meat of the sea turtle, when cooked, rather resembles veal, although it is darker. When I first went to sea in 1937 on the ocean liner De La Salle, *we took these turtles on board alive in the Venezuelan and Colombian ports. Thus on each voyage we were able to serve true sea turtle consommé and blanquettes of sea turtle—a superb dish.*

  During the voyages of the France, *the shells of the sea turtles were auctioned off to the crew on shore, since we never shipped live turtle. Our consommé was made with canned turtle, which we bought in New York, but it became increasingly difficult to find.*

6 cups Classic Beef Consommé or
Clear Double Beef Consommé
Few sprigs of fresh parsley
1 sprig each fresh rosemary,
savory, and thyme
Pinch of dried marjoram
Pinch of dried sage
2 bay leaves
1 teaspoon coriander seeds
1 teaspoon whole peppercorns
⅓ cup cherry brandy
2 cups canned turtle soup with
meat added
Salt

In a large saucepan, combine the consommé with the herbs and spices. Simmer, uncovered, 15 minutes, then strain through a fine sieve, discarding the solids. Return to a clean saucepan. Stir in the brandy and turtle soup; season to taste with salt. Simmer 15 minutes, then serve.

Consommé Oxtail Clair
(Clear Oxtail Soup—South African Specialty)

Classic Beef Consommé, made
with 1 oxtail (cut into 2-inch
pieces) instead of beef shin
1 bay leaf
1 sprig fresh thyme
Few sprigs of fresh parsley
Freshly ground pepper
¼ cup arrowroot or cornstarch
1 carrot, peeled and finely diced
1 white turnip, peeled and finely
diced
2 small leeks (white part only),
chopped
⅓ cup Madeira wine

Preheat oven to 450 degrees. Prepare the consommé as directed, but first roast the oxtail and bones with the bay leaf, thyme, and parsley, and pepper to taste in a hot oven for 1 hour before cooking with water to cover. Strain; remove and reserve oxtail pieces, discarding other solids.

Prepare Clear Double Beef Consommé; measure 6 cups of consommé for this recipe. Stir in arrowroot and cook, stirring constantly, until consommé is thickened. Add the vegetables, Madeira, and oxtail meat (removed from the bones and diced) and simmer, covered, until the vegetables are tender, about 10 to 15 minutes. Serve in cups.

Consommé des Gladiateurs
(Oxtail Soup with Barley)

Classic Beef Consommé, made
with 2 oxtails (cut into 2-inch
pieces) instead of beef shin
⅓ cup fine barley
2 cups water
Salt
6 pigeon, quail, or small chicken
eggs, poached

After consommé is cooked, strain. Remove and reserve oxtail pieces; discard other solids. Prepare Clear Double Beef Consommé; measure 6 cups of consommé for this recipe.

Add the barley to the water and simmer 15 minutes, or until tender. Drain and add to the clear consommé. Add the oxtail meat (removed from bones and diced) and reheat. Season to taste with salt. Serve in cups with the poached eggs as garnish.

Consommé à la Siamoise
(Consommé with Cucumbers and Rice)

6 cups Classic Beef Consommé or
   Clear Double Beef Consommé
Few sprigs of fresh parsley
1 bay leaf
1 sprig fresh thyme

1 large seedless cucumber, or
2 regular cucumbers, peeled
Salt
¼ cup uncooked rice
2 tablespoons butter

In a medium saucepan, combine the consommé with the parsley, bay leaf, and thyme. Simmer, uncovered, 15 minutes, then strain through a fine sieve. Set aside.

Using a melon baller, cut balls from the peeled cucumber. Put the cucumber balls in a saucepan and add a little water (about ¼ cup). Sprinkle with salt and simmer until the water has evaporated. In another saucepan, cook the rice in boiling salted water 15 minutes or until tender. Drain and rinse with cold water.

Add the rice and cucumbers to the consommé. Season to taste, then simmer until hot. Serve in cups.

Petite Marmite du Vert-Galant
(Chicken Soup with Vegetables)

6 cups Chicken Consommé
1 bay leaf
1 sprig fresh thyme
   Few springs of fresh parsley
1 cup julienne strips of carrots
1 white turnip, peeled and diced

1 stalk celery, sliced
1 leek (white part only), sliced
1 cup shredded green cabbage
Salt
Thin slices of French bread

Prepare consommé adding bay leaf, thyme, and parsley. When consommé is cooked, strain and reserve chicken; discard other solids. Remove skin and bone from chicken and dice for 1½ cups cooked chicken. Add chicken and vegetables to consommé and simmer, covered, 15 minutes or until vegetables are tender. Season to taste with salt. Serve in an earthenware tureen with bread slices on the side.

Consommé Belle Gabrielle
(Consommé with Chicken and Shrimp)

24 shrimp
¾ cup Marsala wine
8 cups Chicken Consommé

3 tablespoons minute tapioca
3 chicken breast halves
Salt

Cook the shrimp in water to cover for 5 minutes, then shell, devein, and dice. Marinate the shrimp in the Marsala for 1 hour.

Meanwhile, combine the consommé, tapioca, and chicken in a large saucepan. Simmer, uncovered, for 15 minutes. Remove the chicken. Skin and bone the breasts and cut the meat into julienne strips. Return the chicken to the consommé, add shrimp and Marsala. Season to taste with salt; heat and serve.

Consommé de Volaille Chancelière
(Chicken Consommé Chancelière)

Chicken Consommé	**3 fresh mushrooms, sliced**
1 truffle, cut into 6 slices	**½ cup shelled fresh peas**
⅓ cup Cognac	**Salt**

When consommé is cooked, strain. Remove breast from chicken, reserving rest of meat for another purpose; discard remaining solids. Skin, bone, and cut chicken breast meat into julienne strips; reserve. Prepare Clear Double Chicken Consommé; measure 6 cups of consommé for this recipe.

Marinate truffle in Cognac for 15 minutes. Add chicken, truffle (and Cognac), mushrooms, and peas to consommé. Simmer, uncovered, 15 minutes, or until peas are cooked. Season to taste with salt.

Consommé de Volaille des Viveurs
(Chicken Soup with Vegetables and Pastry Sticks)

Clear Double Chicken	**1 egg yolk**
Consommé	**¼ cup grated Parmesan cheese**
Celery leaves from 6 stalks	**3 stalks celery, trimmed and**
celery	**cut into julienne strips**
bay leaf	**Salt**
1 sprig fresh thyme	**Dash of cayenne**
8 ounces Puff Pastry	

Prepare consommé adding celery leaves, bay leaf, and thyme. Strain and discard solids; measure 6 cups consommé for this recipe.

Preheat oven to 350 degrees. Roll puff pastry into a 10-inch square, then brush with egg yolk and sprinkle with cheese. Cut into ½-inch-wide strips. Bake in a moderate oven for 10 to 15 minutes, or until puffed and brown. Cool and set aside.

When ready to serve, add celery strips to soup and simmer 5 minutes until tender but still crisp. Season to taste with salt and cayenne. Serve with pastry sticks.

Consommé de Volaille Murillo
(Chicken Consommé with Crème Royale)

8 cups Chicken Consommé,	**4 white turnips**
slightly warmed	**2 tablespoons uncooked rice**
4 egg yolks	**½ cup fresh shelled peas**
2 large carrots	**Salt**

Preheat the oven to 300 degrees. Beat together 1½ cups of the consommé and the egg yolks. Pour the mixture into a heavily buttered 8-inch square glass baking dish. Bake in a slow oven for 30 minutes. Cool the custard, then chill several hours; cut custard into diamond-shaped pieces.

Using a melon baller, cut balls from carrots and turnips.

In a large saucepan heat the remaining consommé. Add the carrots, turnips, and rice and simmer 15 minutes, or until tender. Add the peas and cook another 5 minutes. Season to taste with salt. Serve in cups, garnished with diamond-shaped egg custard pieces.

Consommé aux Nids Salanganes
(Bird's Nest Soup)

Looking forward to a menu of Chinese specialties in Hong Kong, I had ordered 25 kilograms (55 pounds) of swallows' nests for the famous Bird's Nest Soup. I had no idea how many nests 25 kilograms might be. Imagine my surprise when I saw them unloading 4 enormous cases. I also had no idea of how expensive they were—the bill came to over 10,000 francs ($2,500). Finally we found that 5 kilos (about 11 pounds) were all we needed. During 1972 we managed to get rid of the surplus, being in no position to refuse the first offer!

4 ounces swallows' nests	Salt
6 cups Clear Double Chicken Consommé	12 pigeon eggs or other very small eggs
Dash of cayenne	2 tablespoons vinegar

Soak nests in cold water for several hours to remove impurities.

Place nests in consommé and bring to a boil, reduce heat, and simmer for 15 minutes. As soon as nests become gelatinous, remove from heat and season to taste with cayenne and salt.

While soup is simmering, poach eggs in salted water with vinegar for 3 minutes. Serve soup in individual bowls with 2 eggs for each serving.

Potage Saoto Babati
(Gingered Broth)

Saoto babati is an Indonesian specialty which we prepared on a cruise according to a recipe given in Robert J. Courtine's book, La Cuisine du monde entier *(Cooking Around the World). This book also gave us a recipe for the Javanese dish known as* Le Sambel de Crevettes de Java *(Sautéed Shrimp in Coconut Milk), but unfortunately on the cruise we had neither coconut milk, shrimp pâté, nor tamarind—some of the very few ingredients missing among the great stores shipped on the* France.

1 pound bacon, in 1 piece	2 small pieces fresh gingerroot
½ cup vegetable oil	2½ cups milk
6 cups water	½ cup white wine vinegar
2 leeks (white part only), minced	Sea salt
3 stalks celery, peeled and minced	4 mill-turns freshly ground pepper

Dice the bacon and blanch in lightly salted water. Drain and sauté in a skillet with oil until brown and crisp. Transfer bacon to a saucepan with a slotted spoon and add 6 cups water. Bring to a boil and skim fat carefully.

Add the leeks and celery to the soup. Wrap the gingerroot in cheesecloth, tie, and add to the soup. Simmer, uncovered, over low heat for about 45 minutes. When the bacon is thoroughly cooked, discard gingerroot and beat in milk. Bring to a boil and add the vinegar. Add salt and pepper to taste. Serve in cups.

Consommé de Volaille Boieldieu
(Chicken Consommé with Quenelles)

5 ounces boneless and skinless raw chicken breast	Salt, cayenne, and freshly grated nutmeg to taste
1 truffle, finely chopped	2 quarts Chicken Consommé
2 tablespoons pâté de *foie gras*	½ cup Marsala wine
2 cups heavy cream or crème fraîche	Freshly ground pepper
2 egg whites, slightly beaten	

Purée the chicken breast, truffle, and *foie gras* in a food processor. Gradually beat in cream and egg whites. Season with salt, cayenne, and nutmeg.

Shape the chicken mixture with 2 spoons into egg-shaped dumplings and place in a well-buttered heavy-bottomed saucepan. Add consommé. Bring to a boil, then lower the heat and simmer 5 to 10 minutes. Stir in the Marsala. Season to taste with salt, if necessary, and pepper.

Note: For a simple version, heat the consommé and add 5 ounces diced, cooked chicken, 1 truffle cut into julienne strips, and 1 ounce diced *foie gras* (sold in cans). Simmer 5 minutes and serve.

CREAM SOUPS

Velouté d'Artichauts Danoise
(Cream of Artichoke Soup with Duck Quenelles)

	Stock:
12 artichokes	10 duck necks
Juice of 1 lemon	1 carrot, chopped
2 potatoes, peeled and diced	2 leeks (green part only)
Salt	Few sprigs of fresh parsley
¼ cup (4 tablespoons) butter	1 bay leaf
1½ cups heavy cream or crème fraîche	1 stalk celery, chopped
6 fresh mushrooms, cut in julienne	1 sprig fresh thyme
strips and sautéed in butter	4 cups water
⅓ cup Marsala wine	1 teaspoon salt

Quenelles:

1 pound duck livers	1½ teaspoons salt
2 egg whites	Dash of nutmeg
2¼ cups heavy cream or crème fraîche	

To prepare stock, combine first 8 ingredients. Add salt and simmer, uncovered, for 1½ hours, skimming foam. Strain and boil stock again until reduced to half its volume. Strain stock through a cheesecloth and discard solids. Set stock aside.

Cut the leaves from artichokes, remove the chokes, and trim bottoms. Rub the bottoms with lemon juice. Quarter bottoms and place with potatoes in a saucepan. Cover with water and salt lightly. Bring to a boil and simmer, uncovered, for 20 minutes, skimming the foam. Pass the entire mixture through a sieve or food mill or process in a blender. Place purée in a saucepan and stir in duck stock, butter, and cream. Set aside.

To make quenelles, place duck livers in a food processor and whirl until smooth. Gradually blend in egg whites, cream, salt, and nutmeg. Bring a large saucepan of water to a boil and then reduce to a quiet simmer. Drop quenelles by heaping tablespoons into the simmering water. Cook 15 minutes, then remove with a slotted spoon.

When ready to serve, place liver quenelles into hot soup, then stir in mushrooms and Marsala. Season to taste with salt and serve.

Velouté d'Asperges Comtesse
(Cream of Asparagus Soup with Sorrel)

2¼ **pounds fresh white or green**
asparagus
2 **quarts Chicken Consommé**
½ **teaspoon salt**
8 **egg yolks**

2½ **cups heavy cream or crème fraîche**
1 **cup chopped fresh sorrel leaves**
¼ **cup (4 tablespoons) butter**
Dash of cayenne

Peel the asparagus, cut off the tips (1½ inches), and tie together in bundles. Cut remaining asparagus stalks into 3 pieces and cook in consommé and salt. Add tips and simmer 5 to 10 minutes, or until just tender. Remove bundles of tips and rinse in cold water to stop cooking process. Press the cooking liquid and remaining asparagus through a sieve or food mill.

Beat the egg yolks with the cream, then gradually add some of the hot soup. Stir egg-cream mixture into remaining soup in saucepan and stir over low heat until thickened; do not allow to boil.

Cook the sorrel leaves and butter in water to cover until wilted. Pour sorrel and liquid into soup. Remove strings from bundles of asparagus and add asparagus to soup. Season to taste with salt and cayenne.

Velouté de Champignons Agnès Sorel
(Cream of Mushroom Soup with Tongue and Chicken)

6 **cups Chicken Consommé**
½ **pound fresh mushrooms,**
trimmed (caps sliced, stems
chopped)
6 **tablespoons butter**
½ **cup flour**
2 **cups (1 pint) heavy cream**
or crème fraîche

½ **cup julienne strips of cooked**
smoked tongue
½ **cup julienne strips of cooked**
chicken
Pinch of cayenne
Salt

Heat consommé. In a separate large saucepan, sauté the mushrooms in the butter for 5 minutes. Sprinkle with flour. Add hot consommé and stir over medium heat until thickened. Add cream, tongue, chicken, and cayenne. Stir and season to taste with salt. Serve in a tureen.

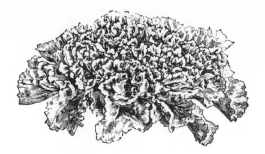

Velouté de Laitue Choisy
(Cream of Lettuce Soup with Croûtons and Chervil)

3 large potatoes, peeled and diced
1 head Boston lettuce
1 tablespoon salt
1 quart heavy cream or crème fraîche

3 tablespoons butter and 3 tablespoons clarified butter
Salt
Freshly ground pepper
3 slices firm white bread, diced
3 sprigs fresh chervil, leaves only

Place potatoes in a saucepan and add either a head of lettuce or the green leaves of several heads. (Reserve the hearts of lettuce for salads.) Add salt and water to cover, bring to a boil, and simmer, covered, for 20 minutes. Press soup through a sieve or food mill, then stir in the cream and regular butter, in small pieces, stirring with a wooden spoon. Season to taste with salt and pepper.

Melt the clarified butter in a skillet and sauté the bread cubes until brown and crisp. Serve soup topped with croûtons and garnished with chervil leaves.

Velouté de Lentilles Premier Consul
(Cream of Lentil Soup)

8 ounces lentils (yellow or orange)
1 medium onion, chopped
1 leek (white part only), chopped
2 tablespoons butter
2 large tomatoes, quartered
2 quarts water or Classic Beef Consommé

Salt and pepper
1½ cups heavy cream or crème fraîche
1 green pepper, diced
¼ cup olive oil
2 tablespoons chopped fresh sorrel leaves
½ cup cooked rice

Soak lentils in water to cover for 2 hours, then drain. In a large saucepan, sauté onion and leek in 1 tablespoon butter until soft but not brown. Stir in lentils and tomatoes. Add water or consommé, salt, and pepper; bring to a boil, lower heat, and simmer, uncovered, for 1 hour, or until lentils are well done. Press soup through a sieve or food mill, replace in saucepan, and stir in cream. Set aside.

Sauté green pepper in oil until soft but not brown. Drain and set aside. Sauté sorrel in remaining butter until wilted, then drain. Stir drained peppers, sorrel, and rice into soup. Reheat and season to taste with salt and pepper.

Velouté de Petits-Pois Fontanges
(Cream of Fresh Pea Soup)

This may well be one of the best of the cream of vegetable soups. Its tender green color is a delight to the eye, and its flavor—enriched with butter and crème fraîche—is bound to please the most demanding gourmets.

1 pound fresh peas in the shell	6 tablespoons butter
2 large potatoes, peeled and diced	1½ cups heavy cream or crème fraîche
Salt	3 tablespoons minute tapioca
	White pepper

Shell the peas. Place them in a heavy-bottomed saucepan, and add potatoes. Pour in water to cover, salt lightly, and simmer covered, about 30 minutes. Force the contents of the saucepan through a sieve or vegetable mill, then pour the mixture into a clean saucepan. Gradually add the butter, in bits, stirring all the while, then add the cream.

Meanwhile simmer the tapioca in lightly salted water for 10 minutes and drain. When ready, stir into the soup. Season to taste with salt and white pepper.

Velouté de Tomates Andalouse
(Andalusian Cream of Tomato Soup)

6 tablespoons butter	2 teaspoons salt
1 medium onion, minced	2 mill-turns fresh pepper
6 large ripe tomatoes, sliced, and seeded	⅓ cup minute tapioca
2 medium potatoes, peeled and quartered	Heavy cream or crème fraîche
	Grated Parmesan cheese

Melt half the butter in a heavy-bottomed saucepan and cook the onion until a pale golden. Add the tomatoes and the potatoes, barely cover with water, then add salt and pepper. Place lid on saucepan and simmer 30 minutes. When done, force soup through a sieve (or purée in a food processor) and stir in remaining butter.

Meanwhile, simmer the tapioca for 10 minutes in lightly salted water, drain, and, when ready, add to tomato mixture. Blend well. Add heavy cream until soup is of desired consistency, reheat, and serve with a bowl of Parmesan cheese.

Velouté de Tortue "France"
(Cream of Turtle Soup à la *France*)

Turtle Consommé with Herbs, using sherry instead of cherry brandy	1½ cups heavy cream or crème fraîche
3 tablespoons rice flour	Salt and pepper
3 tablespoons water	1½ cups shelled tiny peas, cooked and drained
6 egg yolks	

Heat consommé. Mix flour and water and stir into consommé until thickened. Simmer 30 minutes, then strain into a saucepan. Beat egg yolks and cream and stir in some of the hot soup. Stir this mixture into remaining soup until soup coats a spoon. Do not allow to boil. Season to taste with salt and pepper. Serve garnished with peas.

Crème de Légumes Glacée Vichyssoise
(Vichyssoise with Vegetables)

4 **medium potatoes, peeled and diced**	**Salt**
4 **stalks celery, chopped**	12 **ounces fresh sorrel leaves, cut into julienne**
2 **onions, chopped**	½ **cup (8 tablespoons) butter**
1 **sprig fresh thyme**	1½ **cups heavy cream or crème fraîche**
1 **bay leaf**	**Freshly ground pepper**
Few sprigs of fresh parsley	
3 **quarts water or Classic Beef Consommé**	

Combine potatoes, celery, onions, thyme, bay leaf, parsley, consommé or water, and salt to taste in a large saucepan. Bring to a boil, lower heat, and simmer, covered, for 30 minutes, or until vegetables are tender; skim foam. Press soup through a sieve or food mill and set aside.

Pour boiling water over the sorrel and drain. Melt the butter in a skillet and sauté sorrel for 5 minutes. Stir cream and sorrel into soup, reheat, and season to taste with salt and pepper.

Crème de Maïs Washington
(American Cream of Corn Soup)

8 **ears corn, or 2 (1-pound) cans cream-style corn**	1 **cup butter**
Salt	2 **cups heavy cream or crème fraîche**
2 **cups milk**	2 **green peppers tinged with red, diced**
3 **large potatoes, peeled and diced**	2 **tablespoons olive oil**

Husk the corn. Bring a large kettle to a boil, add a pinch of salt and the milk, then add corn. Boil the ears for about 15 minutes. Remove the corn and let cool. Slice off the kernels with a knife and chop coarsely.

Place potatoes in a large saucepan and add water to cover. Salt sparingly and simmer, covered, for 30 minutes. Add corn and stir. Press the soup through a fine sieve or food mill into another saucepan. Add butter in small pieces, stirring with a wooden spoon, then add the cream.

Sauté the green peppers in olive oil without letting them brown. Drain and add to the cream of corn mixture. Season to taste with salt, then serve.

Crème de Volaille Germiny à l'Oseille
(Cream of Chicken Soup with Sorrel)

6 cups Chicken Consommé	1½ cups heavy cream or crème fraîche
½ bay leaf	1 cup chopped, cooked sorrel leaves
1 sprig fresh thyme	2 tablespoons butter
6 egg yolks	Salt

Heat consommé with bay leaf and thyme until boiling. Remove herbs. In a bowl, beat together egg yolks and cream. Gradually beat in 2 cups of the hot consommé, then stir this mixture into remaining consommé. Cook until mixture coats a spoon, but do not allow to boil. Stir in sorrel, butter, and salt to taste. Serve in bowls.

Crème de Volaille Mulligatawney
(Mulligatawny Soup)

6 cups Chicken Consommé	⅓ cup flour
1 bay leaf	Milk from 1 coconut (see Note)
1 sprig fresh thyme	1½ cups heavy cream or crème fraîche
1 onion, chopped	1 teaspoon curry powder
3 whole cloves	1 cup cooked long-grain rice
½ cup (8 tablespoons) butter	Salt

Combine consommé, bay leaf, thyme, onion, and cloves and boil for 5 minutes. While soup is cooking, in a large saucepan, melt butter and stir in flour to make a roux. Stir over low heat for 5 minutes but do not brown. Strain consommé into roux and whisk until smooth and thick. Add coconut milk, cream, curry powder, and rice. Simmer 15 minutes or until piping hot. Season to taste with salt.

Note: To prepare coconut milk, crack open a coconut and pour off the clear liquid into a bowl; use for another purpose or discard. Remove coconut meat from shell and peel off brown skin. Chop meat and place in a blender with 2 cups water. Whirl in blender, then strain mixture through cheesecloth. Squeeze out all the juice and discard pulp. The creamy liquid is the milk.

Soupe à l'Onion Gratinée au Traminer
(Alsatian Onion Soup with Cheese)

One evening the onion soup, gratinéed under the broiler, was served in special earthenware bowls. To judge from the numbers of orders for the soup coming into the kitchen, it was very well received!

½ cup (8 tablespoons) butter
1 tablespoon vegetable oil
3 large onions, minced
2 quarts Classic Beef Consommé
Salt
3 mill-turns white pepper

2 cups Gewürztraminer wine
Crusty bread, preferably a long,
thin French baguette
2 cups (½ pound) grated Gruyère
cheese

In a heavy-bottomed saucepan, melt the butter, add the oil, and cook the onions slowly, stirring often. When pale yellow and thoroughly cooked, pour in the consommé. Season with salt and pepper and add wine. Bring to a boil and simmer for 30 minutes.

Cut the bread into thin slices on the bias and dry them in a moderate oven (350 degrees), the door left slightly open.

Pour the soup into individual bowls up to ¾ inch from the top. Float the dried bread on top and sprinkle with a generous coating of grated cheese. Place the bowls on a baking sheet and brown slowly under the broiler or in a very hot oven (500 degrees) until bubbly. Serve hot.

Thourin Roumanille
(Cream of Onion Soup with Pasta)

6 cups Classic Beef Consommé or
Chicken Consommé
¼ cup (4 tablespoons) butter
2 large onions, minced
2½ cups dry white wine
Salt
3 mill-turns freshly ground white
pepper

2 ounces vermicelli, broken
into 2-inch pieces
6 egg yolks
1¼ cups crème fraîche or heavy cream
6 tablespoons grated Swiss or
Gruyère cheese (optional)

Heat consommé in large saucepan. While consommé is heating, melt butter in skillet and sauté onions until soft but not brown. Stir onions and drippings into consommé. Stir in the wine, salt to taste, and the pepper. Simmer, uncovered, 20 minutes. Add the vermicelli and simmer 10 to 15 minutes longer, or until vermicelli is tender. Beat the egg yolks with cream; slowly beat in 1 cup of the hot soup. Pour this mixture into the remaining soup. Cook, stirring, until thickened and the mixture coats a spoon, but do not allow to boil. Taste for seasoning. Serve in cups, sprinkled, if desired, with grated cheese.

Niccolini Parfumé au Chianti
(Italian Wine Soup)

6 tablespoons butter
2 onions, finely chopped
6 cups Chicken Consommé
2 cups Chianti wine
2 ripe tomatoes, peeled, seeded, and diced

Salt
Freshly ground black pepper
¼ loaf French bread, preferably stale
1¼ cups grated Parmesan cheese

Melt 4 tablespoons of the butter in a skillet and sauté onions over low heat. Transfer onions to a saucepan when they have given up their juice and have taken on a pale gold coloring; add consommé and wine.

Put tomatoes in a saucepan; add remaining butter and 1 teaspoon salt. Sauté over low heat for about 10 minutes, then add the diced tomatoes to the consommé and wine mixture. Season with salt and pepper; simmer for 10 minutes.

Cut the French bread into thin slices and toast lightly.

Fill individual terra-cotta bowls three-fourths full with the soup, float 1 or 2 slices of bread on the surface, and sprinkle with grated cheese. Broil or bake in a hot oven (450 degrees) for 5 to 6 minutes, or until golden brown. Serve immediately.

Soupe de Feijãos
(Portuguese Bean Soup)

1 pound kidney beans
2 large potatoes, peeled and diced
3 leeks (white part only), chopped
¾ cup butter

1½ cups heavy cream or crème fraîche
Salt and pepper
½ cup (8 tablespoons) clarified butter
12 slices French bread
1 clove garlic, sliced in half

Soak beans in cold water for 6 hours. Drain and place in a large saucepan, then add water to twice the depth of the beans. Add potatoes and leeks, bring to a boil, reduce heat, and simmer, covered, for 1½ to 2 hours, or until beans are well done. Skim foam as it forms, and add water from time to time to keep up the level of the liquid. Press the bean mixture through a sieve or food mill, then replace in saucepan and stir in butter and cream. Reheat until bubbly, and season to taste with salt and pepper.

Melt the clarified butter in a skillet and sauté bread until brown and crusty on both sides. Rub slices with garlic. Serve soup topped with bread slices.

Potage de Gombos à l'Antillaise
(Antilles Okra Soup)

Okra is the fruit of a plant, which grows in the Antilles, recognizable by its yellow blossoms. This soup, also known as a gumbo, was a regular item on the ships of the Compagnie Générale Transatlantique. Jean Jacquière, head soup cook on the France, *and Emile Frentzel, who had the same job on the* Antilles, *both made a masterpiece out of it.*

Skill in preparing broths, cream soups, and consommés does not come to every cook. The saying is that good rôtisseurs are born, not made; and the same might be said of the potager—the soup cook.

2 pounds fresh okra (ends trimmed), peeled, and diced
8 ounces ground veal round or loin
4 ounces ground fresh ham
2 stalks celery, minced
1 large onion, minced

2 large, ripe tomatoes, peeled, seeded, and diced
8 cups Classic Beef Consommé
1 cup cooked rice
Dash of cayenne
Salt

Soak okra in cold water for 1 hour.

Mix veal, ham, celery, onion, tomatoes, and consommé in a saucepan. Simmer, uncovered, 10 minutes, then add drained okra and simmer, covered, for 20 minutes, or until okra is tender.

Stir rice into soup, reheat, and season to taste with cayenne and salt.

Potage à l'Arachide
(African Peanut or Ground Nut Soup)

½ cup (8 tablespoons) butter
⅓ cup flour
6 cups Clear Double Chicken Consommé
1½ cups chopped cooked chicken

½ cup finely chopped roasted unsalted peanuts
1½ cups heavy cream or crème fraîche
Salt
Dash of cayenne

In a saucepan, melt the butter and stir in flour. Blend over low heat for 5 minutes but do not brown. Stir in consommé and whisk until thickened. Add remaining ingredients, adding salt and cayenne to taste. Simmer 10 minutes. Serve.

Gazpacho

Andalusian gazpacho is an absolutely delicious thick soup which is highly refreshing in hot weather. Often during the dog days on a summer cruise we used to serve chilled cream soups and consommés, and this gazpacho was one of the favorites. What's more, it's also easy to make.

½ cup olive oil
1 onion, minced
1 clove garlic, minced
5 ripe tomatoes, peeled, seeded, drained, and diced
1 green pepper, diced
3 cucumbers, peeled and diced

Salt
⅓ cup red wine vinegar
Dash of cayenne
6 medium-sweet pickles, sliced
24 thin slices toasted French bread (baguette)

Heat the olive oil and sauté the onion and garlic until soft but not brown. Add the pulp of 3 of the tomatoes, the green pepper, and the cucumbers. Cover with water and add salt to taste. Simmer, uncovered, for 30 minutes.

Press soup through a sieve or food mill or whirl it in a blender. Stir in vinegar, salt, and cayenne to taste. Cool and then refrigerate until icy cold. Serve topped with remaining tomato pulp and pickle slices, and French bread.

Bouillabaisse du Vieux Port
(Bouillabaisse)

In France bouillabaisse is typically a southern dish. To make a truly fine, full-flavored bouillabaisse, you must use only shoal fish—poissons de roche—as well as all those ingredients so characteristic of Provençal cooking: fennel, olive oil, garlic, sweet red and green peppers, thyme, and bay leaf. Saffron is the only ingredient which is not native to the South of France, and the reason for its use in bouillabaisse may be that Marseilles has been an important spice port for centuries; consequently it was easy for cooks to obtain. At any rate, it is thanks to all these ingredients that culinary harmony reaches its peak in this fish soup, so dear to the hearts of Marius and Olive, the Laurel and Hardy of Marseilles folklore.

1 **sea bass, about 2 pounds**	1 **bay leaf**
1 **grouper, about 2 pounds**	1 **sprig fresh thyme**
1 **red mullet, about 2 pounds**	1 **teaspoon aniseed**
1 **red snapper, about 2 pounds**	1 **bulb fresh fennel**
1 **haddock filet, about 1 pound**	8 **large tomatoes, 4 quartered and**
1 **pollack filet, about 1 pound**	**4 peeled, seeded, and diced**
1 **small eel, about 2 pounds**	10 **cloves garlic, pressed**
1 **tablespoon (1 ounce) saffron**	1 **teaspoon sea salt**
1 **tablespoon salt**	2 **sweet green peppers, sliced**
1½ **teaspoons freshly ground pepper**	**in julienne strips**
1½ **cups olive oil, plus additional**	2 **sweet red peppers, sliced in**
for croûtons	**julienne strips**
5 **onions, quartered**	**Dash of cayenne**
3 **leeks (green and white parts**	⅔ **cup Pernod**
separate)	1 **long French bread (baguette),**
Few sprigs fresh parsley	**sliced on the bias**
2 **stalks celery, leaves intact**	**Sauce Rouille**
and sliced	

Scale, clean, wash, and filet the 7 fish. Dice the filets coarsely and place in a bowl with the saffron, salt, and freshly ground pepper. Mix well and set aside.

Cook the bones and heads of the fish in 1 cup of the olive oil over low heat. Add half of the onions, greens of 2 leeks, parsley, celery with leaves, bay leaf, thyme, aniseed, fennel, the quartered tomatoes, and half the garlic. Simmer in the oil for 20 minutes, then add water to cover. Season with sea salt and additional pepper. Bring to the boil, reduce heat and simmer, uncovered, for 1 hour. Strain this court-bouillon through a sieve or cheesecloth; this will serve as the stock for the bouillabaisse.

Sauté the remaining onions, garlic, whites of 3 leeks, and peppers in remaining olive oil until soft but not brown. Add remaining tomatoes, and let simmer for 15 minutes over low heat.

Add the reserved fish filets and pour in the court-bouillon. Bring to the boil and simmer over low heat for 15 minutes.

Correct the seasoning, which should be fairly spicy, and add salt and cayenne. Stir in Pernod and simmer additional 5 minutes.

Moisten slices of French bread with olive oil and toast under the broiler or in a hot oven. Rub with remaining garlic.

Serve soup in a tureen and float bread slices on surface. Top with Sauce Rouille.

Note: A cooked lobster or spiny lobster tail, cut into rings with shell intact, or a few crayfish tails can be added to the bouillabaisse if desired.

Sauce Rouille

Purée 3 cloves of garlic with 1 hot red pepper. In a bowl, moisten 1 cup of bread crumbs with 4 tablespoons of water. Combine crumbs with garlic purée and then drizzle in 5 tablespoons of olive oil, beating well. If the mixture is too thick, thin it with some of the soup broth.

Bourride Provençale
(Provençal Fish Soup with Sauce Aïoli)

Bouillabaisse	**Olive oil**
1½ cups Sauce Aïoli	**Garlic**
1 French bread (baguette), cut into thin slices	

Use fish filets (not the eel or fish heads) when preparing the Bouillabaisse and omit the saffron. When soup is hot but not boiling, stir in Sauce Aïoli. Brush bread slices with oil and toast on both sides under broiler. Rub with garlic. Serve soup topped with toast slices.

Pistou du Pays Provençal
(Provençal Vegetable Soup with Garlic, Basil, and Herbs)

½ cup white beans (navy or pea)	**½ teaspoon fresh basil**
¼ cup diced fresh ham fat	**2 quarts water**
2 medium carrots, chopped fine	**2 teaspoons salt**
2 small white turnips, minced	**¼ teaspoon pepper**
2 leeks (white part only), minced	**1 ounce (about ½ cup) vermicelli,**
1 celery heart, minced	**broken into 2-inch pieces**
1 potato, peeled and diced small	**½ cup grated Swiss or Gruyère**
2 cloves garlic, chopped	**cheese**
1 large tomato, peeled, seeded, and diced	

Soak beans for 1 hour, then drain.

Render ham fat in a skillet and then sauté vegetables and garlic until soft but not brown. Add tomato to vegetables, along with beans and basil. Add water, salt, and pepper. Bring to a boil, lower heat, and simmer, covered, for 1 hour.

Add vermicelli to soup and simmer another 10 minutes, or until tender. Adjust seasonings and serve topped with grated cheese.

Borscht Lithuanien au Fumet de Caneton
(Lithuanian Borscht with Duckling Consommé)

1 duckling about 3 to 4 pounds
½ cup water
Salt and pepper
6 cups Clear Double Chicken Consommé
2 leeks (white part only), cut in julienne strips
2 medium carrots, cut in julienne strips
2 stalks celery, peeled and cut in julienne strips
2 medium beets, cooked and peeled
Dash of cayenne
1 cup sour cream

Preheat the oven to 350 degrees, then roast duckling for 1 hour in a heatproof pan. Cool.

Pour fat off duck and discard. Add ½ cup water to pan, then place pan on top of stove and bring to a boil, loosening all brown particles. Set aside.

Bone the duckling legs and remove the breast. Cut the meat in large pieces. Set aside. Prepare the consommé adding the duckling giblets, pan juices, and carcass along with the chicken bones. Strain and discard solids.

Cook the leeks, carrots, and celery in boiling salted water, then drain. Cut beets into julienne strips. Put duckling meat and cooked vegetables (except beets) into consommé. Season to taste with salt and cayenne. Serve soup topped with sour cream and julienne beets.

Bisque de Homard Cleveland
(Lobster Bisque with Bourbon)

2 tablespoons vegetable oil
Heads and claws of 2 lobsters
1 carrot, chopped
1 stalk celery, chopped
1 onion, chopped
⅔ cup Cognac
2 cups dry white wine
4 cups Fish Stock
Bouquet garni (parsley, celery leaves)
2 tomatoes, quartered
1 tablespoon tomato paste
10 whole peppercorns
Few sprigs fresh parsley
1 bay leaf
1 sprig fresh thyme
Salt
½ cup (8 tablespoons) butter
¾ cup heavy cream or crème fraîche
½ cup cooked rice
⅔ cup bourbon
Dash of cayenne

Heat the oil in a skillet and brown the lobsters. When they are red, add the carrot, celery, and onion. Brown lightly and pour Cognac over lobster; set aflame. When flames die, stir in wine and stock. Add bouquet garni, tomatoes, tomato paste, peppercorns, parsley, bay leaf, and thyme. Salt lightly, allowing for seasoning of the fish stock. Bring to a boil, lower heat, and simmer, covered, for 1 hour.

Remove the lobster heads and claws and pound the shells until finely crushed, then add them to the soup. Simmer 5 minutes, then strain through several layers of cheesecloth, pressing firmly to remove all juices.

Stir in the butter, cream, rice, and bourbon. Simmer 10 minutes, then season to taste with salt and cayenne.

Note: Tails of lobster can be poached separately, and half of the diced meat added to the soup. This soup can also be made with shrimp or crayfish.

Eggs

4

Les Oeufs en Cocotte Bridaine
(Eggs en Cocotte with Beef Tongue)

12 thin slices cooked beef tongue	½ cup Sauce au Madère
12 eggs	Chopped fresh tarragon

Preheat oven to 400 degrees. Generously butter 12 small ½-cup ramekins. Place a slice of tongue in the bottom of each, cut to the size of the baking dish. Break an egg on top of the tongue.

Arrange the 12 ramekins in a large pan and pour in water to two-thirds their height. Cover the pan and cook in a hot oven for about 6 minutes. Remove from the oven and place ramekins on a round platter. Spoon some sauce on each and sprinkle with tarragon. Serve 2 to each person.

Les Oeufs en Cocotte Chanoinesse
(Eggs en Cocotte Chanoinesse)

36 medium shrimp, about 2 pounds	12 eggs
1 quart Court Bouillon	1 cup crème fraîche or heavy cream
2 tablespoons butter	2 truffles, sliced

Preheat oven to 400 degrees. Poach the shrimp in Court Bouillon for 5 minutes, then shell and devein. Sauté shrimp with butter for 1 minute in a small skillet.

Butter 12 ramekins, then spoon in shrimp and break an egg into each. Arrange the ramekins in a large pan and pour in water to two-thirds their height. Cover the pan and cook in a hot oven for about 6 minutes.

While eggs are baking, simmer cream until thickened. Lightly steam the sliced truffles and add them to the reduced cream.

Remove ramekins from oven and place on a round platter. Spoon some of the cream on each ramekin. Serve 2 to each person.

Les Oeufs au Plat Catherinette
(Baked Eggs with Tomato and Eggplant)

1 medium onion, chopped	1 large, very ripe tomato, peeled, seeded, and diced
¾ cup oil	Salt
1 clove garlic, chopped	Pinch of cayenne
1 medium eggplant, peeled and diced	¼ cup (4 tablespoons) butter
	12 eggs

Sauté the onion in 1 tablespoon of the oil until translucent, adding the garlic after the onion has cooked for awhile.

Sauté eggplant in remaining oil, then add eggplant and tomato pulp to the pan with the onion and garlic. Salt lightly and add cayenne. Bring to a boil, reduce heat, and simmer gently until all the juice from the tomato has evaporated. Stir the ingredients well with a wooden spatula.

Preheat oven to 350 degrees. Butter 6 individual casseroles and break 2 eggs into each. Melt butter and spoon over eggs. Bake in a moderate oven to taste (well done, medium, or loose). Spoon some tomato–eggplant mixture on each side of the eggs. Serve immediately.

Les Oeufs au Plat Ermenonville
(Baked Eggs with Smoked Ham and Mushrooms)

6 thin slices smoked ham
¼ cup (4 tablespoons) butter
12 eggs

12 fresh mushrooms, peeled, trimmed, and minced

Preheat oven to 350 degrees. Sauté the ham briefly in 1 tablespoon of butter, then transfer to 6 well-buttered individual casseroles. Break 2 eggs into each and bake in a moderate oven for 12 to 15 minutes or until whites are firm.

Meanwhile, sauté mushrooms in remaining butter until golden. When eggs are done, spoon mushrooms onto eggs in each dish and serve.

Les Oeufs Farcis au Plat Amélie
(Baked Eggs with Morels)

3 shallots, minced
1 tablespoon oil
1 large or 2 medium carrots, peeled and finely chopped
2 stalks celery, peeled and finely chopped
12 eggs

1 pound morels or button mushrooms, trimmed
¼ cup (4 tablespoons) butter
1½ cups crème fraîche or heavy cream
Salt and pepper

Preheat oven to 350 degrees. Sauté shallots in oil over low heat. Put carrots and celery in a small saucepan and barely cover with water. Bring to a boil, skimming carefully, then reduce heat and simmer until the water has evaporated.

Grease 6 small ¾-cup ramekins and spoon sautéed shallots and the cooked vegetables into bottoms. Break 2 eggs over the vegetables in each dish and bake in a moderate oven for 15 to 20 minutes or until whites are firm and yolks are soft.

Meanwhile, sauté morels in butter until wilted. Add cream and simmer until thickened. Season with salt and pepper. When eggs are ready, spoon sauce over.

Les Oeufs Pochés Belle Otéro
(Poached Eggs with Potatoes and Chicken)

6 large Idaho potatoes
3 egg yolks plus 12 whole eggs
2 quarts water
1 tablespoon vinegar
6 fresh mushrooms, peeled, trimmed, and diced
2 tablespoons butter, heated until lightly brown
Juice of 1 lemon

Salt
1 cup crème fraîche or heavy cream
1 cup diced cooked chicken breast
2 tablespoons chopped truffles
Pinch of cayenne
½ cup grated Gruyère cheese

Bake the potatoes, remove the skins, and force the pulp through a sieve or food mill (fine gauge) into a bowl. Beat the egg yolks into the potato purée and keep the mixture warm.

Poach the whole eggs by heating water and vinegar until simmering. Break each egg separately into a bowl, being careful not to break the yolk, and slip into the simmering water. Let the eggs poach for 3 minutes, then take them out carefully with a slotted spoon and plunge into cold water to stop the cooking. Trim edges.

Brown the mushrooms in butter, then sprinkle with lemon juice to keep them from darkening; salt lightly.

Preheat oven to 450 degrees or heat broiler. Simmer crème fraîche until thickened, then add chicken, mushrooms, and truffles. Correct seasoning with cayenne and mix well.

Set 2 poached eggs each on heatproof plates. Using a pastry bag with a large fluted tip, decorate the dish with the potato-and-egg mixture, making rosettes around the poached eggs. Cover each egg with a spoonful of chicken mixture, then sprinkle with the cheese. Brown lightly under the broiler or in a hot oven for 5 to 6 minutes. Serve on a large, round platter covered with a paper doily.

Les Oeufs Frits Ali-Bab
(Fried Eggs Ali-Bab)

12 slices bread	1 cup Sauce Nantua
½ cup (8 tablespoons) clarified butter	1 lobster tail or ⅓ pound shrimp, cooked and diced
Oil as needed	2 large truffles, sliced
12 eggs	

Cut the bread into 12 thin slices and trim so as to form ovals. Brown lightly in butter.

Heat oil in a skillet to a depth of ¼ inch and add an egg. Using 2 spatulas or wooden spoons, keep egg from spreading to preserve an oval shape. Cook until desired (hard, medium, or loose), then remove and keep warm; repeat for remaining eggs.

Place slices of toast on a platter, lay an egg on each. Mix Sauce Nantua with lobster or shrimp and spoon over eggs. Decorate each egg with a slice of truffle.

Les Oeufs Frits Hortillone
(Fried Eggs with Mixed Vegetables)

12 eggs	½ pound cooked green beans, cut into 1-inch pieces
¾ cup corn oil	1 cup shelled fresh peas
2 medium carrots, diced and cooked	1 cup crème fraîche or heavy cream, heated
2 turnips, diced and cooked	Salt

Fry eggs, 2 at a time, in oil ¼ inch deep in a small skillet. Flip them over like a pancake to brown on both sides. Meanwhile, mix vegetables and crème fraîche and simmer until thickened.

Put eggs on 6 hot plates, together with a portion of vegetables mixed with cream. Season to taste with salt and serve.

Les Oeufs Frits Camus
(Fried Eggs with Brains and Eggplant)

2 calf's brains
Salt
Vinegar
1 onion, studded with 4 whole cloves
Bouquet garni (fresh parsley, bay leaf, thyme)
1 large eggplant, cut into ½-inch-thick slices

Oil
Flour for dusting
¼ cup (4 tablespoons) butter, heated until brown
1½ cups Sauce au Madère
¼ cup finely chopped, peeled, and seeded tomato
12 eggs

Soak calf's brains in cold water for 2 hours. Wash carefully and remove filaments of blood and membranes from outside. Poach in water containing a little salt, a small amount of vinegar, onion, and bouquet garni. Bring to boil, reduce heat, and simmer for 10 minutes. Let them cool in the cooking liquid and, when cold, drain on a kitchen towel. Cut each into 6 slices.

Cut 12 small oval slices of eggplant using cookie cutter and brown them in oil, ¼ inch deep. Dust the brains with flour and brown in a skillet with butter. Mix Sauce au Madère with tomato. Fry eggs in a skillet with a little oil.

Put 2 slices of eggplant on each plate and set an egg on each. Arrange 2 slices of brains on the side and spoon the sauce over eggs. (This dish can also be served without sauce.)

Les Oeufs Brouillés Offenbach
(Scrambled Eggs with Shrimp, Anchovies, and Tuna)

12 eggs
Salt and pepper
½ cup (8 tablespoons) butter

Garnish:

6 cooked shrimp, shelled, deveined, and chopped
2 tablespoons butter
6 anchovy filets, packed in oil, diced

1 can (6 ½ ounces) tuna, packed in oil, drained and crumbled
6 tablespoons Sauce Tomate

Break the eggs in a mixing bowl, beat lightly, and season to taste with salt and pepper. Melt butter in a double boiler and pour in the eggs. Cook over simmering water, stirring constantly with a wooden spoon until the eggs have reached the consistency you prefer (loose, firm, well done). Put the equivalent of 2 eggs into each of 6 1-cup ramekins.

Briefly sauté shrimp in butter. Add the anchovy filets and tuna and heat gently while stirring. Spoon some of the mixture over each of the eggs, then cover with Sauce Tomate.

Note: The eggs can also be scrambled over low heat.

Omelette Brayaude
(Omelet with Smoked Pork, Potato, and Cheese)

12 eggs
2 teaspoons salt
3 mill-turns freshly ground
  white pepper
4 ounces smoked or salt pork,
  in 1 piece

2 medium potatoes, cooked, peeled,
  and sliced thinly
1 cup grated Gruyère cheese
1 cup crème fraîche or heavy
  cream

Break the eggs into a bowl, season with salt and pepper, and beat briskly with fork or whisk.

Skin pork and cut into julienne strips. Divide between 2 large skillets, and fry until crisp. Add potatoes and brown over low heat. Raise heat and add half the beaten eggs to each skillet. Cook without stirring until brown on the bottom and moist on top.

Place a plate over omelet pan and invert. Slide omelet from plate, uncooked side down, back into skillet. Lightly brown the other side and remove, flat, to a round heatproof plate. Repeat with second omelet.

Preheat oven to 450 degrees or heat broiler. Sprinkle cheese over the omelets and broil until golden or bake in very hot oven for 5 or 6 minutes.

Meanwhile, simmer cream until thickened. Spoon cream around the omelets and serve.

Omelette Piperade
(Pepper and Mushroom Omelet)

2 green or red sweet peppers
4 fresh mushrooms
2 large, ripe tomatoes
12 eggs
2 teaspoons salt

4 mill-turns freshly ground
  pepper
½ cup olive oil
Few sprigs of fresh parsley,
  chopped

Cut peppers and mushrooms into julienne strips. Peel, seed, and dice the tomatoes. Break eggs into a bowl and beat briskly with a fork or whisk. Season with salt and freshly ground pepper.

Sauté the pepper, then the mushrooms, in 2 tablespoons of olive oil; when they begin to brown, add the tomato pulp and parsley. Salt lightly and simmer over low heat for about 15 minutes, or until the juice of the tomato has evaporated. Let cool.

Add tomato mixture to the beaten eggs, blending all ingredients well. Heat remaining olive oil in 2 large skillets. When the oil is quite hot, add half the egg mixture to each pan. Cook without stirring until eggs are brown on bottom and moist on top. Roll up each omelet into a large cigarlike cylinder and transfer to a long platter. If the omelet has not rolled well, push it into shape using a napkin.

Omelette des Moissonneurs
(Harvesters' Salt Pork Omelet)

4 ounces salt pork
2 large potatoes, cooked but
   still firm
¼ cup olive oil
12 eggs

Salt
3 mill-turns freshly ground
   white pepper
1 tablespoon finely chopped fresh
   parsley

Cut small lardons from the salt pork and poach in boiling water to cover for 5 minutes. Drain.

Peel and dice the potatoes, then sauté with oil in 2 skillets. Add the pork and cook until browned.

Beat eggs with salt, pepper, and parsley. Cook as for Omelet with Smoked Pork, Potato, and Cheese. Serve on round platters.

Omelette à la Normande
(Normandy Omelet)

12 eggs
3 tablespoons confectioner's
   sugar
2 apples, peeled, cored, and
   sliced

⅓ cup superfine sugar
2 tablespoons water
¼ cup (4 tablespoons) butter
⅔ cup Calvados, warmed

Break the eggs into a bowl and beat with fork or whisk, seasoning with half the confectioner's sugar.

Cook the apple slices briefly in a saucepan with 2 tablespoons of superfine sugar and water.

Prepare 2 omelets in 2 large skillets, using butter and eggs. Divide apples and place on top of omelets. Roll into a cigarlike cylinder and transfer to a long platter. Sprinkle with the remaining confectioner's sugar and baste with Calvados. Light the liqueur and serve flambé.

Les Oeufs Mollets Grisélidis
(Boiled Eggs with Cauliflower, Peas, and Carrots)

1 small cauliflower
1 pound shelled fresh peas
¼ cup (4 tablespoons) butter
   Sugar
12 eggs
2½ cups crème fraîche or heavy
   cream

Salt
Pinch of cayenne
3 carrots, peeled and cut into
   olive-shaped pieces
Pinch of paprika

Simmer cauliflower for about 20 minutes in lightly salted water. Drain, let cool, and separate the flowerets with a kitchen knife.

Boil the peas for 15 minutes in salted water, using an uncovered saucepan. Drain, then mix with half the butter. Sweeten with a pinch of sugar.

Simmer eggs for 6 minutes, then plunge into cold water to stop cooking. Peel and keep the eggs warm in lightly salted warm (tepid) water at the side of the heat source.

Simmer 1 cup of the crème fraîche in a small saucepan until thickened. Add the flowerets and simmer over low heat until hot. Salt lightly and add the barest pinch of cayenne. Simmer remaining crème fraîche until thickened.

Meanwhile, cover carrots with water in a saucepan, salt lightly, and add remaining butter. Bring to a boil, reduce heat, and simmer until the water has evaporated; let the carrots glaze without browning.

Line 6 shallow 1-cup casseroles with the creamed cauliflower; set 2 eggs on each. Season thickened crème fraîche with salt and paprika, then spoon over eggs. Serve peas and carrots on either side of the eggs.

Les Oeufs Farcis Fadette

(Stuffed Eggs with Chicken and Mushrooms)

12 eggs	Salt
2 chicken wings, cooked and boned	Juice of ½ lemon
6 large, fresh mushrooms, trimmed and chopped	¾ cup crème fraîche or heavy cream
2 tablespoons butter, heated until golden	Pinch of cayenne
	Pinch of grated nutmeg
	Sauce Mornay

Simmer the eggs for 15 minutes in water, then cool in cold water. Peel, cut in half lengthwise, and remove yolks; reserve egg whites.

Force the yolks through a sieve into a bowl. Mince chicken. Sauté mushrooms in butter, then salt lightly and sprinkle with lemon juice; simmer until liquid is absorbed. Boil cream until thickened to consistency of thick sour cream.

Using a wooden spatula, fold the sieved yolks, chicken, and mushrooms into the cream. Season with salt, cayenne, and nutmeg.

Preheat oven to 450 degrees or heat broiler. Set the egg whites on a well-buttered ovenproof platter or on individual egg plates. Using a pastry bag with a round tip, stuff the egg whites with egg-yolk mixture. Cover each egg half with a little Sauce Mornay. Place under the broiler and broil until golden or bake in a hot oven for 5 to 6 minutes.

Les Oeufs Farcis Oudinot

(Stuffed Eggs Oudinot)

12 eggs	2 tablespoons finely chopped truffles
6 large, fresh mushrooms, about 4 ounces	2 cups crème fraîche or heavy cream
¼ cup (4 tablespoons) butter	½ cup finely grated Gruyère cheese
Salt and pepper	
Juice of ½ lemon	

Simmer the eggs for 15 minutes in water to cover and cool them in cold water. Shell and cut in half lengthwise. Remove the yolks and force through a fine sieve; reserve egg whites.

Prepare a mushroom duxelles by peeling, trimming, and chopping the mushrooms. Sauté in butter, salt, and pepper, then sprinkle with lemon juice to keep them from discoloring. Cook until liquid is absorbed and cool.

Mix the duxelles with the sieved yolks and the truffles. Using a pastry bag with fluted tube, force the stuffing into the egg whites.

Preheat oven to 450 degrees or heat broiler. Simmer crème fraîche until thickened. Place the stuffed eggs on 6 heatproof plates and cover with cream, sprinkle with cheese, and broil until golden or bake in a hot oven for 5 to 6 minutes.

Les Oeufs Farcis Nissarde
(Eggs Nissarde)

12 eggs
2 cups crème fraîche or heavy cream
6 large, fresh mushrooms, trimmed and minced
3 tablespoons butter
Salt
Juice of ½ lemon
1 onion, minced

1 large tomato, peeled, seeded, and diced
Freshly ground pepper
1 tablespoon minced fresh chives
1 tablespoon chopped fresh parsley
1 large eggplant
Flour for dusting
¾ cup olive oil
1 cup grated Gruyère cheese

Hard cook the eggs 10 minutes. Cool thoroughly in cold water, peel, and cut in half lengthwise; remove yolks. Set the whites on a platter and sieve the yolks. Set aside.

Simmer crème fraîche until you have 1½ cups. Place mushrooms in a saucepan with 2 tablespoons butter, salt, and lemon juice. Bring to the boil, stirring with a wooden spatula. When the liquid has completely evaporated, remove from heat and stir in ½ cup of the cream.

Sauté onion in remaining butter until translucent. Add tomato and season lightly with salt and pepper. Cook over low heat until the liquid has evaporated and mixture is very thick. Remove from heat and sprinkle with chives and parsley, mixing well.

Peel and cut the eggplant into ¾-inch slices. Using a cookie cutter, cut out 12 2-inch rounds of eggplant. Flour rounds and brown in a skillet with hot olive oil.

Preheat oven to 450 degrees. Mix the reserved yolks, mushrooms, and onion–tomato mixture in a bowl. Using a pastry bag with a round tip, stuff the egg whites with this mixture. Put 2 eggplant rounds in each of 6 shallow casseroles and set 2 stuffed eggs on top. Cover the eggs with remaining cream, sprinkle with cheese, and broil gently until golden or bake in a hot oven for 5 to 6 minutes; serve hot.

Les Oeufs au Gratin Antonin Carême
(Eggs au Gratin Antonin Carême)

12 eggs	Salt
6 fresh mushrooms, peeled, trimmed, and minced	4 cups Sauce Suprême
2 tablespoons butter	1 cup grated Gruyère cheese

Preheat oven to 450 degrees or heat broiler.

Hard cook the eggs for 10 minutes. Cool in cold water, peel, and, using a wire egg-cutter, cut them into equal slices.

Cook mushrooms in butter without browning, salt lightly, and add 3 cups Sauce Suprême; mix well.

Divide 1 cup of the Sauce Suprême into 6 ramekins and arrange the egg slices in each. Cover the slices with the sauce, sprinkle on the cheese, and place under the broiler until brown or bake in a hot oven for 5 to 6 minutes.

Les Oeufs Mollets Aubergiste
(Boiled-Egg Tarts with Ham and Mushrooms)

2 onions, minced	6 3-inch tart shells (Tart Pastry), prebaked
½ cup (8 tablespoons) butter	
6 fresh mushrooms, minced	6 thin slices Bayonne or Smithfield ham
2 tablespoons Sauce Tomate	
12 eggs	1 tablespoon finely chopped fresh parsley

Sauté onions gently in half the butter until translucent but not browned. Add mushrooms; when cooked and liquid has evaporated, stir in Sauce Tomate.

Simmer eggs in water to cover for 7 minutes, then shell carefully. Set 2 eggs into each tartlet and top with mushroom mixture.

Sauté ham lightly in remaining butter, and place 1 slice on each portion. Pour the butter in which the ham has been heated over the tartlets and sprinkle with parsley.

Croquignolles Savoyardes
(Savoy Cheese Croquettes)

4 cups Sauce Béchamel	Salt
2 cups diced Gruyère cheese	Pinch of cayenne
6 egg yolks plus 4 eggs, well beaten	1 cup sifted all-purpose flour
	2 cups dry bread crumbs
8 ounces cooked fresh ham, diced	Oil for deep-frying, heated to 375°
	6 sprigs fresh parsley

Heat Bèchamel and add cheese, egg yolks, and ham. Season with salt and cayenne. Pour the mixture into a well-buttered bowl and let it cool.

When the egg mixture is cold, and using well-floured hands, roll the mixture into 1-inch balls.

Place beaten eggs in a bowl and salt lightly. Roll the croquettes in flour, dip into egg, and roll in bread crumbs. Set croquettes in 2 large deep-drying baskets and fry in 2 batches until golden brown. Drain on absorbent paper, then garnish with parsley; serve on a round platter with a napkin folded into an oval shape.

Soufflé au Parmesan
(Parmesan Cheese Soufflé)

5 tablespoons butter
½ cup flour
2 cups milk, heated until steaming
1 teaspoon salt
Pinch of grated nutmeg

Pinch of cayenne
10 eggs, separated
1½ cups grated Parmesan cheese, plus thin slices of Parmesan, cut into ovals

Melt butter in a saucepan. Stir in flour and blend with a whisk. Cook roux over low heat for a few minutes, without allowing to brown. Still whisking, add milk. Bring to a boil and cook over low heat until very thick. Season with salt, nutmeg, and cayenne. Remove from heat.

Preheat oven to 425 degrees. Beat the yolks into the seasoned sauce, whisking vigorously. Bring almost to a boil, then remove from heat, pour into a bowl, and let cool.

Beat the egg whites until stiff. Blend one-quarter of them into the batter, using a rubber spatula. This should be done gently, lifting the batter so as not to break the stiffness of the whites. Fold in remaining egg whites and the grated Parmesan, still being careful to handle the mixture gently.

Butter well the sides of a 1½-quart soufflé dish. Make a foil collar 2 inches high around edge of dish and tie on with string. Pour in the soufflé batter, filling almost to the brim. Smooth the surface with a spatula, then decorate with Parmesan slices arranged like the points of the compass. Bake in a hot oven for about 20 minutes, with the dish on a rack. The soufflé should rise to about double its original height. To avoid excessive browning, put a disk of aluminum foil on the top.

All soufflés should be eaten immediately after removing from the oven. This timing is for a French-type soufflé which is crusty outside, creamy inside. For an American-style soufflé, bake another 15 minutes, or until a knife inserted into center comes out clean. Remove collar and serve.

Variations

Spinach Soufflé

Prepare a basic soufflé batter as in the preceding recipe, but replace the Parmesan cheese with 1 cup finely chopped and drained cooked spinach.

Artichoke Soufflé

Prepare a basic soufflé batter. Cook 6 artichoke bottoms until tender, purée, and then cook over low heat until dry and thick. Cool. Use this purée in place of the Parmesan cheese.

Mushroom Soufflé

Prepare a basic soufflé batter. Cook 1 pound minced mushrooms in 2 table-spoons butter and then cook over low heat until dry. Cool. Use this purée in place of Parmesan cheese.

Ham Soufflé

Prepare a basic soufflé batter, salting rather more lightly than normally to compensate for the saltiness of the ham. Fold 1 cup minced boiled ham into the batter before baking the soufflé. Omit Parmesan cheese.

Quiche du Pays Lorrain
(Quiche Lorraine)

8 ounces Puff Pastry	3 cups crème fraîche or heavy
5 ounces bacon, sliced	cream
2 cups grated Swiss	Salt
or Gruyère cheese	Pinch of grated nutmeg
3 egg yolks plus 1 whole egg	Pinch of cayenne

Preheat oven to 350 degrees. Use the pastry to line the bottom and 1 inch up the edge of a 9-inch springform pan. Prick bottom heavily with a fork.

Cook the bacon strips until just crisp. Break into large pieces and place in shell. Sprinkle with cheese, then bake the crust in a moderate oven for 5 minutes. Remove from oven.

Beat together the yolks, whole egg, and cream. Salt lightly, taking into account the saltiness of the bacon and the cheese, and season with the nutmeg and cayenne. Pour into shell and bake in moderate oven for about 30 to 35 minutes or until puffed and brown. Remove sides of pan.

Serve the quiche piping hot on a round platter covered with a napkin folded into an oval shape.

Poultry

5

CHICKEN

Poularde Bressane Poêlée au Champagne
(Roast Chicken with Champagne)

1 small roasting chicken, about 4½ pounds	½ cup crème fraîche or heavy cream
Salt and freshly ground pepper	¼ cup Sauce Suprême
1 strip pork fat or bacon, blanched	2 large tomatoes, peeled, seeded, and diced
½ cup (8 tablespoons) butter	2 pounds fresh spinach, trimmed
1 carrot, chopped finely	Pinch of freshly ground nutmeg
1 onion, chopped finely	2 teaspoons Sauce Demi-Glace
1 stalk celery, chopped finely	Few drops of Madeira wine
⅔ cup Cognac	4 slices smoked beef tongue, minced
1¾ cups brut Champagne	3 cups Rice Pilaf
	6 slices truffle

Preheat the oven to 400 degrees.

Season chicken inside and out with salt and pepper. Truss chicken and cover breast with a strip of pork fat; tie with a string.

Melt 1 tablespoon butter in a skillet and sauté carrot, onion, and celery until wilted. Line the bottom of a roasting pan with the vegetables and set in the chicken. Cover the pan and roast chicken in a hot oven for about 1 hour, basting very often with pan juices and making sure that chicken does not overbrown.

Remove chicken to a heatproof platter. Flame with Cognac, then let it rest in a warm oven. Pour off excess fat from the baking pan and place on top of stove. Add Champagne, crème fraîche, and Sauce Suprême. Bring to a boil, scraping up brown particles, then simmer for 20 minutes, skimming whenever a film forms on the surface. Strain this sauce through a sieve and replace in baking pan. Keep warm over low heat.

Melt 1 tablespoon of butter in a skillet and sauté tomatoes until the juice from the fruit has evaporated. Add this tomato sauce to the baking pan, stirring gently with a spoon. Whisk in ¼ cup of the butter, cut into small pieces. The sauce must be very smooth and velvety.

Cook the spinach and press out the liquid with your hands. Chop coarsely. Season with salt and a little nutmeg. Add the chopped spinach to the remaining butter and cook over low heat until dry.

Heat the Sauce Demi-Glace and Madeira in a saucepan and add tongue. Cook for a few minutes until thickened.

Butter 6 small baba molds well and fill with the spinach. Using the handle of a wooden spoon, make a small hole in each portion of spinach and fill with the tongue mixture. Set the molds in a flat container filled with hot water to keep them warm.

Pack the Rice Pilaf into another 6 buttered baba molds.

Place the chicken on a long platter and pour over the sauce in the baking pan. Unmold the spinach and rice molds and place them around the edge of the platter, garnishing each rice mold with a thin truffle slice.

Poularde du Louragais Farci Rôti Périgourdine
(Roast Chicken Stuffed with Truffles)

1 small roasting chicken,
  about 4½ pounds
Salt
Freshly ground white pepper
Few drops of Cognac
1 pound meaty bacon, minced
4 ounces fresh *foie gras*,
  coarsely diced
4 ounces truffles (4 slices,
  remainder diced)
1 strip pork fat or bacon,
  blanched

1 cup melted butter
½ cup dry white wine
2½ pounds new potatoes,
  peeled and cooked
24 cèpes, trimmed and
  quartered
1 shallot, chopped
2 tablespoons finely chopped
  fresh parsley
2 cups Sauce Périgueux

Preheat the oven to 350 degrees. Slit the chicken along breastbone, remove breastbone and ribs, and season cavity with salt, pepper, and Cognac. Fill cavity through the breast opening with a mixture of minced bacon, *foie gras,* diced truffles, a pinch of salt, and 3 mill-turns pepper. Place 2 truffle slices under the skin on each side of the breast. Sew opening closed, then place 2 truffle slices under skin on each thigh and truss chicken. Place strip of pork fat over breast skin and secure with a string.

Season chicken with salt and freshly ground pepper, brush it with ¼ cup of melted butter, and place in a heatproof roasting pan; roast in a moderate oven for about 1½ hours. Baste frequently, and let chicken rest in the oven for several minutes after cooking.

Place chicken on a platter and keep warm; remove the trussings. Pour off excess fat in the roasting pan. Add wine to pan, place pan on top of stove, and cook, scraping up brown particles. Strain and keep sauce warm.

Brown new potatoes in ¼ cup of butter and then sauté cèpes in remaining butter along with shallot. Garnish chicken with potatoes and cèpes, and sprinkle with parsley. Coat the chicken with the strained pan juices and serve with Sauce Périgueux.

Coquelet de Basse-Cour Farci et Rôti à l'Anglaise
(Stuffed and Roasted Chicken, English Style)

6 small, young chickens or game hens, fresh or frozen Salt Freshly ground white pepper 4 shallots, minced ⅔ cup butter 10 chicken livers, diced 2 tablespoons oil	2 cups soft, fine bread crumbs Several sprigs fresh parsley, chopped 6 sheets caul or thinly sliced fresh pork fat 1 cup Clear Double Chicken Consommé 12 thin slices bacon, cooked until crisp

Thaw chickens if frozen. Preheat the oven to 375 degrees. Remove giblets and sprinkle each inside and out with salt and pepper.

Sauté shallots in 2 tablespoons of butter until soft but not brown. Sauté livers lightly in very hot oil; keep livers rare. Season livers with salt, drain, then mix with bread crumbs, shallots, and parsley. Season with salt and a few turns of white pepper. Stuff the chickens with the liver mixture. Sew openings closed and truss solidly; wrap each in a sheet of basting fat and tie with a string.

Place chickens in heatproof dish and roast in a hot oven for about 45 minutes, turning and basting frequently. When the chickens are cooked, remove from dish and let rest for several minutes in a warm place. Add consommé to the dish and place on top of stove. Bring to a boil, scraping up all brown particles. Strain liquid through a sieve and keep hot.

Remove the basting fat and trussing cord from birds and arrange them in a cocotte and cross 2 strips of bacon on each. Spoon sauce over chickens. Melt remaining butter until golden brown, then spoon over birds. Serve the cocotte on a long platter covered with a napkin folded in an oval shape.

Poussin de Métairie Farci Rôti Virginie
(Roasted Stuffed Chicken with Virginia Smoked Ham)

6 small, young chickens or game hens, fresh or frozen Salt Freshly ground white pepper ⅔ cup corn oil or French olive oil 6 shallots, minced ¾ cup butter 2 cups fine dry bread crumbs	2 tablespoons finely chopped fresh parsley 6 thin slices fresh pork fat or caul 3 cups Wild Rice Pilaf 1 cup dry white wine 1 cup crème fraîche or heavy cream 12 thin slices Virginia ham

Thaw chickens, if frozen. Preheat oven to 375 degrees. Sprinkle each inside and out with salt and pepper. Remove the livers and chop, then sauté in 2 tablespoons of oil.

Sauté the shallots lightly in a mixture of remaining oil and ½ cup of butter. Add the bread crumbs in sufficient quantity to ensure that the oil and butter are fully absorbed by the crumbs. Blend in the parsley and the sautéed livers.

Season the stuffing well with salt and pepper, then use the mixture to stuff chickens. Sew or skewer openings, and truss firmly. Wrap each in a very thin sheet of fat and secure with a string. Season the birds with salt and roast in a hot oven for about 40 minutes, basting frequently. When done, remove from the oven and let rest several minutes in a warm place.

Set the Pilaf in a large cocotte or other appropriate dish. Place the chickens on the rice and set aside.

Pour wine into roasting pan and place pan on top of stove. Bring to a boil, scraping up all brown particles. Stir in crème fraîche and simmer until thickened. Strain sauce through a sieve, then pour onto the chickens. Quickly brown the ham in the remaining butter, then place 2 slices over each bird.

Poularde Nantaise Farcie Pochée Crébillon
(Braised Chicken Crébillon)

2 small chickens, about	4½ pounds carrots, carved
2 pounds each	into ovals like pigeon's eggs
Salt and freshly ground pepper	1 onion, studded with 4
3½ pounds fresh mushrooms	whole cloves
3 quarts + ½ cup water	2 to 3 leeks (green part only)
2 cups butter	Few sprigs of fresh parsley
Juice of ½ lemon	2 stalks celery, sliced
6 egg yolks, beaten	2 pounds fresh asparagus
	4 cups Rice Pilaf

Wash and dry chickens. Sprinkle each inside and out with salt and pepper. Reserve giblets and necks.

Peel, trim, and wash the mushrooms, then braise them in a saucepan with ½ cup water, ½ teaspoon salt, ½ cup butter, and lemon juice to keep them from discoloring. Cook, uncovered, until all liquid has evaporated. Cool mushrooms and then mince. Put mushrooms in a bowl and stir in egg yolks; season to taste with salt.

Stuff the chickens with the mushroom mixture, then sew openings closed. Truss well with string and wrap each separately in cheesecloth tied at the ends. Put chickens into a large, heavy-bottomed pot and add remaining water and a pinch of salt. Wrap these in another cheesecloth and add along with the reserved giblets and necks, onion, leeks, parsley, and celery. Bring to a boil, reduce heat, and simmer lightly for about 30 minutes, skimming foam as needed.

Trim asparagus and braise in ⅓ cup of butter until tender but still firm. Spread Rice Pilaf on a long serving platter. Drain the chickens and remove the cheesecloth. Pour some braising liquid over rice, then surround with the carrots and asparagus. Melt remaining butter and serve in a sauceboat. The remaining broth can be served in bowls or reserved for future soups.

Coq au Vin Sauté à l'Auxerroise
(Chicken in Red Wine with Onions, Bacon, and Mushrooms)

Coq au Vin, generally served at dinner, was always a favorite dish with the passengers. At about 10 a.m., I would go to the great salon with the principal saucier to give a demonstration of this regional specialty—but with a certain apprehension. We would all mount the orchestra stand, our only equipment a chopping board, two small saucepans, and an alcohol burner used for doing the Crêpes Suzette at the table. There was always a big crowd, and we were warmly welcomed.

We would cut up the chicken and brown the pieces. The high point of the demonstration was flaming the marc de Bourgogne. *A huge blue flame would mount up, and the crowd would break into applause. Many would accept the invitation to taste the sauce with their fingers, as I recommended, and there would soon be a long line in front of our little table. We were the stars, and had to autograph a good number of menus at the end of the show!*

1 **large broiler-fryer, about** **4½ pounds** **Salt and freshly ground white** **pepper**	*Marinade:*
½ **cup (8 tablespoons) butter**	1 **bottle (⅘ quart) dry red wine**
2 **cups water**	1 **large onion, chopped**
⅔ **cup brandy or** *marc de* **Bourgogne**	1 **carrot, chopped**
2 **large onions, minced**	1 **stalk celery, chopped**
8 **ounces salt pork or bacon,** **blanched and cut into cubes**	1 **sprig thyme**
12 **small white onions**	1 **bay leaf**
1 **tablespoon confectioner's sugar**	**Few sprigs of fresh parsley,** **chopped**
10 **fresh mushrooms, quartered** **Beurre Manié (optional)**	1 **clove garlic, crushed**

Cut the chicken into drumsticks, thighs, and breasts; cut breast in half lengthwise. Sprinkle chicken with salt and pepper. Combine the ingredients for marinade, and marinate the chicken pieces for 12 hours.

Cut the wings, neck, and gizzards into small pieces. Sauté lightly in 1 tablespoon of butter. Add water, salt lightly, and bring to a boil. Lower the heat and then simmer for 30 minutes. Strain this broth and reserve.

Preheat the oven to 350 degrees. When ready, drain chicken and strain and reserve marinade. Dry the pieces with paper towels, then cook lightly in ¼ cup of butter until golden brown. Place chicken in a baking pan and, while the chicken is still hot, flame it with brandy.

Sauté onions lightly in 2 tablespoons of butter in the same pan in which you browned the chicken pieces. When the onions are translucent but not browned, add marinade, bring to a boil, and simmer until almost dry. Purée the mixture in a food mill or food processor, and add the reserved broth.

Season chicken and pour in sauce. Cover chicken and bake in a moderate oven for 30 minutes. Meanwhile, fry salt pork cubes until crisp. Add white onions and sugar and sauté lightly. Sauté mushrooms in remaining butter.

After cooking chicken, skim the fat from the sauce. Remove the chicken and arrange pieces in a small cocotte or other appropriate dish. Bind the sauce lightly with a Beurre Manié if necessary; the important thing is that the sauce should not be too thin. Cover the pieces of chicken with the sauce and add the bacon, small onions, and mushrooms.

Note: This is usually served with thin noodles (taglierini), cooked *al dente* and tossed in additional butter. If desired, sprinkle dry bread crumbs, which have been lightly browned in butter, over chicken.

Poulet en Fricassée Vallée d'Auge
(Chicken Fricassée with Calvados)

1 broiler-fryer, about 3½ pounds	Pinch of sugar
1 teaspoon salt	4 ounces fresh green beans,
¼ teaspoon white pepper	cut into 1-inch pieces
½ cup (8 tablespoons) butter	½ cup fresh peas
½ cup Calvados, warmed	12 small white onions, peeled
6 medium carrots,	4 cups crème fraîche or
peeled and quartered	heavy cream
4 white turnips, peeled	2 mill-turns freshly ground
and quartered	black pepper
	Minced fresh chervil

Remove the legs from chicken and cut in half at the joint; remove the breast and cut in half lengthwise. Season with salt and pepper, then sauté the pieces in a large skillet briefly—without browning—in ¼ cup butter. Flame with Calvados.

Using a sharp knife, round off the corners of the carrot and turnip pieces. Put into separate saucepans, cover each with water, salt lightly, and add a pinch of sugar and the remaining butter. Bring to the boil and cook without lowering heat until the liquid is completely evaporated. Remove from heat.

Bring some well-salted water to the boil and cook green beans for 10 minutes. Add peas and cook another 5 minutes. Drain and reserve. Poach onions in lightly salted water for 5 minutes.

Add the carrots, turnips, beans, peas, and onions to the pan with the chicken. Add the crème fraîche, season to taste with salt and pepper, bring to a boil, reduce heat, and simmer for about 30 minutes or until chicken is tender.

Pile the pieces of chicken up into a pyramid on a large platter and cover with the sauce and vegetables. Sprinkle with chervil.

Poularde Dorée à la Kiev
(Chicken Kiev)

6 chicken breasts, with wings attached	*Chive Butter:*
Salt and freshly ground white pepper	1 pound butter, softened
4 eggs	1 clove garlic, minced
Flour for dusting	2 tablespoons minced fresh chives
1½ cups fine bread crumbs	2 tablespoons minced fresh parsley
Oil for deep frying	Salt and freshly ground white pepper

Cut off the first 2 joints of the wing on each breast and discard. Skin the breasts and remove the rib bones and shoulder bone. Leave the wing bone intact. Flatten the breast meat with a cleaver so that it is as thin as possible. Season with salt and pepper and set aside.

Blend the butter with the garlic, chives, parsley, salt, and pepper. Shape the butter into a series of 6 cigar-shaped rolls or fingers. Chill butter if it begins to get too soft to handle. Place 1 butter finger on each breast and wrap the meat around it. Seal the edges.

Beat the eggs and season with salt and pepper. Dust the chicken with flour, then dip in the egg. Drain, then roll each breast in the bread crumbs, pressing each with your hand to make sure crumbs adhere. Repeat a second time.

Heat frying oil to 375 degrees. Arrange the chicken breasts in a basket and deep fry for about 20 minutes. When golden brown, drain on absorbent paper. Serve on a long platter covered with an oval-shaped napkin.

Coquelet de Métairie Grillé Languedocienne
(Grilled Chickens with Tomato Sauce)

Cooks broil chickens much less than they used to. Maybe the reason is that chicken today hasn't the flavor it had in the good old days and is likely to turn out drier than before. The breading used in this recipe makes the final product more succulent. The potatoes which go with it are prepared according to one of the simplest recipes known. The fresh tomato sauce, which in my opinion is indispensable, gives a happy Mediterranean color to the dish.

6 small, young chickens or game hens, fresh or frozen	½ cup French olive oil
¼ cup corn oil or French olive oil	1 clove garlic, crushed
Salt and freshly ground pepper	2 tablespoons chopped fresh parsley
3 eggs	1 bunch watercress
1 cup bread crumbs	2 cups Sauce Tomate
2½ pounds potatoes, peeled and sliced ½ inch thick	1 tablespoon lemon juice

Thaw chicken, if frozen. Preheat the oven to 400 degrees and prepare grill. Separate the legs from the chickens by cutting on either side of the body. Slit each along the back, open out, and remove the rib cage and breastbone. Flatten the breasts with a meat pounder or cleaver. Brush pieces generously with oil and sprinkle with salt on both sides. Put them side by side in a shallow roasting pan and roast lightly for 10 minutes in a hot oven, turning from time to time. Remove from oven and cool.

Beat eggs and season with a pinch of salt and pepper. Dip the chicken pieces in the beaten egg, then in the bread crumbs. Press firmly with your hand to make crumbs adhere. Arrange the chickens on the rack of a charcoal brazier and grill 8 inches above gray coals for about 7 to 8 minutes on each side. (These may also be done under the broiler.)

Sauté potatoes in olive oil until golden brown. Add garlic and sprinkle with parsley. Continue to sauté without allowing the garlic to brown. Cover a platter with these potatoes, and top with chicken. Garnish with watercress and serve with hot Sauce Tomate mixed with lemon juice.

Brouchettes de Foies de Volailles Grillées
(Chicken Livers en Brochette)

18 chicken livers, about 1½ pounds
1 teaspoon salt
6 mill-turns freshly ground white pepper
½ cup oil
12 medium, fresh mushrooms, trimmed and washed
Lemon juice
6 thick slices pre-cooked smoked ham, cut into 1½-inch cubes
Rice Pilaf

Mustard Butter:
2 cups butter
1 tablespoon Dijon-style mustard
2 tablespoons flour

Carefully remove fat, sinews, and any green pieces from each liver. Cut each liver in half, season with salt and pepper, and sauté in ⅓ cup of oil until livers are lightly browned. Put them into a lined sieve, preferably with cheesecloth, and let cool.

Prepare coals for grilling or preheat broiler. Rub each mushroom cap with lemon juice to keep from darkening. Place the mushrooms, livers, and ham cubes on skewers as follows: First a mushroom cap, then 6 chicken livers alternating with 6 ham cubes, ending up with a second mushroom cap. Oil skewers lightly with remaining oil, using a pastry brush, and grill over charcoal or in a broiler, turning from time to time and cooking to your taste (rare, medium, or well done).

In a saucepan, mix butter, mustard, and flour. Stir until melted and thickened.

Place brochettes on a long serving platter and cover with the Mustard Butter. Surround with Rice Pilaf.

Farce à Gratin
(Chicken Liver Spread)

10 chicken livers	**Pinch of freshly ground pepper**
4 ounces ground pork fat	**1 bay leaf**
½ teaspoon salt	**Leaves of 1 sprig thyme**

Wash the livers carefully.

Melt the pork fat over low heat until completely rendered. Pass the fat through a fine sieve into a heavy skillet. Add the chicken livers seasoned with salt, pepper, bay leaf, and thyme. Cook over extremely low heat or at the side of the heat source for 20 minutes.

Let cool and force through a fine sieve or purée in a food processor. Place into a crock, cover, and chill until needed. **Makes about 1 cup**.

DUCK

Caneton d'Aylesbury Rôti aux Oranges
(Roast Duckling with Orange)

The Roast Duckling à l'Orange was a very popular dish. We therefore prepared it often on the France, in a quantity never equaled on any other liner. During the North Atlantic voyages, the dish was served in both first and tourist classes. We carried 1,699 people in tourist class on each crossing, so for a single meal we had to roast 400 ducklings. That meant an enormous job for the rotissiers who were on duty in the afternoon. They would set the 400 ducklings out in a 20 x 20-foot square on giant pans. As I watched the cooks season and prepare this flock, I imagined what it would be like if they were still alive and loose in our kitchens!

2 ducklings, about 4 pounds each, fresh or frozen	*Stock:*
1 teaspoon salt	**1 carrot, diced**
Small pinch of cayenne	**1 onion, diced**
½ cup dry white wine	**1 stalk celery, diced**
12 small navel oranges	**2 tablespoons olive oil**
2 tablespoons white wine vinegar	**1 quart water**
1¾ cups confectioner's sugar	**Salt**
1 tablespoon potato flour or cornstarch	**Several sprigs of fresh parsley**
⅔ cup Cognac or Grand Marnier	**1 bay leaf**
4 paper frills	**1 sprig fresh thyme**

Thaw ducklings, if frozen. Preheat oven to 450 degrees. Remove giblets, cut the wings at the joint, then finely chop the bony sections of the wings and the 2 necks. Put wings and necks in an ovenproof dish, together with carrot, onion, and celery. Stir in olive oil. Roast in a very hot oven for 30 minutes. Stir frequently.

Transfer the above to a saucepan and cover with water. Salt lightly, and add parsley, bay leaf, and thyme. Bring to a boil and let simmer, uncovered, over medium heat for 1 hour; skim foam as needed. Strain through a fine sieve and reserve this stock as base for the sauce.

Preheat oven again, this time to 350 degrees. Truss the ducklings and place on a rack in a heatproof roasting pan. Season with salt and cayenne. Roast in a moderate oven for about 1½ to 2 hours; turn and baste until they are well roasted and crusty. Place ducklings on a platter and keep warm. Pour off all grease in the roasting pan and add white wine. Add the reserved stock. Place pan on top of stove and boil, scraping up any meat particles in pan. Strain pan juices and set aside.

Remove the orange part of the outer skin (the zest) from 6 of the oranges and cut into julienne strips with a sharp paring knife. Extract the juice from these oranges and put it in a small saucepan. Add vinegar and 1¼ cups of confectioner's sugar. Bring to a boil and cook until you have reduced the juice to a golden caramel with a honeylike consistency. Put the julienned orange skin in another saucepan and barely cover with water. Bring to a boil for 5 minutes, then drain. Stir potato flour into orange peel, add the caramel, the roasting pan juices, and the Cognac, and season with a pinch of cayenne. Simmer, stirring occasionally, for 30 minutes.

Preheat oven to 450 degrees. Peel remaining oranges, being careful to remove all the white membrane, then cut into quarters so that the segments remain connected at the bottom, opening out into a fan. Place the quartered oranges on a heatproof platter, sprinkle with remaining confectioner's sugar and glaze them under the broiler or in a very hot oven for 12 to 15 minutes.

Decorate tops of ducklings with the oranges, attached with decorative attelets (skewers). Place paper frills on the ends of the drumsticks. If desired, a few orange segments can be added to the sauce. Spoon sauce over duckling or serve over pieces after carving.

Roast duckling goes well with tiny green peas cooked in butter or with Dauphine Potatoes.

Caneton de Long Island Rôti à l'Ananas Frais
(Roast Long Island Duckling with Pineapple)

2 **Long Island ducklings, about 4 pounds each, fresh or frozen Duck stock (see Roast Duckling with Orange Sauce)**
1 **fresh pineapple**

1¼ **cups confectioner's sugar**
⅔ **cup kirsch**
Potato flour
¼ **cup superfine sugar**

Thaw ducklings, if frozen. Preheat the oven to 350 degrees. Prepare a duck stock as for Roast Duckling with Orange Sauce, using onion, carrot, celery, and bouquet garni.

Peel a ripe pineapple, taking care to preserve its rounded form. Cut into ¾-inch-thick slices, removing the core with a small cutter. Poach the pineapple slices in a Pyrex dish in just enough water to cover, sweetened with ½ cup of the confectioner's sugar. Remove slices with a slotted spoon and dry them well on a paper towel. Pour the cooking liquid into a saucepan and add remaining confectioner's sugar. Boil until a browned caramel forms with a honeylike consistency. Stir in half the duck stock.

Roast the ducklings in a moderate oven for 1½ to 2 hours, or until brown and crusty. Remove from pan and place on platter. Turn off heat and then place platter into the oven with door open. Pour off the fat from the roasting pan. Add remaining stock, place on top of stove, and boil, scraping up all particles. Combine the liquid with the stock mixed with caramel. Simmer the mixture for 30 minutes until reduced to half its volume. Stir in kirsch and then, measuring liquid, add 1 tablespoon potato flour for each cup of liquid. Strain the sauce through a fine sieve.

Preheat oven again, this time to 450 degrees, or heat broiler. Arrange 6 pineapple slices on a platter, sprinkle with superfine sugar, and caramelize under the broiler or in a hot oven for 10 to 12 minutes. Cube the remaining pineapple slices and add them to the sauce. Simmer for a few minutes to blend flavors.

Put the ducklings on a long serving platter, breast to breast. Place 3 slices of pineapple on top of each duckling and spoon sauce over birds. Serve with peas cooked in butter and lightly sprinkled with sugar.

Caneton Rouennais Rôti aux Beignets, Augerons
(Roast Duckling with Apple Fritters)

4 large cooking apples
⅔ cup Calvados
2 ducklings, about 4 pounds each, fresh or frozen
1 teaspoon salt
¼ teaspoon freshly ground white pepper
1 cup water or duck stock (see Roast Duckling with Orange Sauce)
4 paper frills

Fritters:
3 cups unsifted all-purpose flour
⅔ cup confectioner's sugar, approximately
1 envelope active dry yeast
2 cups lukewarm milk
3 eggs, well beaten
Oil for deep-frying

Peel and core apples, leaving them whole. Cut each apple crosswise into 6 round slices and put slices in a shallow bowl or Pyrex pie pan; marinate for 2 hours in Calvados.

Thaw ducklings, if frozen. Preheat oven to 350 degrees. Roast the ducklings seasoned with salt and pepper in a moderate oven for 1½ to 2 hours. When they are done, turn off oven. Remove ducklings from roasting pan and let rest on a platter for 30 minutes with the oven door open. Pour off fat from the roasting pan, add water, place on top of stove, and boil, scraping up all brown particles. Strain and keep sauce hot.

To prepare fritters, mix flour and sugar. Dissolve yeast in milk. Add eggs, yeast, and milk to flour and beat until smooth. Allow batter to rise in a warm place for 1 hour. Heat the oil to 360 degrees. Dip each apple slice in the batter and deep-fry for 6 or 7 minutes. Drain on absorbent paper, then roll in additional confectioner's sugar.

Arrange the ducklings on a long serving platter and spoon the pan juices over them. Circle the ducklings with the apple fritters and decorate the drumsticks with paper frills.

Caneton Braisé au Chambertin
(Duckling Braised in Wine)

The plump, white-fleshed American duckling invariably delighted our American passengers but was generally unappreciated by the Europeans. This gave headaches to the rotissiers, who had to ask each waiter the nationality of the passenger he was serving! It is best, in preparing this dish, to use Burgundy and to use exactly the quantity of wine specified in the recipe.

1 **duckling, about 4 pounds,**	1 **cup butter**
fresh or frozen	12 **slices firm white bread**
Salt and freshly ground pepper	1 **cup Chicken Liver Spread**
3 **cups good Burgundy wine,**	2 **cups duck stock (see Roast**
preferably Chambertin	**Duckling with Orange Sauce),**
⅔ **cup** *marc de Bourgogne* **or**	**thickened, if desired,**
Cognac	**with Beurre Manié**
12 **large, fresh mushrooms**	1 **truffle, thinly sliced**

Thaw duckling, if frozen. Preheat oven to 400 degrees. Season cavity with salt and pepper. Roast in a hot oven for 30 minutes, basting often with pan drippings, and then remove from oven while still underdone.

Pour off the fat from the roasting pan and add 1 cup of wine. Place pan on top of stove and boil, scraping up all brown particles, until liquid is reduced by half. Remove drumsticks, thighs, and breasts from duck and place them in a buttered saucepan. Cut up the remaining carcass and flame it with *marc de Bourgogne*. Set aside.

Wash and stem flute mushroom caps. Sauté in half the butter until golden brown, then simmer for 30 minutes over very low heat.

Have oven at 400 degrees. Cut bread into heart-shaped pieces, heat remaining butter, and brown croûtons on both sides. Spread croûtons with chicken liver spread and bake in a hot oven for 5 minutes. Cover duckling in saucepan with stock and reheat. Put drumsticks and thighs on a round platter and top with the breasts. Add mushrooms. Place croûtons around duckling and garnish with truffle slices.

Serve with thin buttered noodles. **Makes 4 servings**.

Caneton Nantais Rôti Dame Catherine
(Roasted Duckling with Prunes)

1 **pound large prunes**	⅓ **cup clarified butter**
2 **ducklings, about 4 pounds**	½ **cup confectioner's sugar**
each, fresh or frozen	2 **slices lemon**
1 **teaspoon salt**	½ **teaspoon ground cinnamon**
¼ **teaspoon white pepper**	¾ **cup water or duck stock**
6 **cooking apples, peeled,**	**(see Roast Duckling with Orange**
cored, and quartered	**Sauce)**

Remove pits from the prunes and soak prunes in water to cover for 6 hours.

Thaw ducklings, if frozen. Preheat oven to 350 degrees. Season cavities of ducklings with salt and pepper and roast in a moderate oven for 1½ to 2 hours, or until brown and crusty. Keep warm. Drain off and reserve fat.

Turn oven up to 450 degrees or heat broiler. Arrange apple quarters in a lightly buttered ovenproof dish, then brush with butter. Sprinkle with confectioner's sugar and broil gently or bake in a hot oven until they have taken on a fine golden color, about 10 to 12 minutes. Keep oven temperature at 400 degrees.

Put the prunes along with soaking water into a saucepan, add more water to just cover, plus lemon slices and cinnamon. Bring to a boil and simmer for 15 minutes. Discard the lemon, drain the prunes, and sauté them in a skillet with ¼ of the duck pan drippings. Place roasting pan on top of stove, add water or duck stock, and cook, scraping up all brown particles. Strain through a fine sieve. Arrange the ducklings on a long heatproof serving platter. Surround with alternating apple quarters and prunes, and spoon pan juices over ducklings. Place in a hot oven for 15 minutes to reheat and serve.

Caneton Chalandais Farci Rôti "France"
(Roasted Stuffed Duckling à la *France*)

2 **ducklings, about 2 pounds**	*Mousse:*
each, fresh or frozen	5 **duckling livers**
Salt	3 **shallots, minced**
Freshly ground white pepper	1 **clove garlic, crushed**
2 **cups Sauce Hollandaise**	1 **tablespoon butter**
½ **cup white wine**	1 **tablespoon finely chopped**
1 **cup crème fraîche or heavy**	**fresh parsley**
cream	⅓ **cup Cognac**
	Salt
Mushroom Purée:	4 **mill-turns freshly ground**
6 **fresh mushrooms, chopped**	**white pepper**
Salt	**Pinch of ground nutmeg**
Pinch of white pepper	¾ **cup crème fraîche or**
2 **tablespoons water**	**heavy cream**
½ **cup crème fraîche or**	1 **cup cooked rice**
heavy cream	

Prepare the mousse. Force the duckling livers through a sieve or purée in a food processor. Sauté the shallots and garlic in butter without browning, then add to the puréed livers, together with parsley, Cognac, salt, pepper, and nutmeg. Blend in crème fraîche and rice. Put the mixture in a 3-cup terrine and place in a pan of water coming half way up the sides. Bring water in pan to a boil, cover, and simmer for 30 minutes over medium heat. Remove from heat and cool.

Thaw ducklings, if frozen. Preheat oven to 350 degrees. Truss and season with salt and pepper, then roast for about 1½ to 2 hours in a moderate oven, basting frequently until brown and crusty. Remove from oven and let rest for a few minutes on the open door of the turned-off oven. Remove duck from pan and set aside pan with drippings.

While duck is roasting, prepare mushroom purée. Simmer mushrooms with salt, pepper, and water until liquid is absorbed. Stir in crème fraîche and simmer until thickened. Purée in food processor or blender.

Turn oven up to 450 degrees, or heat broiler. Separate the breasts from from the wing joints with a fileting knife. Scallop the breasts on the bias, getting 6 scallops per breast. Using heavy kitchen shears, remove the breast and rib bones. Clean the cavities well and stuff with cooled duckling mousse. Replace the breasts, restoring the natural shape to the fowl. Cover the top of the ducklings with mushroom purée. Spoon over a layer of Sauce Hollandaise and brown under the broiler or in a hot oven for 8 to 10 minutes. Meanwhile, pour off fat in roasting pan and add white wine and crème fraîche. Place on top of stove and boil, scraping up all brown particles. Pass sauce through a fine sieve.

Arrange the ducklings, neck to neck, on a long serving platter and surround with Rice Pilaf molds. Serve sauce alongside, possibly with peas (cooked in natural juices, thickened with Beurre Manié) as the vegetable.

Caneton Nantais Braisé aux Navets Nouveaux
(Braised Duckling with New Turnips)

2 ducklings, about 4 pounds each, fresh or frozen	6 tablespoons butter
Salt	2 tablespoons sugar
Freshly ground white pepper	¾ cup sweet white wine
½ cup corn oil or French olive oil	¾ cup duck stock (see Roast Duckling with Orange Sauce)
12 small white turnips, cut into balls	4 paper frills

Thaw ducklings, if frozen. Preheat oven to 400 degrees. Truss the ducklings securely and season with salt and pepper. In a casserole over low heat, brown on all sides in oil. Braise, covered, in a hot oven, basting often, for 1½ hours or until brown and crusty.

Meanwhile, put the turnip balls into a saucepan and cover with water. Add butter, salt, and sugar. Bring to a boil, reduce heat, and simmer until liquid has evaporated and the turnips become well browned and glazed. Remove and keep warm.

Add wine to braising casserole and bring to a boil. Pour in stock and simmer 5 minutes, then add turnip balls and simmer additional 5 minutes.

Remove the trussing string from the ducklings and place ducklings on a long carving platter. Surround them with turnips. Spoon a small amount of the braising liquid over ducklings and place remaining sauce in a sauceboat. Slip paper frills on the ends of the drumsticks and serve.

Caneton Duclairois en Salmis à la Rouennaise
(Salmis of Duckling à la Rouennaise)

 2 ducklings, about 4 pounds
each, fresh or frozen
Salt and freshly ground pepper
Beurre Manié
 6 slices firm white bread
 3 tablespoons clarified butter
12 large fresh mushrooms, washed
trimmed, and fluted
Chopped fresh parsley

Stock:
 ½ cup butter
 1 onion, chopped
 1 carrot, chopped
 1 stalk celery, chopped
 ⅔ cup Cognac, warmed
 2 cups dry red wine
 2 cups water
Salt and freshly ground pepper
Bouquet garni (1 bay leaf, 1 sprig
fresh thyme)

Thaw ducklings, if frozen. Remove livers and reserve. Remove wings and truss.

Prepare the stock. Cut necks and wings into small pieces and brown well in half the butter, together with onion, carrot, and celery. Flame with Cognac, then add wine and water. Season well with salt and pepper. Add bouquet garni and bring to a boil. Skim foam carefully and continue simmering, uncovered, for 1 hour. Strain through a fine sieve and reserve.

Preheat oven to 400 degrees. Season the ducklings with salt and pepper, and roast in a hot oven for 1 hour, basting frequently, until medium rare. Let cool slightly, then pour off fat from roasting pan and add 1 cup of the stock. Place roasting pan on top of stove and simmer, scraping up all brown particles. Strain liquid into remaining stock.

Remove thighs and breasts from the ducklings, and separate the drumsticks from the thighs. Put drumsticks, together with breasts, in a well-buttered large saucepan or Dutch oven.

Grind the carcasses in a mortar, food processor, or meat grinder and add to the stock. Bring to a boil and simmer for 30 minutes, then pass the stock through a fine sieve again, pressing well. Stir Beurre Manié into stock and blend over low heat until thickened. Pour sauce over duckling in saucepan.

Cut bread into heart-shaped pieces, brush with clarified butter, and toast lightly under the broiler.

Brown mushrooms lightly in a skillet with remaining butter until brown, then sauté over low heat for 20 minutes.

Press the reserved duck livers through a fine sieve or purée in a food processor and add them to a saucepan. Simmer duckling in the sauce to the point where the skin is separated from the meat. Remove from heat and correct seasoning.

Pile duckling pieces in center of large platter and surround with mushrooms. Dip the points of the croûtons in the sauce, then into chopped parsley, and set them around the duck in a pyramid. Serve sauce on the side, perhaps with buttered noodles.

SQUAB

Pigeonneau de Nid Rôti Bûcheronne
(Roast Squab with Chanterelles)

6 squab or game hens, fresh or frozen
6 slices basting fat or bacon
1 teaspoon salt
⅔ cup Cognac
½ cup Port wine
3 pounds chanterelles
⅔ cup butter
2 mill-turns freshly ground white pepper
1 pound new potatoes
12 glazed onions (see Squab with Glazed Vegetables)
5 ounces thinly sliced proscuitto or Bayonne ham, cut in thin strips

Thaw squab, if frozen. Preheat oven to 400 degrees. Truss squab, then wrap in thin slices of basting fat. Sprinkle with salt and roast in heatproof pan for 25 minutes in a hot oven, turning and basting frequently. Remove squab from oven and transfer to a platter and keep warm. Let rest several minutes.

Add Cognac and Port to the roasting pan, place on top of stove, and boil, scraping up all brown particles. Strain juices through a fine sieve.

If chanterelles are dried, soak in warm water for 30 minutes. Trim the stems and wash carefully in several changes of water. Sauté over moderate to high heat in half the butter, heated until brown. Season with 2 pinches of salt and pepper; brown thoroughly.

Cook potatoes, then peel and sauté in remaining butter until brown. Scatter potatoes and onions around squab. Sprinkle prosciutto over, then spoon pan juices on top. Surround with chanterelles.

Variation

An alternative way of preparing this dish is to serve the squab stuffed. Prepare the stuffing, then spoon it into each squab. Sew or skewer openings and roast as above.

Stuffing:

1 pound bacon, blanched and diced
2 cups stems and trimmings from chanterelles
2 shallots, chopped fine
1 clove garlic, minced
¼ cup coarsely chopped truffles
Salt and freshly ground pepper

Mix bacon with chanterelles, shallots, garlic, and truffles; add salt and pepper to taste and serve.

Pigeonneau de Nid en Compôte St.-Germain
(Squab with Glazed Vegetables)

6 squab or game hens, fresh or frozen	*Stock:*
Salt	1 onion, chopped
¼ teaspoon white pepper	1 carrot, chopped
1 cup softened butter	1 stalk celery, chopped
1 cup sweet white wine	2 cups water
24 small white onions, peeled	Salt
¼ cup confectioner's sugar	Several sprigs of fresh parsley
6 large carrots	1 bay leaf
2½ pounds fresh green peas, shelled	1 sprig fresh thyme

Thaw squab, if frozen. Truss squab, then set aside and prepare stock. Slice the necks and mix with onion, carrot, and celery. Place under broiler until brown. Put the necks and vegetables into a saucepan with water, salt, parsley, bay leaf, and thyme. Boil the stock until reduced by half, skimming foam as needed. Pass through a fine sieve and discard solids.

Preheat the oven to 400 degrees. Season the squab with salt and pepper, then put in a heatproof pan. Brush with ¼ cup of the butter and roast in a hot oven for 20 minutes, basting frequently. Remove from pan, take off the trussing string, and put the squab into a large saucepan. Add wine to roasting pan, place pan on top of stove, and boil, scraping up brown particles. Pour pan juices over the squab.

Turn oven up to 450 degrees, or heat broiler. Poach the onions in lightly salted water for 10 minutes. Drain, dot with ¼ cup of butter, and sprinkle with sugar. Glaze under the broiler or in a hot oven for 5 to 6 minutes, until golden brown.

Cut each carrot into 4 pieces and shape pieces into ovals the size of olives. In a saucepan, combine carrots, ¼ cup of butter, and water to cover. Cook until water has evaporated and carrots are glazed.

Add onions, peas, and carrots to squab, cover with the reserved stock, bring to a boil, and reduce heat and simmer, uncovered, for 30 minutes. Place squab on serving platter and stir remaining butter into sauce. Season with salt and pepper, and spoon sauce over squab.

Pigeonneau de Nid Rôti sur Canapé
(Roast Squab on Toast)

6 squab or game hens, fresh or frozen	1 cup Chicken Liver Spread
8 ounces fat bacon or basting fat, thinly sliced	⅔ cup dry white wine
Salt	6 strips bacon, cooked until crisp
Freshly ground white pepper	1 bunch watercress, washed and trimmed
1 loaf French bread	3 lemons, sliced in half in zigzag cuts
½ cup (8 tablespoons) clarified butter	

Thaw squab, if frozen. Preheat oven to 400 degrees. Truss squab, then wrap each in basting fat and secure with string. Season with salt and pepper, then roast in a hot oven for 40 minutes, turning and basting often.

Turn up oven to 450 degrees. Cut a loaf of French bread on the bias into large, thick slices. Brush slices generously with butter and toast on both sides under the broiler or in a hot oven. Spread each slice with Chicken Liver Spread, then place under the broiler again or in a hot oven for a few minutes or until golden. Arrange the slices on a long serving platter. When the squab are roasted, remove and discard fat. Remove trussing string and put each squab on a slice of toast.

Add wine to roasting pan, place on top of stove, and boil, scraping up brown particles. Pass the sauce through a fine sieve. Put a bacon strip on each squab, securing it with a decorative attelet (skewer). Place a generous bouquet of watercress in the middle of the platter and a half lemon next to each squab. Spoon the strained pan juices over the birds, and serve with a dish of French-Fried Potatoes Pont-Neuf or Fresh Peas Country Style.

Pigeonneau Biset Grillé Crapaudine
(Grilled Squab with Sauce Diable)

6 squab or game hens, fresh or frozen	1 hard-cooked egg, sliced
¼ cup oil	12 small rounds of truffle
1 cup clarified butter mixed with 2 tablespoons Dijon-style mustard	2 cups Sauce Diable
Salt	3½ pounds potatoes, prepared as for Straw Potatoes
Freshly ground white pepper	1 bunch watercress, cleaned, trimmed, and divided into 2 bunches
3 cups fine, dry bread crumbs	

Thaw squab, if frozen. Preheat oven to 400 degrees. Make 2 incisions close to the body to release the legs but leave them attached. Make an incision on each side of the breast from the wings to the end of the body. Flatten the birds with the hand into the shape of a toad. Brush them with oil and brown in a hot oven for 18 minutes, turning them from time to time. Then brush squab with butter-mustard mixture. Season with salt and pepper and coat with bread crumbs, pressing to make sure breading adheres.

Prepare the coals or preheat the broiler. Grill the squab on both sides gently for 15 minutes, 8 inches above gray coals or place in broiler. Put the grilled birds on a long serving platter and keep warm.

To make the "toad's eyes," put the white part of 2 egg slices in the middle of each side of the filets. Add 2 small rounds cut from a truffle in the center to make the eyes of each "toad." Place Straw Potatoes around the squab and garnish with a bunch of watercress at either end of the platter. Serve with Sauce Diable.

Pigeonneau Biset Sauté Minute
(Sautéed Squab)

6 squab or game hens, fresh or frozen
Salt
4 mill-turns freshly ground white pepper
1 cup butter
1 medium onion, chopped
⅔ cup Chicken Consommé
Few drops of Cognac
Juice ½ lemon
12 large fresh mushrooms, minced
1 tablespoon chopped fresh parsley

Thaw squab, if frozen. On each bird, remove the thighs and drumsticks, and separate breast from carcass by slitting lengthwise. Bone the breasts. Season all sections with salt and pepper. Heat ⅓ cup of butter until golden brown, and sauté squab. When the pieces are well browned, add onion and sauté until translucent. Add consommé, Cognac, and lemon juice. Bring to a boil, reduce heat, and simmer for 10 minutes. Remove from heat and stir in ⅓ cup of butter, 1 tablespoon at a time, stirring constantly.

Heat remaining butter until golden brown and sauté mushrooms. Stir into sauce and season to taste. Place the squab on a serving platter and top with the sauce. Sprinkle with parsley just before serving.

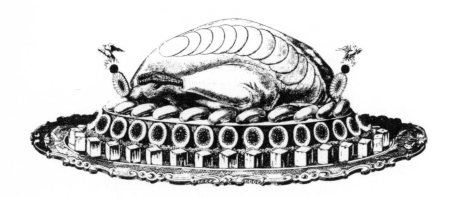

OTHER POULTRY

Grouse Écossaise Rôtie avec Bread Sauce
(Roast Scottish Grouse with Bread Sauce)

6 grouse, about 1 pound each
Salt and freshly ground pepper
6 slices caul fat
⅔ cup bourbon, warmed
½ cup dry white wine
¼ cup (4 tablespoons) butter
1 loaf French bread, cut in large 2-inch-thick bias slices
Chicken Liver Spread
1 bunch watercress, washed and trimmed

Sauce:
½ cup fine white bread crumbs
2 cups milk
1 onion, studded with 4 whole cloves
2 pinches of salt
Pinch of grated nutmeg

Thaw grouse, if frozen. Preheat oven to 400 degrees. Sprinkle birds with salt and pepper. Wrap them in fat but wrap the drumsticks in oiled parchment paper or foil; truss. Roast the grouse in heatproof pan in a hot oven for 30 minutes (for medium-rare) or 45 minutes (for well done). Remove grouse from oven, keeping the lard on the birds, which should be crusty. Remove trussing strings and flame with bourbon. Remove birds from pan and keep warm.

Pour off the fat from the roasting pan and add wine. Place on top of stove and boil, scraping up brown particles. Strain pan juices and set aside. Butter bread slices and toast lightly on both sides under the broiler. Spread a generous layer of chicken liver on the bread and heat in a hot oven for several more minutes, or until slightly melted. Set the slices of bread on a long serving platter and place the grouse on them. Heap half the watercress at either end of the platter, and spoon pan juices over birds.

For bread sauce, combine bread crumbs with milk. Simmer in saucepan, along with onion, salt, and nutmeg for 5 minutes. Remove onion and serve in a sauceboat.

Salmis de Perdreaux à la Solognote
(Partridge Salmi Sologne)

6 partridges, fresh or frozen	2 cups dry red wine
Salt and freshly ground pepper	4 cups water
½ cup (8 tablespoons) butter	2 tablespoons flour
3 shallots, chopped	12 large fresh mushrooms, washed
1 carrot, chopped	and cut in fluted shape
2 stalks celery, chopped	3 slices firm white bread
1 clove garlic, chopped	¼ cup (4 tablespoons) clarified butter
Bouquet garni (bay leaf, sprig	Chopped fresh parsley
of fresh thyme, rosemary	1 truffle, sliced
leaves)	
⅔ cup *marc de Bourgogne* or	
Cognac, warmed	

Thaw partridges, if frozen. Preheat oven to 450 degrees. Truss the birds, season with salt and pepper, and roast in a hot oven for 10 minutes (the juices should run red) in a lightly buttered roasting pan turning and basting frequently.

Let birds cool. Using a sharp knife, remove thighs and breasts and put them in a well-buttered saucepan. Cut carcasses and necks into pieces and put them back in the roasting pan. Add shallots, carrot, celery, garlic, and bouquet garni. Replace in hot oven and roast 30 minutes. When the ingredients are well browned, remove the pan and add *marc de Bourgogne*; set aflame. Add wine and water, place on top of stove, and bring to a boil. Reduce heat and simmer, uncovered, for about 1 hour. Strain the stock through a sieve and discard solids. Mix ¼ cup of the butter with the flour and add it to the stock, stirring until thickened.

Heat remaining butter until golden brown and sauté mushrooms lightly. Add mushrooms to the partridge thighs and breasts, pour stock over the birds, bring to a boil, and reduce heat and simmer for about 20 minutes.

Cut bread into triangles. Brush slices on both sides with clarified butter and broil until golden. Dip the tips into the sauce, then into a dish of chopped parsley. Place partridge on a deep platter and alternate croûtons with truffle as a garnish.

Cailles Farcies de la Suisse, Normande
(Roasted Stuffed Quail with Apples)

I don't remember where I learned this recipe for stuffed quail. We prepared the dish for the first time during the 1972 cruise, and the sauciers and pastry cooks brought off this tour de force *much to the satisfaction and admiration of the passengers.*

12 quail, fresh or frozen
1 frying chicken, about 3 pounds
2 teaspoons salt
  Pinch of ground nutmeg
2 cups crème fraîche or heavy cream
3 egg whites, lightly beaten
12 thin slices basting fat or bacon

¼ teaspoon freshly ground pepper
½ cup Calvados, warmed
1 cup semi-sweet white wine
12 very large cooking apples, cored and peeled
3 pounds Puff Pastry dough
4 egg yolks, beaten with 2 tablespoons water

Thaw quail, if frozen. Remove breastbone and rib bones.

Cut the thighs and breasts from chicken; skin and bone them and remove the sinews. Finely grind the chicken meat, then force through a sieve with a wooden pestle or purée in a food processor. Season with 1 teaspoon salt and nutmeg. Put the mixture in a bowl set onto shaved ice and, using a spatula, blend in crème fraîche and egg whites. Let cool for 2 hours.

Preheat the oven to 400 degrees. Using a pastry bag and large nozzle, stuff the quail with chicken mixture. Sew up, truss, and wrap each bird in a thin sheet of basting fat, tying with string. Season the quail with remaining salt and the pepper, lay them on their sides in a heatproof pan, and roast in a hot oven for 20 minutes, turning and basting frequently.

Remove pan from the oven and flame the quail with Calvados. Remove from pan, and set aside. Drain off the fat from roasting pan and add wine. Place on top of stove and boil 2 to 3 minutes, scraping up particles, then sieve into a saucepan. Set aside. Hollow out apples until the holes are large enough to each hold a quail. Place a bird in the cavities, first removing basting fat and trussing string. Roll pastry dough to a ⅛-inch thickness and wrap quail and apple in dough, molding it into an apple shape. Using a fluted oval cookie cutter, cut 2 "apple leaves" from the dough and mark them with a knife point to give the impression of veins in a leaf. Roll little cylinders of parchment paper or foil and insert these little chimneys into each apple between the "leaves." Using a pastry brush, paint whole apple with the egg yolk mixture.

Have oven at 375 degrees. Put the apples on greased cookie sheets and bake for about 20 to 30 minutes in moderate oven. When the pastry is nicely browned, turn off heat and let the quail rest in oven for 15 minutes, then pour roasting pan juices in through the parchment tubes. Cover a long serving platter with a napkin folded into an oval shape, place the quail on the platter, remove the chimneys, and serve.

Cailles Farcies Braisées "France"
(Stuffed Braised Quail à la *France*)

12 plump quail, fresh or frozen	*Stock:*
4 pounds seedless green grapes	¼ cup oil
1 cup dry sherry	1 onion, chopped
½ cup Port wine	1 carrot, chopped
8 ounces fresh *foie gras*, diced	1 stalk celery, chopped
4 ounces truffles, diced	Bouquet garni (bay leaf, celery
⅓ cup Cognac	leaves, sprig of thyme, rosemary
⅓ cup Madeira wine	leaves)
Salt	1 teaspoon salt
Freshly ground white pepper	Freshly ground white pepper
12 vine or grape leaves	Beurre Manié
12 thin sheets basting fat	
1 cup fine brandy, warmed	

Thaw quail, if frozen. Peel the grapes, if desired. Marinate them in a mixture of sherry and Port wine for 30 minutes. Drain and reserve both grapes and marinade. Marinate the *foie gras* and truffles in a mixture of Cognac and Madeira for 10 minutes. Drain and reserve *foie gras*.

Preheat oven to 400 degrees. Using a sharp knife, remove breast and rib bones. Season the cavities lightly with salt and pepper. Stuff with *foie gras*, sew up, and truss the quail firmly, then wrap each first in a vine leaf, then in a sheet of fat tied with a string. Season again with salt and pepper, set the quail on their sides in a heatproof roasting pan, and roast in a hot oven for about 20 minutes, turning and basting frequently.

Fry the necks, rib bones, and breast bones in oil in a skillet, together with the onion, carrot, and celery. When the mixture is richly browned, drain and put into a saucepan. Add the bouquet garni, salt, and water to cover. Bring to a boil, skimming foam carefully, then simmer until reduced by half. Sieve, then thicken the quail stock with Beurre Manié. Season sauce with salt and pepper, and simmer for about 15 minutes.

When the quail are done, remove from oven and untruss; remove fat. Put them in a saucepan and pour in brandy; set aflame. Drain fat from roasting pan and add grape marinade. Place pan on top of stove and boil until reduced by half.

Place quail on a large serving platter and sieve the roasting pan juices over the birds. Serve sauce separately. A good side dish is Wild Rice Pilaf.

Suprême de Pintadeau Fermier Doré Belle-Otéro
(Boneless Breast of Guinea Hen with Stuffed Tomatoes)

6 young guinea hens, fresh or frozen	2½ pounds fresh spinach, washed and trimmed
2 cups milk	Pinch of ground nutmeg
Salt and pepper	2½ pounds small new potatoes, cooked and peeled
¼ cup all-purpose flour	½ cup Port wine
⅓ cup (6 tablespoons) clarified butter	1 teaspoon tomato paste
12 firm, ripe tomatoes	12 paper frills
½ cup (8 tablespoons) butter	

Thaw guinea hens, if frozen. Remove the breasts and tips of the wings. Skin the breasts and tie wing bones in place. Soak in milk for 2 hours.

Chop remaining bones and parts and cover with water. Simmer, uncovered, for 1 hour. Strain stock through a sieve and bring back to a boil; reduce until you have ½ cup.

Preheat oven to 400 degrees. Drain breasts, season with salt and pepper, then coat with flour. Sauté breasts in clarified butter over very low heat for 10 minutes, then transfer to a covered roasting pan and place in a hot oven. Turn breasts while roasting to assure browning, and roast for 20 to 25 minutes.

Scoop out the pulp and seeds from tomatoes to make shells about ½ inch thick. Discard seeds and juice, and dice pulp. Cook pulp briefly in a saucepan until very soft; set shells aside.

Heat half the butter in a skillet until brown, and sauté the spinach until cooked. Season with salt and nutmeg, then mix spinach with tomato purée and stuff into tomato shells. Sauté potatoes in remaining butter until lightly browned.

Combine stock with wine and tomato paste and simmer for 5 minutes. Season with salt and pepper.

Arrange breasts on a long serving platter, surrounded with the tomato shells alternating with potatoes. Spoon sauce over hens and place frill on each wing.

Suprêmes de Pintadeau Doré "France"
(Boneless Breast of Guinea Hen à la *France*)

3 guinea hens, fresh or frozen	1 cup Chicken Consommé
2 cups crème fraîche or	Beurre Manié
heavy cream	6 fresh artichoke hearts
Salt	1 large bunch asparagus, tips only
Pinch of cayenne	6 slices firm white bread
Pinch of ground nutmeg	¼ cup (4 tablespoons) clarified butter
3 egg whites, slightly beaten	1 can (4 ounces) sweet pimientos,
2 tablespoons chopped truffles	drained and cut into large pieces
1¼ cups butter	6 paper frills
1 cup Port wine	

Thaw guinea hens, if frozen. Remove skin from breasts, cut off wing tips, and truss remaining wing bones to breasts; remove the breasts and cut in half. Using a sharp knife, make an incision in breasts to form a small cavity; set breasts aside.

Skin and bone remaining parts and remove any sinews. Discard bones. Grind meat very fine in a food processor or meat grinder, 3 or 4 times. Place in a bowl set over shaved ice and, stirring constantly with a spatula, blend in the crème fraîche, a small amount at a time, plus the salt, cayenne, and nutmeg. Mix thoroughly, force through a sieve, and then add egg whites and truffles. Using a pastry bag and large round nozzle, stuff the cavities of the breasts with the mousseline.

Heat ¼ cup of the butter until brown over low heat, and sauté the breasts, checking to see that the stuffed inner part of the meat is well done. Keep warm on a platter.

Add wine and consommé to pan and bring to a boil, scraping up brown particles. Thicken with Beurre Manié, then sieve sauce into a double boiler and blend in, a little at a time, ½ cup of butter. Keep warm.

Sauté artichoke hearts in ¼ cup butter; sauté asparagus tips in remaining butter. Cut bread into heart-shaped pieces, brush on both sides with clarified butter, and broil until golden.

Arrange the breasts on the heart-shaped croûtons. Place artichoke hearts, pimiento pieces, and asparagus tips around them and cover with the sauce. Place a paper frill on each wing bone.

Ballottine de Dindonneau Truffée et Braisée, aux Marrons de l'Ardèche

(Ballottine of Turkey with Chestnuts)

1 small turkey, about 6 to 7
    pounds, fresh or frozen
1 teaspoon salt
¼ teaspoon freshly ground
    pepper
1 onion, chopped
1 carrot, chopped
1 stalk celery, chopped
2 tablespoons lard
1 cup dry white wine
    Braised Chestnuts

Stuffing:
8 ounces chopped lean pork
8 ounces chopped pork fat
1 cup Madeira wine
¼ cup chopped truffles
    Salt and pepper

Thaw turkey, if frozen. Marinate the pork and pork fat for 2 hours in Madeira. Drain and reserve liquid; add truffles, salt, and pepper to meat and mix well with the hand.

Cut off the first 2 joints of the wings and discard. Remove breasts from the turkey (with remaining wing joints still attached). Skin and bone turkey, and remove sinews from thighs and drumsticks. Chop rib and breastbones and set aside. Make an incision lengthwise in the side of each breast, spread the flesh open, and flatten with the side of a cleaver into a large, thin sheet. Season with salt and pepper.

Preheat oven to 350 degrees. Shape stuffing into 2 rolls, as long as the flattened breasts. Place a roll of stuffing on each breast, then roll each up and cover with a small sheet of parchment paper moistened with a little water. Tie securely with string.

Sauté onion, carrot, and celery in lard without letting vegetables brown. Put into the bottom of a small heatproof roasting pan and on this place the turkey rolls, thighs, and bones. Cover and roast in a moderate oven for 1¼ hours, basting from time to time and turning over pieces for even browning. Turn off oven, let rest on the open door for 30 minutes. Remove rolls, drumsticks, and thighs and keep warm. Add reserved marinade and white wine to roasting pan, place on top of stove, and boil, uncovered, until reduced by half. Sieve into a double boiler and skim the fat off carefully. Keep warm.

Remove string and paper from the turkey breasts. Slice the drumsticks and thighs and arrange them on a long serving platter. Place slices of turkey breast on sliced turkey. Arrange the chestnuts around edge and cover with the sauce.

Fish

6

Sole Meunière de la Manche Frite Saint-Honorat
(Sole Meunière Saint Honorat)

6 whole sole, 12 ounces each	Oil for deep-frying, heated to 360°
2 cups milk	2 ripe tomatoes, peeled, seeded, and
½ cup flour	diced
4 eggs, well beaten	2 tablespoons butter
Salt, pepper	1 cup Sauce Béarnaise
1½ cups dry bread crumbs	1 teaspoon salt
	Deep-Fried Parsley

Clean and skin the fish, keeping the heads attached. Slice the 2 filets from the dark side leaving them attached and open them out like lapels on a suit. Break the spine with attached vertebrae in several places so that when the sole has been fried it can be pulled out in pieces easily.

Dip the fish in milk, then in flour, then into eggs seasoned with salt and pepper. Coat fish with crumbs, pressing with the heel of the hand to make sure they adhere. Roll back the filets to separate them from the spine, then deep-fry for about 10 minutes. Drain on a kitchen towel, then remove the pieces of spine. Place on a platter and keep warm. Sauté tomato pulp in butter, then stir in Sauce Béarnaise. Season to taste with salt, then spoon mixture into cavities of fish.

Serve the fish on a long platter covered with a napkin folded in a rectangle and surrounded with parsley.

Filets de Sole de la Manche Étuvés Coquelin
(Poached Filets of Channel Sole Coquelin)

Sole is one of the most highly prized of all fish, and many recipes have been created over the centuries. To my mind, Poached Filets of Channel Sole Coquelin is one of the best ways to present this fish. The red of the tomato contrasts admirably with the creamy yellow of the sauce, with the whiteness of the sole, and with the rosy pink of the lobster or crayfish. It may be garnished with either a slice of truffle or lobster. A few small croissants provide a happy complement.

1 lobster tail or 12 crayfish	8 ounces Salmon Mousseline
½ cup Cognac	2 quarts Court Bouillon
12 large tomatoes	2 cups Sauce Vin Blanc
Salt	Triangles of baked Puff Pastry
6 small filets of sole, about 2	
pounds	

Preheat oven to 350 degrees. Wash and dry the sole.

Poach lobster tail for 10 minutes and cut into thin slices. (If you are using crayfish, remove the shells from the tails, discard heads.) Marinate lobster in Cognac for 10 minutes.

Thinly slice off the tops of the tomatoes, gently squeeze out the juice and seeds, and drain on a rack. Salt the insides, replace the tops, place on a buttered baking sheet, and bake in a moderate oven for 15 minutes. Remove tomatoes and raise oven temperature to 400 degrees.

Spread Salmon Mousseline on the filets. Roll them up and place in a generously buttered pan. Add Court Bouillon to cover, then cover with the pan lid and poach in hot oven for about 10 minutes. Keep fish warm; increase oven temperature to 500 degrees.

Scoop out tomatoes and arrange on a long platter. Insert a rolled filet into each tomato, replace the tops, and decorate with a slice of lobster meat or crayfish tail. Coat with Sauce Vin Blanc and put under broiler or in very hot oven for 5 to 6 minutes, or until golden brown. Surround the stuffed tomatoes with small triangles of puff pastry.

Note: If you wish a simpler recipe, replace the Salmon Mousseline with a poached oyster.

Délices de Sole Étuvés Castiglione
(Baked Sole Filets with Shrimp and Mussel Sauce)

12 **large fresh mushrooms, peeled**	1 **sprig fresh thyme**
½ **cup (8 tablespoons) butter**	**Few sprigs of fresh parsley**
Juice of 1 lemon	12 **shrimp**
2 **ripe tomatoes, peeled and**	12 **small sole or flounder filets, about**
seeded	**3 pounds**
Salt and white pepper	4 **egg yolks**
1 **pound mussels, washed and**	½ **cup dry white wine**
beards removed	**Chopped fresh parsley**
1 **quart Fish Stock**	
1 **bay leaf**	

Cook mushrooms in lightly salted water with 2 tablespoons of the butter and the lemon juice for about 10 minutes. Dice tomatoes, season lightly with salt and pepper; place in saucepan and add 2 tablespoons of butter. Bring to a boil, and simmer gently for 10 minutes. Set aside.

Cook mussels in a covered pot with 1 cup stock mixed with bay leaf, thyme, and parsley until they open. Let them cool, then remove from shells, carefully reserving cooking juices. Boil juices until you have ½ cup, then strain. Set aside.

Poach shrimp about 7 minutes in 1 cup of stock. Drain shrimp and reserve poaching juices. Cool shrimp and remove shells. Boil reserved liquid until you have ½ cup. Set aside.

Fold filets in half and arrange side by side in a buttered ovenproof pan. Add 2 cups stock, bring to a boil, reduce heat, and simmer gently for about 10 minutes. Keep warm; reserve poaching liquid.

Prepare a sauce using the remaining butter, egg yolks, white wine, and cooking juices from the mussels and the shrimp; mix well. Simmer sauce until it is the consistency of heavy cream, then add tomatoes, mussels, and shrimp. Season with salt and pepper.

Put the fish on a long serving platter, top each filet with a mushroom. Spoon the sauce over fish and sprinkle with parsley.

Délices de Sole Étuvés Grandousier
(Sole with Shrimp Bordelaise)

3 filets of sole, about 6 ounces each

1 pound fresh mushrooms, washed, trimmed, and minced

1½ cups dry white wine

⅔ cup brandy

Salt

1½ cups butter

½ teaspoon paprika

1 large ripe tomato, peeled, seeded, and diced

6 artichokes, cooked and quartered

Triangles of Puff Pastry, baked

Chopped fresh parsley

Shrimp Bordelaise:

2¼ pounds large shrimp, shelled and deveined

¼ cup (4 tablespoons) butter

6 tablespoons olive oil

1 peeled carrot, chopped finely

1 stalk celery, chopped finely

3 shallots, chopped finely

⅔ cup Cognac, warmed

½ cup dry white wine

1¼ cups crème fraîche or heavy cream

Salt

Pinch of cayenne

First prepare the Shrimp Bordelaise. Sauté shrimp in butter and olive oil. When they turn pink, add carrot and celery. Sauté 2 to 3 minutes, then add shallots and sauté another 2 or 3 minutes. Add Cognac, set aflame, and add wine and crème fraîche. Salt and add cayenne lightly, bring to a boil, reduce heat, and simmer 20 minutes.

Wash the fish thoroughly, fold in half, and put in a well-buttered pan. Spread mushrooms over fish, add wine and brandy, and season lightly with salt. Bring to a boil, reduce heat, cover, and simmer gently for about 10 minutes. Drain juices into a saucepan and arrange filets on a long serving platter covered with a napkin to absorb liquid. Keep warm.

Boil the cooking juices until reduced by half. Beat in 1 cup of the butter, cut into small pieces, using a whisk. Season with paprika. Set aside.

Sauté tomato lightly in 2 tablespoons of butter and a pinch of salt. Cook until very thick, then stir into sauce. Sauté artichokes in remaining butter.

Cover the fish with the sauce and surround with alternate bouquets of parsley, Shrimp Bordelaise, artichokes, and Puff Pastry.

Délices de Sole de la Manche "France"
(Stuffed Sole Filets à la *France*)

6 round slices lobster, poached

1 tablespoon Cognac

6 filets of sole, about 3 pounds

2 cups Fish Stock

1 cup dry white wine

6 egg yolks

⅔ cup clarified butter

Pinch of cayenne

2 cups Sauce Américaine, simmered until very thick

1 truffle, cut into 6 slices

Mousseline:

12 ounces skinless and boneless whiting

2 cups crème fraîche or heavy cream

3 egg whites, slightly beaten

1 teaspoon salt

¼ teaspoon white pepper

Marinate lobster in Cognac for 10 minutes. Drain and set aside. Prepare the whiting mousse according to instructions for Salmon Mousseline.

Wash filets well. Put the fish on a flat surface. Use a pastry bag with a large fluted tip and apply the mousse to the full length of each filet. Roll up each filet and arrange in a buttered ovenproof pan. Barely cover with fish stock, together with wine. Bring to a boil, reduce heat, and simmer gently for about 10 minutes. Drain the filets on a kitchen towel and place them on a long serving platter. Keep warm.

Boil the poaching liquid until reduced to 1 cup. Cool, then beat in egg yolks, whisking vigorously. Beat in clarified butter very slowly. Correct the seasoning with cayenne. Heat over simmering water until thickened.

Cover each filet with Sauce Américaine. Place a medallion of lobster on top, and coat with the second sauce. Top with a slice of truffle on each filet.

Délices de Sole Honfleuraise Étuvés Normande
(Sole with Oyster Sauce)

6 **filets of sole or flounder,**	*Sauce:*
about 3 pounds	½ **cup (8 tablespoons) butter**
Salt	½ **cup flour**
5 **cups Fish Stock**	2 **dozen oysters, shucked**
4 **slices firm white bread**	12 **stems from large mushrooms,**
¼ **cup (4 tablespoons) clarified**	**minced**
butter	6 **egg yolks**
	⅔ **cup crème fraîche or heavy cream**

Wash the filets. Melt butter for sauce in a saucepan and stir in flour. Cook this roux over gentle heat for several minutes without letting it brown. While beating briskly with the whisk, slowly add 2½ cups stock. Bring to a boil, reduce heat, and simmer for 20 minutes. Pass the sauce through a fine sieve and set aside.

Fold fish filets in half and put in a well-buttered pan. Salt lightly and add remaining stock. Poach fish for about 10 minutes, then drain and keep warm.

While fish is poaching, put oysters in a small saucepan with their juices. In another saucepan, mix sauce and minced mushroom stems. Salt lightly, bring to a boil, and simmer for 10 minutes. Strain, adding sauce to oysters. Heat to boiling.

Cut about a dozen croûtons from the bread in the shape of an *N* and brown them in clarified butter.

Mix egg yolks and crème fraîche. Beat a cup of the hot sauce into the egg mixture, return to sauce, and simmer, without boiling, until thickened. Season to taste with salt.

Arrange sole on a platter, overlapping filets. Cover with the sauce and arrange croûtons around edge.

Délices de Sole de Douvres Étuvés au Whisky
(Poached Dover Sole with Whiskey Sauce)

10 filets of sole, about 3 pounds	Flour for dusting
Salt	1 egg
3 tablespoons Sauce Vin Blanc	2 cups fine, dry bread crumbs
⅔ cup whiskey	Oil for deep-frying, heated to 360°
⅔ cup crème fraîche or heavy cream	1 bunch curly parsley

Wash fish and cut each filet in half lengthwise. Fold 12 of the pieces in half again and put into a well-buttered pan. Salt lightly and add water to cover. Cover with buttered parchment paper or foil and poach for about 10 minutes. When the filets are done, remove and keep warm.

Boil the cooking juices until reduced by half, then pour this liquid into a pan, add Sauce Vin Blanc, and simmer for about 15 minutes. Strain the sauce, then stir in whiskey and crème fraîche.

Prepare the remaining filets as for Fried Sole with Sauce Gribiche, using flour, egg, and bread crumbs; deep-fry in oil. Preheat oven to 450 degrees or heat broiler. Arrange the poached filets on a long heatproof serving platter. Cover with the whiskey sauce, then brown under the broiler or in very hot oven until golden. Garnish with deep-fried sole alternated with bouquets of parsley.

Goujonnettes de Sole Frites Sauce Gribiche
(Fried Sole with Sauce Gribiche)

6 filets of sole, about 3 pounds	3 lemons, sliced
Salt	Deep-Fried Parsley
3 tablespoons flour	2 cups Sauce Gribiche
3 eggs, lightly beaten	
1½ cups fine bread crumbs	
Oil for deep-frying, heated to 360°	

Cut the filets into 1-inch-wide strips, season with salt, roll in flour, dip in beaten egg, then roll in bread crumbs. Make sure the strips are completely covered with bread crumbs.

Place the fish in a frying basket and lower into hot oil. Cook gently until golden, then drain on paper towels and sprinkle with salt.

Arrange the fish on a round platter covered with a napkin or paper doily. Surround with lemon slices and serve with Sauce Gribiche on the side.

Turbot Gravellinois Poché Sauce Moutarde
(Poached Turbot with Sauce Moutarde)

The turbot, as always, made a great hit. I think the best way to prepare this fine fish is to poach it and serve it with Hollandaise or a Mousseline Sauce—and it goes without saying that the turbot must be fresh! When fresh, the flesh is lightly pearled, while when frozen the color is whitish. We served turbot as steaks for tables accommodating five passengers. Above this number the turbots were served whole, a great delight not only to the palate but to the eye as well.

1 whole turbot, about 3½ to 4 pounds (or sole or flounder)	Several sprigs of fresh parsley
4 lemons, cut in half	3 to 4 leeks (green part only), sliced
1 teaspoon sea salt	Deep-Fried Parsley
2 bay leaves	Sauce Moutarde
1 sprig fresh thyme	

Clean the turbot, keeping the head intact. Wash the fish carefully in cold running water and rub the light side with half a lemon. Put the fish on the rack of a fish poacher. Cover with water and add the sea salt, bay leaves, thyme, parsley, leeks, and the lemon half used to rub the turbot. Cover, bring to a boil, then reduce heat to a very gentle simmer known as "shivering." Poach for about 30 minutes. Cut remaining lemon halves to make notches with zigzag cuts.

　　　Remove fish and drain, then put it on a serving platter covered with a napkin folded into a rectangle. Garnish with remaining lemon halves and Deep-Fried Parsley. Serve with Sauce Moutarde.

Variations

Poached Turbot with Sauce Mousseline

Prepare as for above recipe, but serve with Sauce Mousseline and accompany with steamed new potatoes.

Poached Turbot with Sauce Riche

Prepare as for Poached Turbot with Sauce Moutarde and serve with Sauce Riche and steamed new potatoes.

Poached Turbot with Sauce Gavarnie

Prepare as for Poached Turbot with Sauce Moutarde and serve with Sauce Gavarnie and steamed new potatoes.

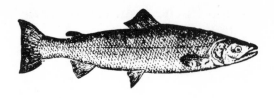

Turbot Saumonné Braisé à la Présidente
(Braised Turbot with Salmon Filets)

This recipe was created on board the France *in honor of the ship's godmother, Mme De Gaulle, when she went on the inaugural cruise to the Canary Islands in 1962. The extremely complex recipe is such as to satisfy the most exacting gourmet. The natural colors, moreover, produce a splendid effect. It was highly praised by Mme de Gaulle and the distinguished passengers invited to the captain's table for the gala dinner.*

1 whole turbot, about 4 pounds
1 small whole salmon, about 1½ pounds
2 cups Muscadet or other dry white wine
Beurre Manié
Salt
Pinch of cayenne
1 cup water

Sole Mousse:
12 ounces sole filets
2 cups crème fraîche or heavy cream
3 egg whites, lightly beaten
Pinch of cayenne

Lobster Butter:
Roe, shell, and coral of 1 lobster
1 cup butter

Garnish:
24 shrimp, cooked, shelled, and deveined
¼ cup (4 tablespoons) butter
6 small oval Puff Pastry shells
12 large mushrooms, fluted

Clean the turbot and remove the 4 filets, using a fish-fileting knife. Remove the dark skin from the 2 back filets, then flatten them with a cleaver. Filet the salmon, skin the belly side, and remove the small bones. Going crosswise, cut each salmon filet into 12 thin slices, or scallops, slightly on the bias. Marinate the turbot filets and salmon scallops for 2 hours in wine. Drain and dry carefully with a kitchen towel. Reserve marinade.

Prepare sole mousse according to instructions in recipe for Salmon Mousseline, using the sole, crème fraîche, egg whites, salt, and cayenne.

Prepare the lobster butter. Finely grind or crush the lobster and combine with the butter. Simmer for 10 minutes over very low heat. Strain butter, pressing out all liquid, then chill. Reheat and pour off the clear butter. Set this butter aside.

Place the fish bones and trimmings into a pot with water to cover. Simmer 30 minutes, then strain. Add Beurre Manié and cook on low heat until thickened. Season to taste with salt and cayenne. Set this fish velouté aside.

Place the turbot filets on a marble surface and spread them with a thin layer of the sole mousse, using a spatula. Reserve remaining mousse. Place the salmon scallops across the top of the mousse and press lightly with the hand. If necessary, secure with toothpicks. Put fish layers side by side into a shallow, well-buttered heatproof pan. Add velouté barely to cover, bring to a boil, reduce heat, and simmer, covered, very gently for about 20 minutes.

Prepare the garnish. Braise the shrimp in 2 tablespoons of butter, then fill pastries. Quickly sauté mushrooms in remaining butter.

Butter a saucepan heavily and fill with reserved marinade and water. Bring to a boil, lower heat, and simmer gently. Mold the remaining sole mousse with a teaspoon into quenelles and place them in the pan. Simmer for 5 minutes, then remove quenelles.

Remove fish filets from pan and arrange side by side down the length of a platter. Surround with quenelles and keep warm.

Combine the quenelle poaching liquid with the velouté in the pan and boil until reduced by half, to the thickness of heavy cream. Divide the sauce into 2 equal parts, each in a separate small saucepan.

Stir 3 tablespoons of the lobster butter into one of the pans. This sauce should be of a fine pink color, contrasting nicely with the natural color of the other. Cover the quenelles and turbot filets with the 2 sauces, alternating between the lobster and the white sauce. Decorate with shrimp-filled pastries and place mushrooms around the fish filets.

Médaillon de Turbot Lorientais Sauté Périnette
(Sautéed Turbot Medallions Périnette)

4 pounds turbot filets	3 hard-cooked egg yolks
3 large, fresh mushrooms, peeled and trimmed	2 tablespoons minced truffles
	1 cup fine, dry bread crumbs
2 tablespoons water	Freshly ground white pepper
Salt	1 lemon, peeled and sliced
⅔ cup clarified butter	Chopped, fresh parsley
Juice of ½ lemon	

Wash filets thoroughly in running water and cut them in half crosswise on the bias.

Braise mushrooms in a saucepan, together with water, salt, 1 tablespoon of the butter, and the lemon juice for 5 minutes. Drain the mushrooms (reserve the liquid), let cool, and then mince. Force the egg yolks through a sieve; mix with mushrooms, truffles, and bread crumbs; season with salt and pepper. Season the turbot with salt, then bread with the mixture, pressing with the hand to ensure good breading.

Brown the filets in a skillet with remaining butter, making sure that the butter is not too hot, since otherwise they would brown excessively before the flesh is properly cooked. Reserve the pan juices. Add reserved mushroom liquid and bring to a boil.

Arrange the filets on a long serving platter and garnish with lemon and parsley. Spoon the combined pan juices over the fish.

Médaillon de Turbot Boulonnais Braisé Bonne Hôtesse
(Braised Stuffed Turbot Medallions)

4½ pounds turbot filets
 1 cup clarified butter
 ⅔ cup dry vermouth

Sauce:
 1 medium onion, minced
 2 tablespoons butter
    Pinch of paprika
 2 tablespoons all-purpose flour
1⅓ cups dry white wine
1⅓ cups Fish Stock
 1 teaspoon salt
 2 mill-turns freshly ground white pepper
 1 bay leaf
 1 sprig fresh thyme
    Several sprigs of fresh parsley

Mousse:
12 ounces whiting filets
 2 cup crème fraîche
 3 egg whites, lightly beaten
 1 teaspoon salt
 ¼ teaspoon pepper

Mussels:
2½ pounds large mussels
 ½ cup water
 1 onion, quartered
 5 to 6 sprigs fresh parsley
 1 bay leaf
 1 sprig fresh thyme
    Flour for dusting
 2 eggs, slightly beaten
    Salt and pepper
 1 cup fine, dry bread crumbs
    Oil for deep-frying, heated to 375°

Clean the filets and cut each into 3 parts on the bias to make 3 medallions. Make an incision lengthwise in side of each filet, shaping a pocket. Set aside.

Prepare sauce. Sauté onion in butter. Add paprika and stir. When the onion is translucent, add flour and cook over low heat without browning. Add wine and stock while stirring constantly with a whisk. Season with salt, pepper, bay leaf, thyme, and parsley. Reduce to two-thirds over gentle heat, then strain the sauce. Keep warm.

Clean mussels, then simmer, covered, with water, onion, parsley, bay leaf, and thyme until opened. Remove the mussels from their shells and dry them on paper towels. Dip in flour, then into eggs, season with salt and pepper, then coat with bread crumbs. Set aside.

Preheat oven to 350 degrees. Prepare a mousse according to instructions in recipe for Salmon Mousseline, using whiting, crème fraîche, egg whites, salt, and pepper. Using a spoon or pastry bag, fill each pocket in turbot with whiting mixture. Place the stuffed filets side by side in a buttered ovenproof pan. Cover with butter and bake in a moderate oven for about 10 minutes. Remove with slotted spoon. Keep warm and reserve the butter in pan.

Deep-fry mussels in oil; when nicely browned, remove from oil and drain on absorbent paper.

Arrange the turbot on a long serving platter. Spoon sauce over fish. Mix the butter in which the fish cooked with the vermouth and simmer until thickened. Arrange mussels around the edge of the platter and spoon vermouth sauce over.

A variation on this dish is to buy whole fish and leave the top filets still attached to the fish, removing the bones with a fish knife and then stuffing the whole fish with poached mussels. You would then replace the filets, place the fish on a rack in a shallow pan, and bake in a hot oven (400 degrees) for about 40 minutes. Serve the fish topped with melted butter.

Suprême de Turbot Ostendais Sauté Aïda
(Turbot au Gratin with Spinach Aïda)

3 pounds turbot filets (or sole or flounder)
Salt
½ cup flour
1 cup butter
¼ cup oil
2½ pounds fresh spinach, trimmed
Pinch of grated nutmeg
¾ cup Sauce Béchamel
½ cup grated Gruyère cheese

Prepare turbot medallions according to instructions in recipe for Braised Stuffed Turbot Medallions. Salt each filet and dip into flour, shaking off excess. Heat half the butter until golden brown; mix with oil and sauté filets.

Meanwhile, cook the spinach in salted water for 5 minutes, press out the water, and then sauté in remaining butter heated until golden brown. Season with salt and nutmeg.

Preheat oven to 450 degrees or heat broiler. Use the spinach as a bed in a baking dish atop which you place the medallions. Cover each medallion with Sauce Béchamel and sprinkle with cheese. Place under the broiler or in a very hot oven until golden brown, about 5 minutes.

Médaillon de Barbue Étuvé Veronique
(Steamed Steaks of Brill Veronique)

When Vincent Auriol, then President of France, was on board the Ile de France *on a trip to the United States, we served Le Medaillon de Barbue Étuvé Veronique at the gala dinner. Gaston Magrin was head chef at the time, and he was warmly commended for the dish by Mme Auriol as they shared a bottle of Champagne at the presidential table.*

1 pound Muscat or other green grapes
1 cup Grand Marnier or Curaçao
6 brill filets, about 3 pounds (or flounder or sole)
2 cups Fish Stock
1 cup butter, in small pieces
Dash of paprika
6 cut-outs of baked Puff Pastry

Peel and remove the seeds from the grapes. Place them in a bowl, cover with ¾ cup Grand Marnier, and marinate for 1 hour.

Cut each filet crosswise in half. Place the filets in a well-buttered pan and cover with stock and remaining Grand Marnier. Lay a piece of buttered wax paper or foil over the pan, bring to a boil on top of stove, lower heat, and simmer gently for about 10 minutes.

Remove the fish from the pan and place on a serving platter; keep warm. Boil the stock until reduced by one-third and strain into a saucepan. Stir in butter, 1 tablespoon at a time, then color the sauce with paprika.

Preheat oven to 500 degrees or heat broiler. Scatter the grapes around the filets. Coat with the sauce and glaze under broiler or in very hot oven for 5 to 6 minutes or until browned. Garnish with small bits of pastry.

Médaillon de Barbue Nordique Sauté Périnette
(Sautéed Brill Medallions Périnette)

This recipe for preparing brill is one of the simplest. It is a very old recipe, but unfortunately it has disappeared from all tables today—except ours, of course!

3 hard-cooked egg yolks	Flour for dusting
2 tablespoons chopped truffles	2 eggs, well beaten
4 large, fresh mushrooms, chopped and braised	1 cup clarified butter
1 cup dry bread crumbs	1 lemon, peeled and sliced
1 teaspoon salt	1 tablespoon chopped fresh parsley
3 pounds brill filets (or sole or flounder)	⅓ cup (5 tablespoons) butter, heated until brown

Force the egg yolks through a sieve, and then mix with truffles and mushrooms. Mix with bread crumbs and season with salt.

Cut each filet into 3 pieces on the bias. Dry fish in a towel, flour lightly, and dip in beaten egg; bread the filets, pressing gently with the hand ensuring uniform breading. Sauté the fish in butter over gentle heat, making sure the butter is not too hot, since brill has firm flesh which must be cooked slowly.

Put the medallions on a long serving platter, garnish with lemon slices, and sprinkle with parsley. Cover with browned butter.

Médaillon de Barbue Nordique Étuvé Havraise
(Braised Medallion of Brill Stuffed with Salmon Mousse)

4 filets of brill, about 3 pounds (or sole or flounder)	1¼ cups clarified butter Deep-Fried Parsley
1 cup Salmon Mousseline	2½ pounds large mussels, fried as in Braised Stuffed Turbot Medallions
3 cups Fish Stock	
6 egg yolks, well beaten	

From each filet, cutting on the bias, prepare 3 slices, then make an incision in the center of each to the top extending practically the entire length of the piece; shape a pocket.

Place mousse in pastry bag with a medium nozzle and stuff the fish slices. Secure with toothpicks. Transfer the fish to a well-buttered baking dish, then add stock barely to cover, bring to a boil, reduce heat, and simmer, covered, over low heat for 15 to 20 minutes. Meanwhile, prepare the mussels.

When fish is done, transfer to a long serving platter and keep warm. Strain cooking liquid into a saucepan and boil until reduced by half. Remove from heat and beat into egg yolks with a whisk. Return to saucepan and stir over low heat until thickened. Remove from heat and slowly beat in clarified butter. Correct seasoning, strain, and use the sauce to cover the fish. Garnish with alternating mounds of Deep-Fried Parsley and Deep-Fried Mussels.

Suprême de Barbue à la Façon des Gastilleurs
(Gourmet's Filet of Brill)

Gastilleurs is an archaic word found in Rabelais, who uses it to mean "gourmet." It is, of course, derived from the word gastric. *This dish was highly complimented by our passengers, many of whom asked me for the recipe.*

4 filets of brill, about 3 pounds
    (or sole or flounder)
4 pounds fresh spinach, trimmed
2 shallots, minced
½ cup (8 tablespoons) butter
8 fresh mushrooms, trimmed and
    left whole
    Juice of 1 lemon
    Salt
2 mill-turns freshly ground white
    pepper

¼ cup Sauce Béchamel
    Pinch of cayenne
2 eggs, well beaten
¼ cup all-purpose flour
    Breading (see Sautéed Brill
    Medallions Périnette)
½ cup (8 tablespoons) clarified butter
    Pinch of grated nutmeg
½ cup grated Gruyère cheese

Cut each filet into 3 slices on the bias, making a total of 12 slices. Flatten slightly with a broad knife, then dry on a towel. Chill.

Cook the spinach for 5 minutes in salted water. Drain and press out the moisture. Cook shallots in 2 tablespoons of the butter without browning. Add mushrooms, lemon juice, ½ teaspoon salt, and pepper. Mix well with a spatula, then cook over low heat until all the liquid from the mushrooms has evaporated. Sitr in Sauce Béchamel and season with cayenne.

Let sauce cool, then spread a layer on half of the fish slices. Cover with the remaining slices and salt lightly. Season egg with salt and pepper, then dust fish with flour, dip in beaten egg, then coat with bread crumbs. If necessary, fix together with toothpicks. Heat the clarified butter until foamy in a skillet and sauté the fish over low heat until golden brown, about 5 to 6 minutes on each side. Keep warm.

Preheat oven to 450 degrees or heat broiler. Heat remaining butter until brown and sauté the spinach, stirring with a fork to separate the leaves. Lightly salt and flavor with nutmeg. When the spinach is hot, put it on a long, heatproof serving platter. Place the fish on top and sprinkle with cheese. Place platter under the broiler or in hot oven for 5 to 6 minutes or until cheese is golden brown.

Saumon de Gave Braisé Castel de Nérac
(Poached Salmon with Crayfish Sauce)

I can highly recommend this method of preparing salmon. The flesh of this fish, which is rather dry by nature, becomes more succulent with the braising and saucing of this recipe. The crayfish garnish is among the richest of sauces and is dramatic in appearance. Aboard the France this dish was usually served on special order at the captain's table for gala dinners.

1 salmon, about 4 pounds, scaled and cleaned
Dry white wine
2 carrots, peeled
2 onions, minced
2 stalks celery, minced
Several sprigs of fresh parsley
2 sprigs fresh thyme
1 bay leaf
1¼ cups butter

12 crayfish
⅓ cup Armagnac, warmed
½ cup crème fraîche or heavy cream
2 ripe tomatoes, peeled, seeded, and diced
3 large, fresh mushrooms, trimmed and diced
Salt and pepper
¼ cup chopped truffles

Wash salmon well and place on the rack of a stainless-steel fish poacher. Add wine to half cover. Mince half the vegetables, combine and add parsley, thyme, and bay leaf and sauté in ¼ cup of butter until golden. Spoon vegetables and herbs over the fish and marinate for 6 hours.

Preheat oven to 350 degrees. While fish is marinating, finely dice remaining vegetables and sauté in ¼ cup of butter without browning. Add crayfish and cook until they take on a pale red color. Flambé with Armagnac, then remove crayfish and set aside. Force the vegetables and cooking juices through a food mill or whirl in a food processor and replace in saucepan.

Push the vegetables off the top to go around the salmon. Butter the salmon lightly, cover the poacher, and poach in a moderate oven for about 35 minutes. Drain off vegetables and pan juices and reserve. Keep salmon warm.

Simmer crème fraîche until reduced by half. Simmer the tomatoes until pulpy. Sauté mushrooms in ¼ cup butter. Add mushrooms and tomatoes to cream, then mix with crayfish sauce. Add salmon poaching liquid, then stir in remaining butter, tablespoon by tablespoon.

Place the salmon on a long serving platter and arrange crayfish around it. Carefully strip off skin on top, cover fish with sauce, and sprinkle with finely chopped truffles.

Saumon Rose de Gave Braisé "France"
(Braised Salmon à la *France*)

This recipe, created on board the France, *was usually served at the captain's dinner in tourist class. We also served it in first class, especially during cruises.*

1 **salmon, about 4½ pounds, scaled and cleaned**	1 **cup butter, in small pieces**
Salt and pepper	6 **fresh mushrooms, washed and trimmed**
2 **onions, chopped**	1 **lobster, about 2½ pounds**
2 **carrots, chopped**	¼ **cup Cognac**
2 **stalks celery, chopped**	2 **ripe tomatoes, peeled, seeded, and chopped**
6 **tablespoons oil**	
Several sprigs of fresh parsley	1 **cup crème fraîche or heavy cream**
1 **sprig fresh thyme**	**Pinch of cayenne**
1 **bay leaf**	**Small crescents of baked Puff Pastry**
2 **cups Chablis wine**	

Preheat oven to 400 degrees. Season salmon with salt and pepper. Sauté onions, carrots, and celery in oil until golden. Place vegetables on the bottom of a fish poacher and add parsley, thyme, and bay leaf. Lay salmon on top. Pour in wine and add ¼ cup of the butter, cut into small pieces. Cover the dish and braise in a hot oven for about 40 minutes, basting frequently.

Meanwhile, flute mushrooms and cook in 2 tablespoons of butter. Poach the lobster, remove from shell, and slice the tail into 6 round slices. Cook tomatoes until pulpy. Simmer crème fraîche until reduced by half.

When the salmon is ready, transfer it to a long serving platter and keep warm. Stir tomato and crème fraîche into the poaching liquid and mix well with a whisk. Stir in remaining butter, 1 tablespoon at a time. Correct seasoning with salt and cayenne.

Arrange the lobster slices on either side of the salmon and place a mushroom atop each slice. Cover salmon with the sauce and surround the dish with pastry crescents.

Darne de Saumon Grillée, Sauce Béarnaise
(Grilled Salmon Steaks with Sauce Béarnaise)

If you wish to grill salmon, the fish must be absolutely fresh. Sauce Béarnaise is the ideal accompaniment, for it makes the flesh more tender and succulent. From my several trips to Scotland, I can state with some authority that cold-water salmon has the best flavor.

1 **whole salmon, about 4 pounds, or 6 2-inch steaks**	**Parslied Potatoes**
Few drops of oil	2 **lemons, sliced**
Salt and freshly ground pepper	2 **cups Sauce Béarnaise**

Prepare coals or heat broiler. Wash the salmon carefully, dry in a towel, and, using a sharp knife, cut into 2-inch-wide crosswise slices; discard head and tail. Brush the steaks with oil, season with salt and pepper, and place on a hot grill 6 inches over a bed of gray coals. (Fish can also be grilled in broiler.) If you wish a pretty grid design on the steaks, lift each one with a spatula and give it a quarter turn. Cook for 10 minutes, gently pushing the coals to the side. Turn and repeat for the other side of the steak.

Place the steaks on a long platter lined with a napkin. Surround with potatoes and place a lemon slice on each steak. Serve with Sauce Béarnaise.

Darne de Saumon Rose Grillée Languedocienne
(Grilled Salmon Steaks with Herbed Butter)

Salt
6 small ripe tomatoes
1 shallot, minced
1 clove garlic, minced
2 teaspoons chopped fresh
  parsley

1½ cups butter
2½ pounds large potatoes
6 salmon steaks, each 1 inch thick
⅓ cup oil

Prepare grill or heat broiler. Put tomatoes in a well-oiled ovenproof dish and brush with oil, sprinkle with salt, and grill under the broiler for 15 minutes or until easily pierced and hot.

Sauté shallot, garlic, and parsley in 1 tablespoon of the butter; cool. Mash 1 cup of the butter until soft, then beat in sautéed vegetables. Shape mixture with wet hands into a roll 1½ inches in diameter. Roll in wet parchment paper and chill until hard. Cut into 6 slices. With a melon baller, cut small balls from potatoes. Boil for 8 to 10 minutes, drain, and sauté until nicely browned in a skillet with remaining butter. Salt lightly.

Transfer the salmon steaks to a long serving platter, arrange the tomatoes and potatoes around them, garnishing each steak with a slice of the butter. Serve immediately.

Saumon Rose du St.-Laurent Sauté Lemaire
(Breaded Salmon Medallions Lemaire)

12 large mushrooms, peeled and
   finely chopped
Juice of ½ lemon
1 cup butter
1 cup crème fraîche or heavy
  cream
Pinch of cayenne
3½ pounds large new potatoes
6 salmon medallions (cut from
  filet)

Salt
Freshly ground white pepper
¼ cup flour
3 eggs, well beaten
1 cup fine dry bread crumbs
2 cups Sauce Normande, flavored
  with ½ teaspoon minced fresh
  tarragon

Cook mushrooms with lemon juice in a saucepan with ¼ cup of butter until all the liquid has evaporated. Cook crème fraîche until it begins to thicken, then stir in the mushrooms. Season with cayenne. Set both aside.

Using a melon baller, cut 30 balls from the potatoes. Wash well to remove excess starch, then using a sieve or a deep-fry basket, blanch the potatoes for 5 minutes in boiling water.

Season salmon with salt and freshly ground pepper. Dredge lightly in flour, dip into beaten egg, and coat with bread crumbs. Heat ⅓ cup of butter until golden brown and sauté fish.

Heat remaining butter and sauté potatoes until tender and brown; salt lightly. Reheat cream.

Line a long serving platter with the cream sauce and place the salmon medallions on it. Put the potatoes in 2 portions at either end of the platter. Pass a sauceboat of Sauce Normande lightly flavored with tarragon.

Médaillon de Saumon Québecois Farci Sauté Gastera
(Stuffed Salmon Medallions)

6 salmon medallions (cut from filet)
2 tablespoons butter
12 large, fresh mushrooms, peeled, trimmed, and chopped
1 teaspoon lemon juice
2 dozen Portuguese, Maine, or Blue Point oysters
2½ pounds mussels
1 bay leaf
Several sprigs of fresh parsley
1 sprig fresh thyme
½ cup dry white wine
1 cup crème fraîche or heavy cream
Salt and freshly ground pepper
Flour for dusting
3 eggs, well beaten
1 cup fine, dry bread crumbs
3 cups Sauce Normande, made with shellfish cooking juices
½ cup (8 tablespoons) clarified butter

Make an incision in the center of the side of each medallion, shaping a pocket for stuffing.

Melt butter in a saucepan and add mushrooms and lemon juice. Bring to boil, reduce heat, and simmer until all the liquid has evaporated.

Scrape and wash oysters and mussels; place in a skillet with bay leaf, parsley, thyme, and wine; cover and cook over low heat. When opened, cool and remove them from the shells.

Boil crème fraîche until reduced by half, and add mushrooms. Season with salt and pepper to taste. Place mixture in a pastry bag with a large round tip and stuff the salmon medallions with the mushroom mixture. Close with toothpicks, sprinkle with salt, then dredge in flour. Dip in beaten egg and coat with bread crumbs. Season with salt and pepper and chill.

Place mussels and oysters into a small saucepan, stir in 1 cup of the Sauce Normande; heat.

Cook the medallions slowly in a skillet in hot clarified butter. Place salmon onto a platter and pour sauce over. Serve with a sauceboat of remaining Sauce Normande.

Mousseline de Saumon
(Salmon Mousseline)

12 ounces boneless and skinless salmon
2 cups crème fraîche or heavy cream
3 egg whites, lightly beaten
1 teaspoon salt
¼ teaspoon freshly ground white pepper

Grind salmon meat to a purée in a mortar or food processor, then put this purée in a bowl set on a layer of shaved ice. Using a spatula, beat in crème fraîche, a small amount at a time, along with egg whites, salt, and pepper.

Use mixture as directed in recipe or shape into quenelles and poach for 15 to 20 minutes in Fish Stock.

Loup de Calanque Braisé "France" ou à la Façon du Chef
(Braised Mediterranean Sea Bass à la *France*)

In French, le bar *is Atlantic sea bass, while* le loup *indicates Mediterranean sea bass. This recipe is certainly the best way to serve this fine fish. It was created aboard the* Ile de France *and met with great success among our guests. Whenever the skipper or his second-in-command invited old faithful customers or VIPs to his table on the Le Hâvre-New York run, we always prepared special meat or fish dishes, and* le bar *was often chosen because of its fine flesh and attractive presentation. This recipe was often followed, and it was invariably hailed with many compliments.*

1 whole sea bass or striped bass, about 4½ pounds
Salt
Freshly ground white pepper
1¼ cups crème fraîche or heavy cream
6 large fresh mushrooms
Few sprigs of fresh chervil, chopped
6 small triangles baked Puff Pastry

Marinade:
2 cups dry white wine
1 carrot, chopped
1 onion, chopped
1 stalk celery, chopped
1 bay leaf
1 sprig fresh thyme

Stuffing:
1 pound fresh spinach, trimmed
1 very ripe tomato, peeled, seeded, and chopped
1¼ cups butter
Salt
1 small lobster (about 2 pounds), or 8 large shrimp
½ pound sea scallops
1 shallot, chopped
1 hard-cooked egg, diced
2 anchovy filets, chopped
1 tablespoon chopped fresh parsley
1 tablespoon dry bread crumbs

Clean the fish, leaving on head and tail, and wash carefully. Dry with a towel and rub the cavity with a little salt and pepper, then set aside.

Prepare stuffing. Cook spinach in boiling salted water for 5 minutes. Drain and squeeze out all the water. Put the tomato, ¼ cup of butter, and a pinch of salt in a small saucepan. Bring to a boil, reduce heat, and simmer gently until juices have evaporated. Remove the shell from the lobster tail or shrimp. Poach together with scallops in salted water to cover for 10 minutes; dice. Sauté shallots in 1 tablespoon of butter in a small saucepan without browning.

Mix the spinach, tomato, shellfish, shallot, hard-cooked egg, anchovy filets, parsley, and bread crumbs. Salt lightly, remembering that the anchovy has already salted the ingredients to a certain extent, and season to taste with pepper. Stuff the bass with this mixture and close up.

Marinate the stuffed bass for 2 hours in marinade.

Preheat oven to 400 degrees. Drain the fish; sieve the marinade, reserving vegetables and liquid separately. Sauté the vegetables of the marinade in 2 tablespoons of the butter briefly without browning. Put the vegetables in the bottom of a fish poacher and put the fish on the rack. Season with salt and a little pepper, and dot the upper surface of the fish with ¼ cup butter. Cover the poacher and braise for 1 hour in a very hot oven. When the fish is cooked, remove to a long serving platter and keep warm.

Maiden entry of the *France* into New York Harbor (***above***). Menu cover for 1973 (***below***).

CENTENAIRE DU VOYAGE DE PHILEAS FOGG

PAQUEBOT FRANCE
CROISIERE AUTOUR DU MONDE

COMPAGNIE GÉNÉRALE TRANSATLANTIQUE

French Line

The *France's* kitchens were very carefully organized.
Little food stood around before the service (*above*);
almost everything was in the refrigerators
ready to be used (*opposite top*).
Only the large pots with the *fonds* and the smaller pots
with the sauces are visible (*above*).

The *sous chefs*, cooks, and helpers wait at their posts
like good soldiers or actors expecting their call. Henri Le Huédé
(second from left, *below*) inspects an eagle sculpted in ice.

A vast refrigerator stocked with meat from all over the world (*above*).

The chefs assemble their dishes (*above*).
Pastry and spun sugar were a great specialty (*below*).

A cooking demonstration (*above*), led by chef Henri Le Huédé, Pierre Franey, and Craig Claiborne. Craig Claiborne (*below*) cuts an elaborate cake on the *France*.

Chef Le Huédé greeting Salvador Dali and the French Ambassador
in the first-class dining room on board the *France* (**above**).

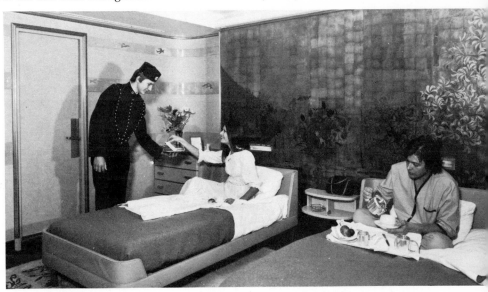

The *France* even managed to make breakfast in bed a culinary delight,
and the ship's perfect service satisfied the most demanding guests.

Crisp linen, shining crystal, beautiful menus,
vintage champagne, and passengers in evening dress
made every dinner a gala occasion (*above*).

The French Ambassador and
Mme Alphand (*above*) arrive for dinner.
Bellboys drill on the stern (*below*).

On board the *France*, the main activity
was—romance (*above*).

Two worlds meet in Tahiti (*opposite below*).

Ernest Hemingway with his favorite bartender (*above left*).
Chef Le Huédé beams at a dinner for the Chevaliers de Tastevin (*above right*).

A flotilla of small craft meets the *France*
on her maiden voyage to the United States.

Strain braising juices into a saucepan, add marinade, and boil until reduced to 1½ cups. Then, stirring with a whisk, blend in ½ cup butter cut into small pieces. Boil crème fraîche until reduced to half and stir into sauce. Flute and braise mushrooms in remaining butter and place them along full length of the fish.

Cover the fish with the sauce, sprinkle with chervil, and circle with pastry triangles.

Bar Argenté de Golfe Braisé ou Rôti Jean-Bart
(Gulf Sea Bass Braised or Roasted)

The silvery Gulf sea bass braised or roasted this way is so delicate that it needs a highly flavored accompaniment such as a mustard sauce to bring out its particular virtues. Deep-Fried Onion Rings provide a happy complement to this dish.

For the smaller tables, the sea bass was served as steaks. For more than eight passengers, the fish was served whole. This was very hard work for the staff, and Léonard Allain, the fish chef, was a key element in its success. He is a remarkable man of small size but large talent.

1 whole sea bass or striped bass, about 4 to 5 pounds	Salt Freshly ground black pepper
2 large onions	6 tablespoons butter
1 carrot	6 shallots
1 stalk celery Sprigs of fresh parsley	3 tablespoons Sauce Velouté (with fish base)
1 bay leaf	1 cup crème fraîche or heavy cream, boiled until thickened
1 sprig fresh thyme	1 teaspoon Dijon-style mustard
3 cups dry white wine, approximately	Deep-Fried Onion Rings

Wash the fish well. Mince 1 of the onions, the carrot, and the celery. Make a bed of the minced vegetables, parsley, bay leaf, and thyme in a large pan. Place the fish on top, pour in wine to cover, and marinate for 2 hours.

Preheat oven to 400 degrees. Drain the fish, dry with paper towels, and place on a roasting pan; season with salt and pepper. Drain the marinating vegetables and strain and reserve wine marinade. Scatter the vegetables around the fish and dot fish with 4 tablespoons of the butter. Bake uncovered in a hot oven for about 35 minutes or until golden, basting often. Strain pan juices and reserve.

While fish is in oven, mince the shallots and sauté until wilted in remaining butter in a heavy-bottomed saucepan. Add the reserved marinade and boil until reduced by half. Stir Sauce Velouté, crème fraîche, mustard, and juices into saucepan. Simmer the sauce over low heat for 20 minutes.

Place the fish on a long platter. Pour the sauce over and surround with clusters of Deep-Fried Onion Rings.

Loup de Calanque Grillé aux Herbes de Lavandou
(Grilled Mediterranean Sea Bass with Herb Sauce)

1 sea bass or striped bass, about 4½ pounds
⅔ cup olive oil
¾ cup crème fraîche or heavy cream
⅔ cup butter, cut in small pieces
Several sprigs of fresh parsley
Parslied Potatoes

Marinade:
3 cups Chablis wine
1 onion, chopped
1 stalk celery, chopped
Several stalks fennel, chopped
1 bay leaf
1 sprig fresh thyme
1 star anise (sold in oriental foods stores)

Clean the fish, leaving on head and tail, then wash thoroughly in several changes of water. Put the fish in a glass or stainless-steel pan and add Marinade to cover. Marinate for about 2 hours.

Prepare grill or heat broiler. Also preheat oven to 400 degrees. Remove the fish from the marinade and brush with oil. Grill 3 to 4 minutes on each side over a hot charcoal fire, moving to give it a diamond-grilled appearance. (This can also be done in a broiler.) Strain the marinade reserving both the vegetables and liquid. Sauté the vegetables in a skillet, with 2 tablespoons of olive oil, taking care not to let them brown. Put sautéed vegetables in the bottom of a fish poacher. Place the bass on this bed, add the marinade, and, without covering the kettle, bake in hot oven for 30 minutes, basting frequently.

When the fish is cooked, remove to a long serving platter and keep warm. Cover fish with a kitchen towel to absorb juices, then strain the poaching liquid into a saucepan and boil until reduced by one-third. Add crème fraîche, boil until reduced to half, then, while stirring with a whisk, slowly blend in butter.

Serve the bass on a platter covered with a folded napkin (in shape of a gondola). Surround the fish with parsley and serve the sauce alongside. Serve with Parslied Potatoes.

Daurade Fraîche Sénégalaise Braisée à la Goréenne
(Braised Red Snapper à la Goréenne)

1 red snapper or porgy, about 3 pounds
6 ripe tomatoes, cut into wedges
Pinch of powdered saffron
2 stalks fennel, minced
Salt
Freshly ground white pepper
½ cup (8 tablespoons) butter, cut into small piecees

3 small limes, peeled and sliced
1 tablespoon chopped fresh parlsey

Marinade:
Juice of 12 small limes
2 cups dry white wine
1 tablespoon each chopped fresh parsley and chives

Clean and scale the fish. Wash thoroughly and put into a stainless-steel or glass pan. Marinate for 6 hours in the lime juice and wine, together with parsley and chives.

Preheat oven to 400 degrees. Drain fish and reserve marinade. In an ovenproof pan, place a bed of tomatoes. Season with saffron and scatter fennel on top. Place the fish atop the vegetables and season with salt and pepper. Boil the marinade until reduced by half and pour it over the fish. Bake fish in a hot oven for about 20 minutes, basting frequently.

When fish is done, remove from pan and place on a long serving platter. Keep warm. Strain the pan juices, pressing liquid out of vegetables, then reheat in a saucepan and stir in the butter. Spoon the sauce over the fish and garnish with lime slices. Sprinkle with parsley and serve.

Daurade Lozida al Dao
(Braised Red Snapper Filets with Olive and Shallot Sauce)

2 red snapper or porgy, filets about 3 pounds	Pinch of grated nutmeg
2 cups Fish Stock	12 each pitted green and black olives
1 cup dry white wine	2 shallots, minced
Juice of 1 lemon	2 tablespoons butter
1¼ cups butter, cut in small pieces	⅓ cup drained capers
	Sprigs of watercress

Wash the filets thoroughly then cut each into 3 slices, on the bias.

Reduce stock by half. Put the fish in a well-buttered, heatproof pan and pour in stock and the white wine to cover. Add the lemon juice, bring to a boil, reduce heat, and simmer for about 15 minutes.

When fish is done, remove from pan and put on a long platter and keep warm. Boil the poaching liquid until reduced by half, then strain into a saucepan. Using a small whisk, blend in butter and add nutmeg. Put this sauce in a double boiler over warm (but not boiling) water cover to keep warm.

Cut olives in half crosswise. Bring them to a boil in lightly salted water, then drain. Sauté shallots in butter, then add the olives, shallots, and capers to hot sauce. Cover the fish slices with the sauce and garnish with watercress.

Daurade Fraîche de Pacifique Braisée Doaumont
(Braised Stuffed Red Snapper with Mussel and Crayfish Garnish)

2 red snapper or porgy filets, about 2 pounds	*Salmon Mousse:*
2 cups Fish Stock	6 ounces salmon filet
6 egg yolks	2 cups crème fraîche or heavy cream
1¼ cups clarified butter	3 egg whites
2 teaspoons chopped fresh tarragon	Salt
Deep-Fried Mussels (see Braised Medallion or Brill Stuffed with Salmon Mousse)	Pinch of cayenne
Crayfish à l'Américaine, using 24 crayfish and cooked as for Lobster à l'Américaine	¼ cup chopped truffles

Clean the filets, and cut each into 3 medallions, on the bias. Cut a pocket in the side of each for stuffing. Prepare mousseline, following general instruction for Salmon Mousseline recipe, then add truffles. Put mousseline into a pastry bag fitted with a large nozzle, and stuff the medallions with salmon mixture. Poach as for Braised Medallion of Brill Stuffed with Salmon Mousse, using the stock for the poaching liquid.

When fish is cooked, drain and reserve the poaching liquid. Arrange fish on a long serving platter and keep warm.

Preheat oven to 450 degrees or heat broiler. Boil the poaching liquid until reduced by half. Remove pan from the heat and let cool slightly, then quickly beat in the egg yolks. Heat mixture in a double boiler or over low heat until well blended and slightly thickened. Stir in the clarified butter, then add tarragon and correct seasoning. Cover fish with the sauce and place under the broiler or in oven to lightly brown. Garnish with alternating Deep-Fried Mussels and Crayfish à l'Américaine.

Truite de Torrent Sautée à la Façon du Héas
(Sautéed Mountain Trout)

6 trout, 8 ounces each	10 fresh mushrooms, minced
Salt	1 cup dry bread crumbs
Freshly ground white pepper	2 hard-cooked eggs, pushed through
½ cup flour	a sieve
1¼ cups butter	1 tablespoon chopped fresh parsley

Clean the trout, leaving the heads and tails intact. Wash in several changes of water, dry, and season with salt and pepper. Flour each fish, shaking off excess flour. Sauté trout until brown in half the butter, turning and basting frequently for 12 to 15 minutes. Remove from skillet and keep hot, reserving the butter in the skillet.

Brown the mushrooms in the butter in which the trout were cooked, salting to taste during cooking. Sauté bread crumbs in remaining butter, then add eggs and parsley. Sauté until crumbs are brown. When the mushrooms are nicely browned, use them to make a bed on a long serving platter. Arrange the trout on the mushrooms and cover with bread crumbs.

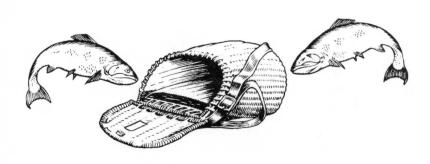

Truites de Torrent Étuvées "France"
(Poached Mountain Trout à la *France*)

6 trout, 12 ounces each	6 fresh mushroom caps, fluted
1 quart Fish Stock	¼ cup (4 tablespoons) butter
1 cup crème fraîche or heavy	Salt
cream	1 tablespoon chopped fresh chives
6 tablespoons Sauce Hollandaise	
Pinch of cayenne	

Clean the trout, keeping the head and tails intact. Wash thoroughly and put the fish on a buttered, heatproof platter or Pyrex dish. Add stock to cover and bring to a boil. Reduce heat until the liquid "shivers" and complete poaching for about 20 minutes.

When done drain the trout, dry on a towel, and arrange on a long serving platter and keep warm. Strain the poaching liquid into a saucepan and boil until reduced to one-fourth. Remove from heat and beat in crème fraîche and Sauce Hollandaise with a whisk. Correct seasoning with cayenne.

Meanwhile, braise mushrooms in butter, salt, and water to cover; cook until all the liquid has evaporated. Put a mushroom cap on each trout, then cover with the sauce and sprinkle with chives.

Lotte de Mer Sautée Girondine
(Sautéed Monkfish Girondine)

4 monkfish filets (angler fish, goosefish), about 1½ pounds	2 shallots, chopped
	½ cup dry white wine
1 quart Court Bouillon	½ cup Madeira wine
Salt	2 large, very ripe tomatoes, peeled,
Freshly ground white pepper	seeded, and chopped
½ cup all-purpose flour	3 slices bread, cut into ½-inch cubes
⅓ cup olive oil	1 tablespoon chopped fresh parsley

Cut each filet into 3 pieces, on the bias. Wash thoroughly, then poach the 12 medallions in court bouillon for 3 minutes.

Drain fish and dry in a towel. Season with salt and pepper, then flour the medallions, shaking each piece to eliminate excess flour. Brown in a skillet in ⅓ cup very hot oil. When the medallions are nicely browned, remove them to a serving platter and keep warm.

Heat the shallots in the pan drippings and, when translucent, add wine and Madeira. Add tomatoes to the skillet, season with salt and pepper, and stir all ingredients gently with a wooden spoon or spatula. Heat to a boil, reduce heat, and simmer for 15 minutes.

While sauce is simmering, fry bread cubes in remaining oil until brown. Spoon sauce around fish and sprinkle croûtons on top. Garnish with parsley.

Rouelle de Thonine au Four à l'Algérienne
(Braised Mediterranean Tuna Steaks)

6 fresh tuna steaks, cut through bone, about 8 ounces each	2 teaspoons chopped fresh chives
3 anchovy filets, each cut in 8 pieces	1 tablespoon chopped fennel
Juice of 8 lemons	6 large ripe tomatoes, peeled, seeded, and diced
⅓ cup olive oil	1 teaspoon saffron threads
¾ cup very dry white wine	1 cup butter, cut in small pieces
2 teaspoons chopped fresh parsley	Salt and freshly ground pepper
	2 lemons, peeled and sliced
	1 tablespoon chopped fresh parsley

Wash tuna carefully, making sure to remove any clotted blood from the bony centers. Using the point of a sharp knife, stud each tuna steak with small segments of anchovy. Place the slices on a long, deep platter or Pyrex dish and moisten with the lemon juice, olive oil, and wine. Sprinkle with a mixture of parsley, chives, and fennel. Turn the tuna several times to cover, then let marinate for about 2 hours.

Preheat oven to 400 degrees. Use tomatoes to line the bottom of a heatproof baking dish. Sprinkle saffron over the tomatoes, then place the tuna on this bed. Strain the marinade into a saucepan, bring to a boil, salt lightly, and boil until reduced by one-third. Cover the tuna with this reduced marinade. Bring again to a boil, cover, and bake in hot oven for about 20 minutes, basting frequently.

When done, transfer the tuna to a long serving platter. Pour the poaching liquid into a saucepan and beat in the butter, stirring constantly with a small whisk. Season with salt and pepper. Cover the tuna with this sauce and garnish each piece with 2 lemon slices and some chopped parsley.

Brandade de Morue Bénédictine
(Baked Potatoes Stuffed with Codfish)

3 pound piece salt cod	Pinch of cayenne
1 bay leaf	6 large Idaho potatoes
1 sprig fresh thyme	3 egg yolks
1 cup soft, fine white bread crumbs	4 slices bread, cut into cubes
¾ cup olive oil	¼ cup (4 tablespoons) butter
4 cloves garlic, crushed	1 clove garlic, chopped
1¼ cups crème fraîche or heavy cream	Few sprigs of fresh parsley

Soak the cod for 12 hours in cold water. Change water several times.

Preheat oven to 350 degrees, then bake potatoes in moderate oven for 1 hour.

While potatoes are baking, drain fish and poach for 10 minutes in water to cover, with bay leaf and thyme. Let cool in the liquid, then carefully remove skin and bones. Finely shred the codfish into a bowl and stir in bread crumbs. Heat the olive oil and garlic in saucepan over low heat. In another pan, heat the crème fraîche until almost boiling, then beat it into olive oil. Remove the garlic and blend the cream mixture into the cod slowly, keeping the mixture smooth. (You can also combine in a food processor.) Season with cayenne and set aside.

Turn oven up to 450 degrees or heat broiler. When potatoes are done, spoon out the mealy part and force it through a food mill, keeping the skins intact for stuffing. Blend egg yolks into potato pulp, beating vigorously with a spatula. Fill the potato skins with the creamed codfish, then, using a pastry bag with a fluted nozzle, pipe a broad border on the surface of the potato around the codfish. Brown under the broiler or bake in hot oven for 5 to 6 minutes. While fish is browning, sauté bread cubes in butter and garlic. Arrange the potatoes on a long serving platter and surround them with croûtons and parsley.

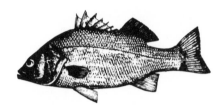

Quenelles de Brochet de Loire "France"
(Pike Quenelles à la *France*)

2 pounds pike filet (or halibut)	Pinch of cayenne
1 pound veal kidney suet	3 shallots, minced
Cream Puff Pastry	1 cup vinegar
8 egg whites, lightly beaten	3 to 4 white peppercorns
Salt	½ cup (8 tablespoons) butter
Dash of freshly ground white pepper	1 cup Sauce Velouté (from fish base)
Pinch of grated nutmeg	1 tablespoon each chopped fresh parsley and chervil

Place fish in a mortar and purée with a pestle until very fine. (This can also be done in a food processor.) Cream suet in a mortar until very smooth. (This can also be done in a food processor.)

Blend the fish and suet together until very smooth, then incorporate pastry dough slowly. Fold in egg whites a little at a time and season with salt, pepper, nutmeg, and cayenne. Mixture must be very smooth, with all ingredients carefully blended.

Flour a marble slab or cutting board and spoon out a heaping tablespoon of the mixture. Shape the mixture into an oval about 2 inches long and ¾ inch in diameter. Continue to shape remaining quenelles.

Bring a large saucepan of water to a boil, add a pinch of salt, and then drop in quenelles and cook for about 15 minutes. Drain and plunge into ice water. When quenelles are thoroughly cooled, drain and dry on paper towels.

Place shallots in a saucepan and add vinegar and peppercorns. Simmer until all but 1 tablespoon of vinegar has evaporated. Stirring with a whisk, gradually blend in butter. Add the velouté and reheat, but do not allow to boil.

Gently reheat the quenelles in a well-buttered saucepan and then place on a serving platter. Cover with sauce and sprinkle with parsley and chervil.

Cuisses de Grenouilles Sautées Provençale
(Sautéed Frogs Legs Provençale)

We often got special orders for frogs legs, and whenever they were on the menu they were a great success. Some restaurants in France and French restaurants abroad call them "nymphs' legs" on their menus, but I never did. The term can be confusing and lead to implications of doubtful taste!

36 frogs legs, thawed if frozen	2 shallots, chopped
Salt	2 cloves garlic, chopped
½ cup all-purpose flour	2 tablespoons chopped fresh parsley
½ cup (8 tablespoons) butter	Juice of ½ lemon
4 mill-turns freshly ground white pepper	

Soak frogs legs in cold water flavored with vinegar for 1 hour. Drain and dry legs on paper towels. Sprinkle legs with salt and roll in flour. Heat half the butter until brown and sauté frogs legs. Season with pepper. When the legs are cooked to a golden brown, add shallots. Shake the pan to mix the shallots well with the legs. When the shallots become translucent, add garlic. Sauté further, then sprinkle with parsley. Mix well by shaking the pan, then add the lemon juice.

Place frogs legs on a serving platter and add remaining butter to pan juices; heat until foamy, then spoon over frogs legs.

Cuisses de Grenouilles Sautées Arlésienne
(Sautéed Frogs Legs Arlésienne)

3 pounds frogs legs, thawed if frozen	Freshly ground white pepper
Salt	2 shallots, chopped
Flour for dusting	3 zucchini, diced
⅓ cup (5 tablespoons) butter	2 tablespoons chopped fresh parsley
	Juice of ½ lemon

Prepare frogs legs as in Sautéed Frogs Legs Provençale. Heat butter until golden, sauté legs until golden brown. Add shallots and zucchini and shake the pan from time to time to mix the ingredients. Continue cooking over low heat for 5 to 6 minutes or until vegetables are tender but still crisp.

Serve the frogs legs in individual skillets. Sprinkle with parsley and lemon juice.

Shellfish

7

LOBSTER

Lobsters were extremely popular both on Atlantic crossings and cruises. On the Atlantic, we of course used principally crustaceans from northern waters. These succulent and tender lobsters, known in France as *homards*, were taken on in extraordinary quantities. At the beginning of one cruise, I ordered 8,000 lobsters in New York. We had never taken on so large a store before, and the suppliers at the port were flabbergasted.

Five hundred lobsters were used to make Sauce Américaine. The remaining 7,500 were poached in the enormous pots called "steams" in our kitchens. They supplied the great buffets on the promenade decks, day and night, ensured availability of the proper garnish for our fish courses, and made it possible to offer two kinds of lobster gratin—Thermidor and Dunkerquoise.

To poach 7,500 lobsters kept our cooks busy, I can tell you. The union representative came to me in protest! The assistant chef, Maurice Foch, former chief *poissonier* of the *France*, organized what he called a rolling squad and within twenty-four hours the job was done. The lobsters were counted, then dispatched to an enormous refrigerated room to await use as needed. And we lost not a single lobster!

Anyone who has never seen the serving of lobster aboard the *France* can scarcely realize what it was like, and I can say without boasting that no restaurant in the world has equalled our record. And every lobster was served on time, no diner having to wait.

Once in Hong Kong we took on thousands of pink spiny lobsters. These are closer to the Caribbean and Mediterranean variety known in France as *langoustes*. All species of this wonderful seafood have their particular points and drawbacks, and the recipes to follow have been divided into the two basic species. Interchanging them will do no great harm and will not damage the authenticity of the recipe.

Homard de l'Atlantique Grillé à la Léonard
(Grilled Atlantic Lobster)

This recipe was created aboard the France *by the head fish cook, Léonard Allain. It was invariably a great hit with the passengers.*

6 uncooked lobsters, each about 2 pounds	⅓ cup fine, dry bread crumbs
	⅔ cup Cognac
1½ cups butter, softened	Deep-Fried Parsley
Salt	Juice of 1 lemon
Pinch of cayenne	
1 teaspoon dry mustard	

Preheat oven to 425 degrees. Cut the lobsters in half lengthwise. Using a sharp knife, remove the intestinal tube extending from the head to the tail and the head sac. Put the lobsters in a heatproof pan.

Mix butter with salt, cayenne, mustard, and bread crumbs. Spread this seasoning evenly over the lobster halves and bake in very hot oven for about

20 minutes. Serve the lobsters on a long platter covered with a folded napkin. Arrange them in pairs, head to head, and garnish with parsley.

Place pan on top of stove and add Cognac and lemon juice. Heat until hot and pour over lobster. Serve, if desired, with additional melted butter mixed with additional lemon juice.

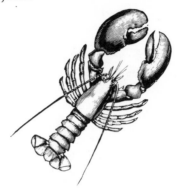

Homard aux Douze Aromates
(Lobster with Twelve Herbs)

3 uncooked lobsters, 2½ pounds each
½ cup oil
½ cup (8 tablespoons) butter
1 teaspoon salt
¼ teaspoon freshly ground pepper
2 carrots, diced
2 leeks (white part only), chopped
1 stalk celery, chopped
3 shallots, chopped
2 onions, chopped
1 clove garlic, chopped

1 teaspoon chopped fennel
1 bay leaf
Chopped fresh parsley
Chopped fresh chervil
1 teaspoon chopped tarragon
1 sprig fresh thyme, chopped
2 cups Fish Stock
2 cups Port wine
⅔ cup Cognac
Pinch of cayenne
⅓ cup crème fraîche or heavy cream

Split the lobsters in half lengthwise. Remove the head sac and the intestinal tube from head to tail. Remove the coral and force through a sieve.

Sauté the lobsters briefly in oil and half the butter; season with salt and pepper. When the shell has taken on a strong red color, remove from pan and set aside. Lightly sauté carrots, leeks, celery, shallots, onions, garlic, fennel, bay leaf, parsley, chervil, tarragon, and thyme in oil and butter used to sauté the lobster; do not allow to brown.

Place the lobsters back into the pan and pour in stock, Port, and Cognac. Season with salt and cayenne. Bring to a boil, reduce heat, cover, and simmer gently for 15 minutes.

Transfer the lobsters to another pan and keep warm. Add the crème fraîche to the pan and simmer the liquid until reduced by half. Mix the coral with remaining butter and whisk vigorously into sauce. Remove bay leaf.

Preheat oven to 450 degrees or heat broiler. Remove the tail meat from the lobsters. Slice each length of tail meat into 3 slices cut on the bias. Replace the meat in the shells and place the lobsters on a long heatproof serving platter. Cover lobsters with the sauce. Place under the broiler or in very hot oven for 5 to 6 minutes or until bubbly.

Petit Homard du Maine à l'Américaine
(Maine Lobster à l'Américaine)

2 uncooked Maine lobsters, 3
  pounds each
1 carrot, chopped
1 large onion, chopped
2 stalks celery, chopped
½ cup oil
½ cup (8 tablespoons) butter
1 cup Cognac, warmed
1 cup dry white wine

1 cup Fish Stock
  Bouquet garni (bay leaf, thyme,
  parsley)
4 large tomatoes, quartered
1 tablespoon tomato paste
  Salt
½ teaspoon cayenne
1 tablespoon flour
  Chopped fresh tarragon

Remove claws and legs from lobsters, making sure to keep the claw joints intact. Slit the shells so they will be easier to remove at the table. Break the heads in half lengthwise, remove the head sac. Remove the coral, reserving it in a bowl. Cut the tail along with the shells crosswise into 3 equal parts.

Sauté the lobsters and chopped vegetables in oil and ¼ cup of butter over high heat until the shells turn red; stir constantly with a spatula. When the vegetables are lightly browned, pour in the Cognac and set aflame. Add wine, stock, bouquet garni, tomatoes, and tomato paste. Bring to a boil, reduce heat, cover, and simmer gently for about 30 minutes. Season heavily with salt and cayenne, since the sauce should be quite sharp.

When cooking is completed, remove lobsters, keep warm, and force sauce through a sieve or purée it in a food processor; pour purée into a saucepan. Blend the coral with remaining butter and the flour, then add it to the sauce and cook until thickened. Add lobster pieces and simmer for a few minutes over low heat. Sprinkle with tarragon just before serving.

Petit Homard de l'Atlantique à la Nage
(Atlantic Baby Lobster with Butter Sauce)

6 small uncooked lobsters, 1½
  pounds each
3 shallots, minced
2 cups butter

Lobster Court Bouillon:
3 quarts water
½ teaspoon salt
2 carrots, chopped
2 onions, diced
1 stalk celery, chopped
  Several sprigs of fresh parsley
1 sprig fresh thyme
2 bay leaves
6 peppercorns
4 cups dry white wine

Combine all ingredients for Court Bouillon and boil for 35 minutes. Plunge the lobsters into the boiling liquid and simmer for about 20 minutes. When cooked, place in 2 tureens with all but ¾ cup of the court bouillon.

Sauté shallots gently in a saucepan with ½ cup of the butter. When translucent but not browned, add reserved court bouillon and stir in remaining butter, 1 tablespoon at a time. Bring to a full boil, and when the butter is blended, remove from heat and pour into a sauceboat

Langouste de Tropiques Étuvée Newburg
(Lobster Newburg)

2 uncooked spiny lobsters, 3½ pounds each
Lobster Court Bouillon (see Atlantic Baby Lobster with Butter Sauce)
⅔ cup Cognac
1 cup Madeira wine
1 cup Fish Stock

2⅔ cups crème fraîche or heavy cream
6 egg yolks
½ teaspoon salt
Pinch of cayenne
¼ cup (4 tablespoons) butter, cut in small pieces
Rice Pilaf

Poach lobsters in Court Bouillon for about 25 minutes. Remove from pot and let cool.

Separate the heads of the lobsters from the tails, remove the shells and the intestinal tube from the center of the tail meat, and cut all the meat into ½-inch-thick slices. Place lobsters in a well-buttered saucepan and pour in Cognac and Madeira. Bring to a boil, reduce heat, and simmer gently for 15 minutes.

Boil stock until reduced to ½ cup. Add stock and 2 cups of the crème fraîche to the sauce. In a bowl, mix the egg yolks and remaining crème fraîche, then beat in some of the hot sauce. When blended, add egg mixture to the sauce and blend well. Season with salt and cayenne and simmer until thickened, but do not boil. Stir in the butter, 1 piece at a time.

Pour lobster mixture into a serving bowl and serve with Rice Pilaf.

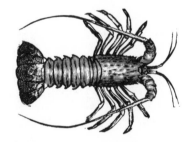

Langouste Rose de Hong Kong Rôtie à la Diable
(Roast Hong Kong Lobster à la Diable)

3 uncooked spiny lobsters, 2½ pounds each
2 cups butter
Salt
Pinch of cayenne
1 tablespoon dry mustard

½ cup fine, dry bread crumbs
⅔ cup Cognac
1 bunch fresh parsley
3 lemons, cut in half and decoratively notched
Melted butter

Preheat oven to 450 degrees. Cut off the claws and legs of the lobsters. Split the lobsters lengthwise and remove the head sacs and intestinal tubes.

Cream the butter until softened and season with a little salt and cayenne. Mix with mustard, bread crumbs, and Cognac.

Using a pastry bag with a large, round tip, top the lobster halves from head to tail with this seasoning. Roast in very hot oven for 15 minutes.

Remove lobsters to a long serving platter and garnish with parsley and lemon. Serve with a sauceboat of melted butter .

Langouste Fraîche de Bonne Espérance Rôtie aux Épices
(Roasted Cape of Good Hope Lobster with Herbs)

3 uncooked spiny lobsters, 3½ pounds each	2 cups butter
Salt	½ cup dry white wine
Cayenne	½ cup wine vinegar
1 teaspoon mixed thyme leaves, basil, rosemary, marjoram	1 tablespoon flour
¾ cup oil	½ cup Fish Stock
2 shallots, chopped	½ cup bourbon, warmed
	1 bunch fresh parsley

Preheat oven to 400 degrees. Cut lobsters lengthwise and remove the head sacs and the intestinal tubes. Place in an ovenproof dish and season with salt, cayenne, thyme, basil, rosemary, and marjoram. Oil the lobsters generously, then roast in hot oven for about 25 minutes.

Briefly sauté shallots in 1 tablespoon of the butter. Add wine and vinegar and boil until 2 tablespoons of liquid are left. In another pan, melt 1 tablespoon of butter and stir in flour. Mix and cook briefly, without browning. Add fish stock and stir until blended. Add shallot mixture and remaining butter, 1 tablespoon at a time. Bring to a boil, stirring briskly with a whisk, and correct seasoning with a little salt and cayenne.

When lobsters are done, remove from oven and pour bourbon over; set aflame. Arrange lobsters on a long serving platter and garnish with parsley. Serve sauce on the side.

Cardinal des Mers au Gratin Thermidor
(Lobster Thermidor)

3 uncooked lobsters, 2½ pounds each	Salt
Lobster Court Bouillon (see Atlantic Baby Lobster with Butter Sauce)	3 shallots, chopped
	½ cup dry white wine
	2½ cups Sauce Béchamel
12 large fresh mushrooms, trimmed and diced	1 tablespoon Dijon-style mustard
1 cup butter	1 cup grated Gruyère cheese
	Sprigs of fresh parsley

Poach the lobsters in the Court Bouillon for about 25 minutes, then cool.

Cut lobsters in half lengthwise and remove the head sacs and intestinal tubes. Remove the meat from the shells and cut into bite-sized pieces. Remove coral and shells. Sauté the mushrooms in ¼ cup of butter without browning; salt lightly. Add diced lobster and coral and sauté gently, stirring occasionally until lobster is cooked.

Sauté shallots lightly in ¼ cup of the butter without browning. Add wine, bring to a boil, lower heat, and boil until liquid has almost evaporated. Set aside.

Preheat oven to 450 degrees or heat broiler. Heat Béchamel and stir in mustard. Combine sauce, shallot mixture, and lobster. Use this mixture to fill the shells. Place on a heatproof platter, sprinkle with cheese, and put under the broiler or in hot oven until golden brown.

Serve lobster on a long serving platter covered with a napkin which has been folded into a rectangle or gondola. Garnish with parsley.

Petite Langouste Rose du Cap au Gratin Dunkerquois
(Grantinéed Cape Baby Lobster à la Dunkirk)

3 uncooked spiny lobsters,
2½ pounds each
Lobster Court Bouillon (see
Atlantic Baby Lobster with
Butter Sauce)
1½ cups Sauce Américaine
3½ pounds fresh mushrooms

Juice of 1 lemon
¼ cup (4 tablespoons) butter
Salt
1 cup crème fraîche or heavy cream
Pinch of cayenne
2 cups Sauce Béarnaise
1 bunch fresh parsley

Poach the lobsters in Court Bouillon for about 25 minutes, then cool. Split from head to tail. Remove the head sacs and the intestinal tubes; remove meat from shells and dice coarsely; reserve shells. Mix the diced lobster with Sauce Américaine.

Trim and chop the mushrooms. Sauté with lemon juice and butter until liquid is absorbed, then season with salt. Add crème fraîche and simmer until thick. Add cayenne.

Preheat oven to 450 degrees or heat broiler. Line the lobster shells with the mushrooms and fill the top with lobster mixture.

Cover with a thin layer of Sauce Béarnaise. Just before serving place under broiler or in hot oven until lightly browned. Arrange the lobsters on a long serving platter covered with a napkin and garnish with parsley.

Croquettes de Homard
(Lobster Croquettes)

3 uncooked tails from 2½-pound
lobsters
½ cup (8 tablespoons) butter
1 cup flour
2 cups Fish Stock
½ cup Sauce Américaine,
simmered until reduced by ½

6 egg yolks
Pinch of cayenne
2 eggs, lightly beaten
1 cup fine, dry bread crumbs
Oil for deep-frying, heated to 375°
1 tablespoon chopped truffles
1 tablespoon Cognac

Shell the lobster tails and remove the intestinal tubes. Dice the meat and sauté about 5 minutes in 2 tablespoons of butter over low heat.

In a saucepan, heat remaining butter and stir in ⅔ cup of flour and the stock. Stir, simmering until thickened. Flavor sauce with reduced Sauce Américaine. Beat ½ cup sauce into the egg yolks, then add to remaining sauce. Pour the sauce over the diced lobster meat and season with cayenne. Spread the lobster and sauce in a shallow pan to a depth of 1 inch. Smooth out the surface and cover with well-buttered parchment paper or foil. Cut slits in the paper so that the cream will cool more quickly and refrigerate for 2 hours.

Flour a cutting board or marble slab, turn lobster cream out on it, and cut into three portions. Flour and roll each third into a cylinder, then cut off 4-inch lengths. Cover these croquettes with remaining flour, dip into lightly seasoned beaten egg, and then coat with bread crumbs. Form each croquette into a stubby cylinder, then deep-fry in hot oil for 8 to 10 minutes or until richly browned. Drain on absorbent paper. Garnish croquettes with truffles and sprinkle with Cognac.

SHRIMP, CRAB, SCALLOPS

Coupe de Crevettes Sauce Audoise
(Shrimp Cocktail with Sauce Audoise)

2 pounds shrimp or prawns	1½ cups Sauce Audoise
Court Bouillon	1 lemon, cut into wedges
6 lettuce leaves	

Poach the shrimp in Court Bouillon to cover, about 7 minutes; drain and let cool. Shell and devein, then chill.

Line cocktail glasses with lettuce leaves. Arrange each portion of shrimp with the tails turned toward the outer edge of the glass and cover with Sauce Audoise. Serve with lemon wedges set onto the rim of the glasses.

Coupe de Camarons Sauce Mousquetaire
(Spanish Prawns with Sauce Mousquetaire)

Camarónes *are very large, pink prawns which are found chiefly in warm waters. They are found all along the shores of the Mediterranean. They can be replaced by the pink and gray shrimp of the Atlantic coast.*

4 pounds prawns or large shrimp	1½ cups Sauce Mousquetaire
Court Bouillon	1 lemon, cut into 6 wedges
6 lettuce leaves	

Poach the prawns in Court Bouillon to cover, about 7 minutes; let cool, then remove the shells. Devein and chill prawns.

Line shellfish cocktail glasses with lettuce leaves, heap the prawns on the leaves, and garnish with Sauce Mousquetaire, topping off with lemon wedges attached to the rim of the dish by a slit.

Crevettes Sautées Bordelaise
(Sautéed Shrimp Bordelaise)

3 pounds large shrimp or prawns	3 shallots, minced
Salt	2 cups crème fraîche or heavy cream
Freshly ground black pepper	Pinch of cayenne
½ cup vegetable oil	Juice of ½ lemon
¼ cup (4 tablespoons) butter	1 tablespoon chopped fresh parsley

Remove the shells from the shrimp. Wash carefully, then remove the intestinal tube which runs from head to tail along the back. Season with salt and pepper.

Saute shrimp in hot oil; when they have taken on a good color, drain into a sieve. Heat butter until foaming and sauté shrimp once again, together with shallots. When the shallots are nicely colored, transfer shrimp and shallots to a medium saucepan, add crème fraîche, and season with salt and cayenne. Bring to a boil, reduce heat, and cook gently until all ingredients are well blended and sauce is thickened, about 10 minutes.

Serve shrimp in a tureen, sprinkled with lemon juice and parsley.

Sambel de Crevettes de Java
(Sambal—Indonesian Shrimp Simmered in Coconut Milk)

2 pounds large shrimp or prawns
2 red bell peppers, chopped
2 large onions, chopped
½ cup vegetable oil
2 cloves garlic, minced

2 cups coconut milk
Bouquet garni (bay leaf, celery, thyme)
Salt
6 cups Rice Pilaf

Shell and devein shrimp. Sauté peppers and onions in oil. When the onions begin to color, add garlic. When the garlic begins to brown, add the shrimp to the skillet. Sauté until the shrimp take on a good color, then transfer to a saucepan. Add coconut milk to cover, put in the bouquet garni, and salt lightly. Cover the saucepan and simmer for 10 minutes. Remove bouquet garni.

Press Rice Pilaf into a lightly oiled 1½-quart ring mold. Unmold and spoon simmered shrimp in the center of the ring and serve.

Crabes Farcies à l'Antillaise
(Antilles Stuffed Crab)

6 blue crabs
Court Bouillon
1 lime, cut in half
2 cups soft bread crumbs
⅔ cup milk
10 shallots, minced
2 tablespoons olive oil
1 clove garlic, chopped
2 tablespoons minced fresh parsley

1 teaspoon chopped fresh leaf thyme
1 small pimiento, minced
Salt
⅔ cup dark rum
1 cup dry bread crumbs
6 tablespoons butter
1 bunch fresh parsley

Poach crabs in Court Bouillon for 20 minutes and let cool. Using a slender knife, remove the meat without damaging the shells. Wash the shells carefully, dry and moisten the insides with lime juice.

Soak soft bread crumbs in milk and then drain and press out liquid.

Sauté the shallots in oil, and when they begin to color, add garlic, parsley, thyme, and pimiento. Add moistened bread crumbs to crabmeat and season with salt. Add rum, stir, and use the mixture to fill the shells. Smooth the surface and sprinkle with dry bread crumbs.

Heat broiler, dot tops of crabs with butter, and place the shells on a bed of coarse salt to keep them from falling over. Place crabs under broiler until golden, about 5 minutes.

Serve crabs on a long serving platter covered with a folded napkin (square or lozenge), with parsley as garnish.

Cocktail de Crabe Sauce Tango
(Crabmeat Cocktail with Sauce Tango)

3 cups flaked cooked crabmeat	Sauce Tango
6 lettuce leaves	6 lemon wedges

Remove any cartilage from crabmeat. Line cocktail glasses with lettuce leaves and heap a portion of crabmeat in each. Garnish with Sauce Tango and attach a lemon wedge by making a slit in each wedge.

Coupe de Fruits de Mer Sauce Chilienne
(Crab and Shrimp Cocktail with Sauce Chilienne)

1¼ pounds shrimp	2 cups Sauce Chilienne
2 cups flaked cooked crabmeat	1 lemon, cut into 6 wedges
1 head Boston lettuce	

Poach the shrimp in water to cover until they turn pink; shell and devein. Crumble the crabmeat and mix with the shrimp. Line each cocktail glass with 2 leaves of lettuce and heap the crab and shrimp mixture onto the lettuce.

Cover with a Sauce Chilienne, and garnish with wedges of lemon on the rims of the glasses.

Coquille St.-Jacques au Gratin "France"
(Scallops au Gratin à la *France*)

We took scallops aboard at Le Hâvre, poached them immediately, and stored them in the cold room. They were served at a stopover in Nassau, following a recipe created on board. We broke all records: 900 Coquilles St.-Jacques were eaten that night! What is more, this actually meant 1,800 scallops since each serving required two scallops.

2 pounds bay or sea scallops	2 cups crème fraîche or heavy cream
4 cups water	Pinch of cayenne
1 tablespoon coarse salt	6 large, fresh mushrooms, trimmed
½ cup dry white wine	and chopped
2 bay leaves	6 scallop shells
Few sprigs of fresh parsley	1 cup (4 ounces) grated Gruyère
1 sprig fresh thyme	cheese
4 large shallots, minced	Few sprigs of fresh parsley
½ cup (8 tablespoons) butter	
2 tablespoons flour	

Wash the scallops. Poach in water to which you have added salt, wine, bay leaves, parsley, and thyme. Simmer for about 15 minutes, then let the scallops cool in the liquid. Drain and reserve liquid. Cut sea scallops into 4 pieces; cut bay scallops in half if large. Strain the poaching liquid into a saucepan and boil until reduced by half.

Sauté shallots in 3 tablespoons of butter until melted, then pour in the poaching liquid and boil until reduced by half. Mix 2 tablespoons of butter with the flour and stir into sauce. Boil the crème fraîche until reduced by half, then stir into the sauce and simmer gently for a few minutes until thickened. Correct the seasoning, adding cayenne. Sauté the mushrooms in the remaining butter and add, along with scallops, to the sauce. Blend all the ingredients and simmer a few more minutes until thickened.

Preheat oven to 500 degrees or heat broiler. Set the shells in a bed of rock salt to keep from tipping. Spoon the mixture into the shells and sprinkle with cheese. Brown in hot oven or under broiler for 5 to 6 minutes. Serve on a long platter covered with a folded napkin and decorate with parsley.

Turban de Coquilles St.-Jacques "France"
(Scallops in Wine Sauce à la *France*)

2 pounds bay or sea scallops
Flour for dusting
½ cup oil
Salt
Freshly ground black pepper
5 shallots, chopped
2 cloves garlic, chopped
1¼ cups Muscadet or other dry
white wine
⅔ cup Cognac
2 large tomatoes, peeled, seeded, and chopped
¾ cup crème fraîche or heavy cream
6 cups Rice Pilaf
1 tablespoon chopped fresh parsley

Wash the scallops in several changes of water, then dry on a paper towel. Flour generously and sauté in very hot oil until browned, about 5 to 6 minutes. Season with salt and pepper. Remove scallops and drain oil leaving only 1 tablespoon in pan.

Sauté shallots and garlic until golden. Add the scallops, Muscadet, Cognac, tomatoes, and crème fraîche. Salt and pepper lightly, then simmer over gentle heat for 5 minutes.

Mold the Rice Pilaf into a 1½-quart crown or ring mold, then unmold onto a serving platter. Pour the scallops into the center of the rice and sprinkle with parsley.

MISCELLANEOUS

Valapa de Poisson de Bahia
(Brazilian Fish and Shrimp)

Valapa is a typically Brazilian dish. The chicken meat can be replaced by chicken consommé, although in its land of origin valapa is almost always served with pieces of chicken in it. This is an extraordinary dish, absolutely delicious, and the fowl blends very well with the fish, in no way compromising the flavor of the valapa. The combination surprises some Americans and Europeans, who sometimes are not used to mixtures of this sort, but it is guaranteed to satisfy the most delicate palate.

1¼ pounds fish filets (turbot, mullet, bluefish, rockfish)	1 clove garlic, minced
¼ cup (4 tablespoons) lard	3 large tomatoes, peeled, seeded, and diced
1 whole chicken breast, skinned, boned, and diced	1 hot pepper, diced
20 large shrimp, shelled and deveined	1 teaspoon salt
1 medium onion, minced	1 bay leaf
	1 sprig fresh thyme
	½ teaspoon dried marjoram leaves

Cut fish filets into 1-inch cubes. Sauté in lard in a large saucepan for 5 minutes. Add the diced chicken breasts, shrimp, onion, and garlic. Brown lightly, then add the tomato pulp and the pepper. Mix well with a wooden spatula and add just enough water to cover. Season with salt, bay leaf, thyme, and marjoram. Bring to a boil, cover, and simmer for 15 minutes.

Remove bay leaf and serve in a deep round dish.

Jambalaya de Damao
(Lobster and Shrimp Jambalaya)

1 medium onion, minced	2 live lobsters, 2 pounds each
1 clove garlic, minced	2 pounds large shrimp
⅔ cup vegetable oil	2 cups raw long-grain rice
¼ cup all-purpose flour	Pinch of cayenne
2 quarts Court Bouillon	Few drops Tabasco sauce
2 large tomatoes, skinned, seeded, and chopped	1 small dried red pepper, crushed
	3 cups Sauce Tomate

Preheat oven to 400 degrees. In a heatproof casserole, sauté onion and garlic in 2 tablespoons of the oil. When they begin to color, add flour, mixing vigorously with a whisk. Cook this roux over low heat for a few minutes, then add Court Bouillon. Stir until thickened, then add tomatoes.

Cut the lobster into large pieces and sauté with shrimp in remaining hot oil until red. Drain, then add to the sauce. Sprinkle in the rice and season to taste with cayenne, Tabasco, and red pepper. Bring to a boil, cover, then bake in a hot oven for 20 minutes, stirring occasionally. Serve Jambalaya with Sauce Tomate on side.

Crêpes de Fruits de Mer au Gratin "France"
(Seafood Crêpes au Gratin à la *France*)

20 shrimp, cooked, shelled, and
   deveined
2 cups flaked, cooked crabmeat
1¼ pounds steamed mussels
8 large, fresh mushrooms, diced
1 cup butter
⅓ cup Cognac
⅓ cup Madeira wine
2 cups crème fraîche or heavy
   cream
1 teaspoon Dijon-style mustard
   Pinch of curry powder
4 cups Sauce Américaine
1 cup grated Gruyère cheese

Crêpes:
2 cups all-purpose flour
3 eggs
   Salt
2 cups milk
   Pinch of grated nutmeg

Make crêpe batter by whisking together flour, eggs, salt, milk, and nutmeg. Beat vigorously, then let mixture rest for 1 hour.

Dice the shrimp, crumble the crabmeat. Remove the mussels from the shells and add to shrimp and crabmeat. Sauté mushrooms without browning in 2 tablespoons of the butter. Add seafood, Cognac, and Madeira and simmer 15 minutes or until liquid has nearly evaporated.

In another saucepan, combine crème fraîche, mustard, and curry powder and boil until reduced by half. When the cream begins to thicken, stir in seafood mixture until thoroughly blended, using a wooden spatula. Salt lightly, taking into account that the shrimp and mussels are already salted. Cool.

Preheat oven to 350 degrees. Prepare 18 7-inch crêpes using batter. Lay them out on a cutting board and spread a heaping spoonful of the filling over the entire surface of each crêpe. Roll the crêpes into cylinders and arrange in a buttered au gratin dish. Cover with Sauce Américaine, then sprinkle with cheese. Bake in moderate oven for 5 to 10 minutes or until bubbly.

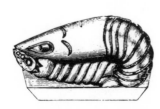

Caviar d'Astrakhan aux Blinis Gretshnevoi
(Blinis with Caviar)

½ cup buckwheat flour
1 envelope active dry yeast
3 cups warm milk
2¼ cups sifted all-purpose flour
3 egg yolks, beaten
4 egg whites, beaten until stiff
⅔ cup crème fraîche or heavy cream, beaten lightly

Garnish:
Sour cream
Caviar
Melted butter
Lemon juice
Chopped hard-cooked egg
Minced onion

Put the buckwheat flour in a large bowl. Stir in yeast and 2 cups of the milk. Cover and let rest for 2 hours in a warm place.

Stir all-purpose flour into buckwheat mixture and add egg yolks and remaining milk. Beat until smooth, and rest again 1 hour. Fold in egg whites and crème fraîche and let rise for about 20 minutes.

Heat griddle and drop batter by tablespoons to make pancakes about 3 inches in diameter. Brown on both sides, then continue to make more blinis, keeping cooked ones warm.

Place blinis on a round platter covered with a napkin. Serve with garnishes.

Meats, Pâtés, and Terrines

8

BEEF

Serving roast ribs of beef on the *France* was a problem. We were roasting sixty sides of beef, which meant thirty forequarters. It took three kitchen helpers the entire afternoon to prepare the ribs and twenty ovens to roast them. The beef had been purchased in New York because American beef is very tender, but I wonder if French beef hasn't perhaps more flavor?

The roasts were not always all consumed. It was very difficult to anticipate how much the passengers would be eating of any one dish, and we therefore had to allow for a fairly wide margin. In any event, whatever was not eaten at dinner was given to the crew. Some foods could not be reused, such as the baked potatoes that passengers ate to combat seasickness, or the hors d'oeuvre served at the buffets on the promenade decks where there was no air-conditioning.

There has been much talk about the great waste in the *France*'s kitchens and the garbage cans full of still-edible food. This was not the case. Someone, who had no way of really knowing, once told me that leftover pastry on the *France* was thrown overboard. I never saw anything of the sort. What I did see, during a cruise to the West Indies, was a kitchen helper throwing bits of bread to the gulls. I told him to stop, for I was certain that had anyone seen him, those bits of bread would soon have become whole loaves.

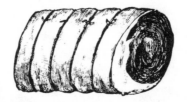

Côte de Boeuf de l'Ohio Rôti Fleuriste
(Ohio Boneless Rib Roast with Glazed Vegetables)

I have always had the reputation of deploring waste of any kind. No cook who ever worked for me would dispute this, and the suppliers at Le Havre will attest to the fact that I was a good manager. Only rarely did I ever go beyond the strict allotment I was allowed and I never exceeded the daily ration which, at that time, had increased from 25 to 30 francs per passenger.

1 rolled boneless rib roast, about 4½ pounds, plus bones Salt 6 large tomatoes Glazed Mixed Vegetables, without tomatoes	6 small potatoes, peeled ¼ cup (8 tablespoons) butter Bunch of watercress, washed and trimmed

Preheat oven to 325 degrees. Have butcher cut bones into large pieces. Prepare roast by trimming off fat and tying meat with string. Season with salt and wrap in aluminum foil. Put bones in bottom of a roasting pan and place meat on top. Cover and roast in a moderate oven for 2 hours for rare (140 degrees), 3 hours for medium (160 degrees) on a meat thermometer. Let roast rest for 1 hour in a warm place.

Meanwhile, prepare tomato shells, as for Grilled Medallions of Mediterranean Sea Bass. Prepare Glazed Mixed Vegetables, omitting the tomatoes. Boil potatoes until tender in salted water, then trim to an egg shape. Cook until brown in butter.

Remove foil and replace the string on the roast with fresh string (a tied roast slices easier) and set it on a long serving platter. Fill the tomato shells with a mixture of vegetables and alternate around the roast with potatoes. Place a bouquet of watercress at each end of the platter.

Filet de Boeuf du Kansas Rôti à la Façon de Virginie
(Filet of Kansas Beef, Virginia Style)

1 beef filet, trimmed, about
   4 pounds
Salt
3 tablespoons butter, melted
¾ cup Madeira wine
3 large potatoes (not Idaho),
   or 6 sweet potatoes, peeled and
   cut into ½-inch slices

Sugar
¼ cup (4 tablespoons) butter
½ cup maple syrup
Rice Croquettes
Sprigs of watercress, washed
   and trimmed

Preheat oven to 500 degrees. Have your butcher remove fat and tendons from the filet. Tie wide end and tuck in the last 4 inches where the tail flattens so that the filet is the same thickness throughout. Tie at 1-inch intervals, then season with salt and place in a shallow, ovenproof roasting pan. Brush with butter and roast in a very hot oven for 1 hour, turning the filet once. Beef will be crusty brown outside, pink inside. Remove from the oven and keep warm.

Place the roasting pan on top of stove. Add wine and bring to a boil, scraping up all brown particles. Sieve the juices into a saucepan and keep warm over low heat. Dust potato slices lightly with salt and sugar, and sauté in butter until tender. Scatter the slices on an oiled baking sheet, coat with the maple syrup, and place under the broiler or in hot oven for 6 to 7 minutes. Remove the strings from the beef, place on a long platter, and surround with potato slices alternating with Rice Croquettes. Coat the filet with the deglazing juices and tuck bunches of watercress at each end of the platter. Cut beef into 1-inch-thick slices.

Filet de Charolais Rôti "Île de France"
(Roast Beef Filet à *l'Île de France*)

1 beef filet, about 4 pounds
2 ounces larding fat
Salt and freshly ground pepper
1½ cups butter, softened
¾ cup Port wine
1 pound carrots, cut into
   large ovals
1 teaspoon sugar
3 pounds large potatoes, peeled

½ cup Classic Beef Consommé, mixed
   with 1 tablespoon Glace de Viande
1 sprig fresh tarragon, chopped
1 pound fresh green beans,
   trimmed and left whole
8 small tomatoes, peeled and
   left whole
3 hard-cooked egg yolks

Trim and lard the beef filet, or ask your butcher to do so. Preheat oven to 450 degrees. Tie filet with string to make even thickness throughout, then season with salt and pepper. Spread the filet with ¼ cup of butter and roast in a heatproof pan in a very hot oven for about 1 hour, turning and basting frequently. Remove from oven and let rest on a platter in a warm place for 15 minutes. Beef will be crusty brown outside and pink inside.

Drain off some of the fat from the roasting pan. Add wine to the roasting pan, place on top of stove, and boil, scraping up all particles. Sieve juices into a saucepan and keep warm. While roast is cooking, prepare vegetables. Put carrots into a saucepan cover with lightly salted water and sugar and add ¼ cup of butter. Boil until the water has evaporated. When nicely glazed by the butter, remove from heat.

Using a melon baller, cut balls from potatoes. Wash well to remove starch, then blanch in lightly salted boiling water for 5 minutes. Drain and sauté potatoes in a skillet in ½ cup of butter until golden brown. When brown, add consommé mixed with Glace de Viande to potatoes and stir to coat. Sprinkle with tarragon, shaking the skillet to ensure even covering by the tarragon.

Cook green beans in boiling water for 15 to 20 minutes, or until tender. Drain and sauté briefly in ¼ cup of butter without letting them brown. Season tomatoes lightly with salt and pepper. Dot each with remaining butter and broil for 5 minutes. Force the hard-cooked yolks through a sieve.

Put the roast on a long serving platter, surrounding it with alternating mounds of potatoes, green beans, carrots, and the grilled tomatoes. Sprinkle tomatoes with the sieved egg yolks, cover the roast with the pan juices, and serve.

Filet de Boeuf de la Marche Rôti Bressane
(Roast Beef Filet Bressane)

1 beef filet, about 4½ pounds
2 ounces larding fat
1 teaspoon salt
⅛ teaspoon freshly ground white pepper
2 large truffles, diced
¾ cup Madeira wine, plus additional for soaking truffles
1 cup Sauce Demi-Glace
8 pitted green olives, blanched and cut in half lengthwise
12 small mushroom caps, fluted
½ cup shelled pistachio nuts, blanched and peeled
½ cup (8 tablespoons) butter
3 pounds small new potatoes, cooked and peeled

Marinade:
2 cups Chablis wine
⅔ cup Cognac
1 onion, chopped
1 carrot, chopped
1 stalk celery, chopped
Few sprigs of fresh parsley
1 sprig fresh thyme
1 bay leaf

Have your butcher prepare and lard beef filet. Prepare marinade and marinate filet for 3 hours. Strain and reserve the liquid. Preheat oven to 500 degrees.

Dry filet with a kitchen towel and put it in a small heatproof roasting pan. Season with salt and pepper, then roast in a very hot oven for 1 hour, turning and basting occasionally. Remove from oven and let the meat rest on a platter in a warm place for 30 minutes. Beef will be crusty brown outside and pink inside.

While meat is roasting marinate truffles in Maderia to cover for 30 minutes. Drain. Add marinade and ¾ cup Madeira to roasting pan; boil on top of stove, scraping up brown particles. Strain into a saucepan and add Demi-Glace. Simmer over low heat for 20 minutes, skimming foam as needed. Add olives and truffles.

Sauté the mushroom caps and pistachio nuts in 2 tablespoons of the butter. Stir mushrooms, nuts, and drippings into sauce. Sauté potatoes in remaining butter until golden brown.

Place the roast on a long serving platter and cover with the sauce. Surround with potatoes.

Coeur de Charolais Rôti Ducs de Bourbon
(Roast Beef Filet Ducs de Bourbon)

1 beef filet, about 3½ to 4½
   pounds
   Larding fat
   Salt
4 mill-turns freshly ground white
   pepper
1 cup butter
3 shallots, chopped
2 pounds small mushrooms,
   trimmed and left whole
2 pounds small new potatoes,
   peeled and cooked
1 teaspoon Glace de Viande,
   mixed with 2 teaspoons water
2 teaspoons chopped fresh
   tarragon leaves

Marinade:
2 cups dry white wine
1 carrot, chopped
1 onion, chopped
1 sprig fresh thyme
   Few sprigs of fresh parsley
1 clove garlic, crushed
1 stalk celery, chopped
4 whole cloves
1 bay leaf

Have beef filet larded and tied by butcher as in the Roast Beef Filet à *l'Ile de France.* Make marinade and marinate the filet for several hours.

Preheat oven to 500 degrees. Drain meat, dry with a kitchen towel, and season with salt and pepper. Reserve marinade and vegetables. Coat the top of the meat generously with ⅓ cup of butter; roast in a heatproof pan in a hot oven for 1 hour for a rare roast, turning and basting frequently. Place roast on serving platter and keep warm.

Place the marinade and vegetables into a saucepan and boil until reduced by one-fourth. Add marinade to roasting pan, place on top of stove, and boil, scraping up all particles. Sieve into a saucepan. Sauté 2 of the shallots for 1 to 2 minutes in 2 tablespoons of butter, then add to sauce. Simmer over low heat for 15 to 20 minutes or until slightly thickened, skimming as needed.

Heat remaining butter until brown and sauté the mushrooms. When they are cooked, add remaining chopped shallot and salt lightly. Mix potatoes with Glace de Viande mixture and sprinkle with tarragon.

Place the roast on a long serving platter and remove the string. Alternate potatoes and mushrooms around it as garnish. Cover the roast with the sauce.

Filet de Charolais Rôti à la Boston
(Filet of Roast Beef, Boston Style)

3 dozen Portuguese oysters or American oysters (Wellfleet, Blue Point, Chincoteague, etc.)	Salt
	5 mill-turns freshly ground white pepper
2 cups dry white wine	½ cup (8 tablespoons) butter, softened
1 bay leaf	2 cups Sauce Hollandaise
1 sprig fresh thyme	Lorette Potatoes
Few sprigs of fresh parsley	Sprigs of watercress, washed and trimmed
1 beef filet, about 3½ pounds	
Larding fat	

Cook the oysters until shells open, about 5 to 6 minutes, with wine, bay leaf, thyme, and parsley in a covered saucepan. Let cool, then remove from the shells, adding the juices to the liquid in the pan. Strain juices through a sieve into a saucepan and boil until reduced by one-fourth.

Preheat oven to 500 degrees. Prepare the beef filet as in the preceding recipes, larding and tying with string. Season with salt and pepper, and spread with butter. Roast as in the preceding recipes, then keep warm.

Drain the fat from pan, and add reserved oyster liquid. Boil on top of stove, scraping up brown particles. Strain liquid into a saucepan, and stir in Sauce Hollandaise and oysters. Heat until bubbly.

Place the roast on a long serving platter. Cover with some of the sauce and surround with Lorette Potatoes. Put bouquets of watercress at either end of the platter. Serve the remaining sauce hot in a sauceboat.

Contrefilet Salessois Rôti avec Yorkshire Pudding
(Roast Beef and Yorkshire Pudding)

1 beef sirloin, about 4 pounds	*Yorkshire Pudding:*
Salt	1 cup sifted all-purpose flour
Freshly ground white pepper	2 eggs
¼ cup (4 tablespoons) butter, softened	½ teaspoon salt
	Pinch of grated nutmeg
1 cup dry white wine	Small pinch of cayenne
Sprigs of watercress, washed and trimmed	1 cup milk
	½ cup finely chopped beef suet

In a bowl, combine flour, eggs, salt, nutmeg, cayenne, and milk. Beat until smooth, then let rest 1 hour.

Preheat oven to 500 degrees. Prepare the roast, leaving only a thin layer of fat on the upper side. Season with salt and pepper and spread roast with butter. Cook in heatproof pan in a very hot oven for about 1 hour, turning and basting frequently for a rare roast.

While meat is roasting, fry fat for pudding until rendered. Remove crisp pieces and fold into standing batter. Pour the hot fat into a 13 x 9 x 2-inch baking pan and add the batter. Bake in hot oven for 15 to 20 minutes, then lower heat to moderate (350 degrees) and bake for another 15 minutes, or until brown and crusty. Remove from oven, cut into squares, and serve immediately with the roast.

When meat is finished, discard fat from roasting pan and add wine. Place pan on top of stove, bring liquid to a boil, scraping up all particles, then strain into a saucepan.

Serve the roast on a long serving platter with squares of Yorkshire Pudding around it. Serve the pan juices in a sauceboat and decorate the platter with bouquets of watercress at either end.

Contrefilet Auvergnat Rôti Armenonville
(Beef Loin Roast Armenonville)

1 beef sirloin, about 4 pounds
Salt
5 mill-turns freshly ground black pepper
1 cup butter
1 cup dry white wine
12 baby artichokes, cooked whole and drained
6 large, ripe tomatoes, peeled, seeded, and chopped

2 shallots, chopped
Juice of 3 lemons
2 tablespoons peanut oil
2 pounds fresh green beans, cut into 1-inch pieces
2 pounds potatoes, cooked, peeled, and quartered

Prepare roast and pan juices with salt, pepper, butter, and wine according to the directions in Roast Beef and Yorkshire Pudding.

Simmer artichokes with tomatoes, shallots, and ¼ cup of butter for 15 minutes. Season with salt and add lemon juice. Heat peanut oil and sauté green beans for 10 to 15 minutes, or until tender yet crisp. Season with salt. Sauté potatoes in remaining butter until brown, then season with salt. Slice and surround beef with mounds of vegetables and spoon pan juices over.

Tournedos de Charolais Grillé Bergerette
(Tournedos Bergerette)

1 cup oil
12 baby artichokes
Juice of 1 lemon
6 small, ripe tomatoes
⅔ cup butter
3 pounds small new potatoes, cooked and peeled

1 tablespoon Glace de Viande
1 small sprig fresh tarragon, chopped
6 filet slices, cut 1½ inches thick
Salt
Freshly ground black pepper
¾ cup Sauce Béarnaise

Heat half the oil and sauté artichokes with lemon juice until easily pierced, about 15 to 20 minutes.

Brush tomatoes with some oil and place in a Dutch oven. Cover and cook over low heat for 10 minutes or until tender, then season with salt.

Heat butter and sauté potatoes until golden. Stir in Glace de Viande and tarragon. Keep warm.

Season and grill the filet in remaining oil, as in Tournedos Rossini. Place filets on platter and remove strings. Surround with vegetables and top each with a rosette (use a pastry bag with a star tip) of Sauce Béarnaise.

Tournedos de Charolais Sauté Rossini
(Tournedos Rossini)

2 truffles, slivered
¼ cup Madeira wine
1 beef filet, about 4 pounds
    Salt and freshly ground pepper
⅔ cup butter
½ cup Port wine
½ cup Sauce Demi-Glace
    or Classic Beef Consommé

6 slices firm white
    bread, cut 1 inch thick
½ cup (8 tablespoons) clarified butter
6 slices fresh *foie gras*, ½-inch thick
    Noisette Potatoes

Marinate truffles in Madeira for 30 minutes. Drain. Cut 1½-inch-thick slices from the filet and tie each with a string to keep round. Season with salt and pepper. Heat 6 tablespoons of butter until brown and pan-broil filets for 5 minutes on each side (for rare steak). Remove steaks and keep warm.

Add wine and Demi-Glace. Bring to a boil on top of stove and scrape up all brown particles. Strain the sauce into a saucepan and beat in remaining butter, cut into small pieces. Keep warm.

Cut large rounds of bread. Heat the clarified butter in a skillet and toast bread on both sides.

Place the toasted bread on a long serving platter and put a filet steak on each. Remove strings. Top each steak with a slice of *foie gras*, then pass dish briefly under the broiler (not long enough to melt the goose liver). Garnish each slice of *foie gras* with truffles and top each portion with sauce. Serve with a side dish of Noisettes Potatoes.

Tournedos de Charolais Grillé Henri IV
(Grilled Tournedos Henri IV)

6 filet slices, 8 ounces each
    Salt and freshly ground pepper
    French-Fried Potatoes Pont-
    Neuf

Sprigs of watercress, washed and
    trimmed
¾ cup Sauce Béarnaise

Prepare coals or preheat broiler. Season and tie slices, as in Tournedos Rossini, then grill 6 inches above gray coals, changing position of the steaks after 2 minutes to make a criss-cross design on each side. They can also be done under the broiler. Ten minutes are needed to cook the steaks to medium-rare.

Prepare French-Fried Potatoes Pont-Neuf using potatoes and oil.

Arrange the steaks on a long serving platter, remove strings, and decorate with a bouquet of watercress at either end. Put French-Fried Potatoes Pont-Neuf around them. Using a pastry bag with a fluted nozzle, place a rosette of Sauce Béarnaise in the center of each steak.

Tournedos de Charolais Sauté Monselet
(Tournedos Monselet)

12 **baby artichokes**	6 **filet slices, about 6 ounces each**
Juice of 2 lemons	**Salt**
¼ **cup vegetable oil**	**Freshly ground white pepper**
1 **teaspoon salt**	1 **cup butter**
2 **pounds carrots, cut into 1-inch**	1 **cup White Veal and Poultry Stock**
pieces	⅔ **cup Madeira wine**
Pinch of confectioner's sugar	4 **ounces thin noodles, cooked**
1 **cup crème fraîche or heavy**	**and drained**
cream	

In a saucepan, combine artichokes, lemon juice, oil, and salt. Cover and braise for 25 to 30 minutes, or until artichokes are easily pierced. Add carrots, remaining butter, sugar, and water to just cover. Simmer uncovered until water is evaporated and carrots are glazed. Simmer crème fraîche until reduced by half. Keep warm.

 Season and pan-broil the filet slices in half the butter in a skillet, as in Tournedos Rossini. Remove steaks and keep warm. Add stock and wine to skillet, boil, scraping up all particles. Strain into a saucepan and keep warm.

 Stir noodles into cream and add salt to taste. Place steaks on serving platter, remove strings, and surround with artichokes, carrots, and noodles. Spoon sauce over steaks.

Filet Mignon de Charolais Sauté Bouquetière
(Pan-Broiled Filet Mignon)

6 **filet mignon, each about**	8 **ounces white turnips, diced and**
8 **ounces**	**cooked**
Salt	8 **ounces fresh green beans,**
Freshly ground white pepper	**left whole and cooked**
1⅓ **cups butter**	8 **ounces fresh peas, cooked**
½ **cup Madeira wine**	6 **small tomatoes**
1 **cup Sauce Demi-Glace**	1 **small cauliflower, poached and**
8 **ounces carrots,**	**broken into bite-sized pieces**
sliced and cooked	6 **toasted bread rounds**

Season and prepare the filet mignon in 6 tablespoons of butter, according to directions in Tournedos Rossini. Remove steaks and keep warm.

 Add wine to pan then bring to a boil, scraping up all particles. Stir in Sauce Demi-Glace and simmer for 10 minutes. Strain into a saucepan, then beat in 4 tablespoons butter, cut into small pieces, with a whisk.

 Mix cooked carrots, turnips, green beans, and peas with ½ cup butter; season lightly with salt. Brush tomatoes with ¼ cup of butter and broil 3 to 4 minutes, or until tender; season with salt. Heat remaining butter until golden, then add cauliflower and toss; season with salt.

 Place steaks on toasted bread rounds on a serving platter. Surround with mounds of vegetables and spoon sauce over.

Filet Mignon de Charolais Sauté Languedocienne
(Filet Mignon with Artichoke Hearts,
Sweet Peppers, Mushrooms, and New Potatoes)

6 medium artichokes
  Juice of 1 lemon
1 teaspoon sea salt
2 tablespoons peanut oil
3 large red-and-green peppers
1 cup olive oil
1 large can (14 ounces) cèpes,
  drained
1 cup + 2 tablespoons butter
2 shallots, chopped
2 sprigs fresh parsley, chopped

3 mill-turns freshly ground white
  pepper
3 pounds small new potatoes,
  cooked and peeled
6 filet mignon, cut 1 inch thick
2 tablespoons clarified butter
½ cup sweet white wine
¼ cup Madeira wine
6 toast rounds
  Sprigs of watercress, washed and
  trimmed

Cut artichokes into quarters and remove chokes. Combine with lemon juice, sea salt, and 2 tablespoons peanut oil and braise for 15 minutes. Clean and dice sweet peppers and sauté in ⅓ cup of olive oil until lightly browned.

Cut the cèpes into quarters. Brown ½ cup butter and sauté cèpes with shallots and parsley, all seasoned with pepper. Sauté potatoes in ⅓ cup of butter until brown; season with salt. Keep vegetables warm.

Season filets and brush with clarified butter. Pan-broil in remaining butter, as in Tournedos Rossini. Remove steaks and keep warm.

Add white wine and Madeira to skillet; boil, scraping all particles, then strain into a small saucepan.

Place toast rounds on serving platter and top with filets. Remove strings. Alternate artichoke hearts—garnished with diced sweet peppers—with mounds of cèpes and potatoes. Top with the sauce and decorate with a bouquet of watercress at either end.

Sirloin Steak au Poivre Sauté à l'Armagnac
(Peppered Steak with Armagnac)

3 pounds boneless sirloin, cut
  into 6 1-inch-thick pieces
1 teaspoon salt
½ cup vegetable oil
2 tablespoons crushed white
  peppercorns
⅔ cup butter
⅔ cup Armagnac, warmed

½ cup dry white wine
¼ cup White Veal and Poultry Stock,
  mixed with 2 teaspoons potato
  starch
  Juice of ½ lemon
  Sprigs of watercress, washed
  and trimmed

Season steaks with salt and brush them generously with oil. Spread peppercorns on both sides of the steaks and allow to marinate for about 2 hours at room temperature.

Brown the steaks in a skillet with remaining oil and ¼ cup of butter over high heat to seal in the juices. Turn the steaks as they cook to taste. When done, pour off all the fat in the skillet, add Armagnac, and set aflame. When flames die, remove steaks from skillet and place on long serving platter. Keep warm.

Add wine to skillet, bring to a boil, and stir, scraping up all brown particles. Add stock, stir until thickened, and strain into a saucepan. Whisk in remaining butter, cut into small pieces, and the lemon juice. Add salt if needed.

Cover steaks with the sauce and decorate the platter with bouquets of watercress at either end.

This steak goes well with French-fried potatoes (regular, soufflés, etc.) or with sliced sautéed potatoes.

Contrefilet Limousin Grillé au Beurre d'Échalottes
(Grilled Sirloin with Shallot Butter)

2 shallots, minced	6 pieces boneless sirloin, each
1 cup butter	8 ounces, cut 1½ inches thick
Salt	¼ cup peanut oil
2 mill-turns freshly ground	Sprigs of watercress, washed
white pepper	and trimmed
Juice of ½ lemon	French-Fried Potatoes Pont-Neuf

Sauté shallots in 2 tablespoons of butter, remove from heat, and let cool. Beat in remaining softened butter, and season with salt, pepper, and lemon juice. Shape butter with wet hands into a roll 3 inches long, then wrap in wax paper. Chill until hard.

Salt the meat and brush with oil. Grill as in Tournedos Henry IV. Keep warm.

Unwrap and cut butter into 6 crosswise slices. Arrange the steaks on a long serving platter and top each with a slice of shallot butter. Put watercress all along the edge of the platter and serve with French-Fried Potatoes Pont-Neuf.

Picadinho à la Brésilienne
(Brazilian Picadinho)

Once when the France *put in at Rio de Janeiro, Miguel de Carvalho, a member of the Confrérie des Gastronomes du Brésil (Confraternity of Brazilian Gourmets), taught me this recipe for* Picadinho à la Brésilienne. *Our passengers, always eager to discover new tropical dishes, gave it a hearty welcome. If you wish, you can add to the ingredients some diced bananas sautéed in oil.*

1 small beef filet, about 2½	2 large tomatoes, peeled,
pounds, cut into 1-inch cubes	seeded, and diced
1 teaspoon salt	Bouquet garni (sprig of fresh
3 mill-turns freshly ground white	thyme, sprig of fresh marjoram,
pepper, or 1 small pinch,	chervil leaves, tarragon leaves)
cayenne	2 tablespoons Worcestershire
¼ cup (4 tablespoons) butter	sauce
1 onion, chopped	2 tablespoons red wine vinegar
1 clove garlic, chopped	6 eggs, poached

Season meat with salt and pepper, then brown in hot butter over high heat. When browned, add onion, garlic, tomatoes, bouquet garni, Worcestershire sauce, and vinegar. Simmer, uncovered, over low heat for 10 minutes. Correct seasoning. Meat will be pink in the center of each cube.

Serve in a deep, round platter or dish, garnished with poached eggs.

Aiguillette de Charolais à l'Anglaise ou à la Ficelle
(English-Style Boiled Beef, or "On the String")

Very few restaurants serve this dish nowadays, and that is too bad, for it's a recipe which provides exceptionally tender beef. It was very popular with passengers on the France, *and many asked for it even on short laps. Although we did not create the dish, it became one of our great specialties. The total number of portions prepared this way on the* France *over its long career cannot be counted, proving that some of the simplest dishes turn out to be the most popular.*

2½ pounds beef brisket
24 carrots, scraped
24 white turnips, peeled
6 large leeks (white part only), trimmed
3 celery hearts
4 cups crème fraîche or heavy cream
¼ cup prepared white horse-radish, or 3 tablespoons grated fresh horseradish

Stock:
2 beef bones, split lengthwise
1 stalk celery, chopped
1 onion, studded with 3 whole cloves
2 carrots, chopped
2 leeks (green part only), sliced
3 quarts water
2 teaspoons salt

The beef should be tied with sufficient string left free so that it can be suspended from a wooden spoon set over the pot during cooking.

Prepare a stock using the beef bones, celery, onion studded with cloves, carrots, and leek greens; add water and salt, bring to a boil, reduce heat, and simmer for 2 hours, skimming foam as needed. Strain the stock into a small, high kettle.

Trim carrots and turnips to the size and shape of pigeons' eggs and wrap them in cheesecloth, tying each securely. Wash leeks and celery hearts thoroughly, and tie into 2 separate bundles in cheesecloth. Put carrots, turnips, leeks, and celery into the stock, bring to a boil, and simmer for 20 minutes. Remove vegetables from stock, tie the meat to the center point of a wooden spoon, and suspend it in the simmering stock by placing the wooden spoon across the kettle, resting on opposite sides of the rim. Cook, covered with foil, for 1 to 1½ hours, or until tender.

Place vegetable in broth and simmer 10 minutes or until tender. Boil crème fraîche until reduced by half, then stir in horseradish. Season to taste with salt. Cut beef into slices and untie vegetables. Serve beef slices and vegetables in a tureen with the broth. Serve sauce in a sauceboat.

Churrarco en Brochette Paulista
(Beef Kebab São Paulo with Pilaf)

2½ pounds boneless sirloin
1 veal bone, chopped
2 medium onions, minced
¾ cup oil
4 cups water
Salt
1 bay leaf
Few sprigs of fresh parsley
1 small sprig thyme
½ teaspoon potato or cornstarch, mixed with 1 tablespoon
water
1 sweet green pepper, seeded
and diced
2 large, ripe tomatoes, peeled,
seeded, and diced

1 small pinch cayenne
18 small, whole white onions,
parboiled for 5 minutes
4 cups Rice Pilaf
Marinade:
2 cups red wine vinegar,
approximately
1 teaspoon salt
2 medium onions, coarsely
chopped
1 bay leaf
1 teaspoon leaf thyme
1 teaspoon cumin
3 mill-turns freshly ground
white pepper

Trim fat and sinews from sirloin. Reserve trimmings. Cut beef into 1½-inch cubes and put cubes into a bowl or other container. Prepare marinade and soak meat for 6 hours. Remove beef cubes and reserve liquid.

Put the reserved trimmings in a saucepan and add veal bone and 1 of the onions. Brown well in ¼ cup oil. Pour in water and add salt, bay leaf, parsley, and thyme. Bring to a boil and cook until reduced by half. Strain the liquid and thicken with potato-starch mixture.

Sauté pepper and remaining onion in 2 tablespoons oil for 5 minutes. Add tomatoes and stock made from beef trimmings and simmer for 20 minutes. Correct seasoning with cayenne.

Boil reserved marinade until only ½ cup is left. Sieve and add this to the sauce, which should be very spicy. Simmer sauce until thickened.

Prepare coals or preheat broiler. Alternate cubes of marinated beef and small onions on 6 skewers. Brush skewers with remaining oil, as well as with the sauce, and grill over hot charcoal fire, turning until brown on all sides. (These can also be done in a broiler.) Cook to taste and serve on a bed of Rice Pilaf.

VEAL

Carré de Veau de l'Allier Braisé Armentierais
(Braised Rack of Veal)

1 6-bone rack of baby veal,
trimmed
1 onion, chopped
1 carrot, chopped
1 stalk celery, chopped
Bouquet garni (parsley, thyme,
marjoram)
1 veal joint, chopped into small
pieces
Salt

Freshly ground white pepper
¼ cup (4 tablespoons) butter, softened
1 cup dry white wine
2 pounds new potatoes, cooked
1¼ cups clarified butter
12 heads Belgian endive
½ cup water
6 slices firm white bread
Chopped fresh parsley
Paper frills

Trim the rack of veal and clean the bones by scraping with a butcher's knife. Preheat oven to 400 degrees.

Prepare a bed of onion, carrot, celery, bouquet garni, and veal joint in a Dutch oven. Truss the veal with 3 strings and season with salt and pepper. Butter the meat side of the rack, then set on the bed of vegetables. Cover and braise for about 1½ hours in a hot oven, turning and basting frequently. Remove from oven and keep in a warm place to rest for about 30 minutes, covered with a damp kitchen towel.

Add wine to the pan juices and place on top of stove. Simmer over low heat for about 15 minutes, then strain, pressing out all juices.

Sauté the potatoes in ½ cup of clarified butter until brown; season with salt. Braise endive in ¼ cup of clarified butter and water in a covered pan for 10 minutes or until tender; season with salt.

Heat oven to 450 degrees or heat broiler. Trim bread slices into rounds. Brush with remaining clarified butter and toast under the broiler or in a hot oven for 5 to 6 minutes.

Remove trussing strings from the veal and set it atop toast on a long serving platter. Circle the veal with potatoes alternating with clusters of endive. Spoon sauce over veal, sprinkle parsley on the endive, and decorate the bone ends with paper frills. This dish should be served very hot.

Longe de Veau de l'Allier Braisée Vallée de Bray
(Braised Loin of Veal à la Bray Valley)

This dish, properly prepared, has earned its place on every table. This indicated cut can be replaced by a boned rack of veal or any other cut which lends itself to braising. The rich and varied garnish goes perfectly with the meat, and the Château Potatoes are indispensable.

1 loin of veal, about 4½ to 5 pounds	⅔ cup butter
1 veal kidney (optional)	1 boned veal's foot and a few veal bones, chopped
1 carrot, minced	12 small onions, peeled
1 onion, minced	1 tablespoon confectioner's sugar
1 stalk celery, chopped	12 fresh mushrooms, trimmed
Few sprigs of fresh parsley, chopped	2 cups Classic Beef Consommé
1 bay leaf	½ cup crème fraîche or heavy cream
1 sprig fresh thyme	Château Potatoes

While your butcher is preparing the loin of veal, have him insert a veal kidney into the loin (first removing all the fat from kidney), roll it up, and tie securely.

Preheat oven to 350 degrees. Sauté carrot, onion, celery, parsley, bay leaf, and thyme in 2 tablespoons of the butter until golden brown. Line the bottom of a braising pot with the mixture and place the veal on it, surrounded with veal foot and bones. Cover the pot and bake in a moderate oven for 1¼ hours, basting often.

Poach onions in lightly salted water for 20 minutes. Drain; place onions in a shallow baking dish and dot with ¼ of the remaining butter and sprinkle with confectioner's sugar. Bake in moderate oven for 15 to 20 minutes or until the sugar has caramelized. Sauté mushrooms in remaining butter until golden.

Remove the loin and veal's foot from the braising pot. Place loin on a long platter and keep warm. Cut the veal's foot into small cubes and place in a saucepan. Add 2 cups consommé to the braising pot, boil until reduced by half, and add the crème fraîche. Simmer for 10 minutes over low heat or until thickened slightly. Strain liquid into a saucepan, season, and keep warm.

Garnish veal loin with the onions, mushrooms, and potatoes. Spoon sauce over veal and serve.

Côte de Veau du Gatinais Sautée Normande
(Sautéed Veal Chops Normande)

6 veal chops, about 8 ounces each	12 cooking apples, peeled, cored,
Salt	and quartered
Freshly ground white pepper	¼ cup (4 tablespoons) butter, softened
⅔ cup butter, heated until brown	¼ cup confectioner's sugar
2 cups crème fraîche or heavy	1 tablespoon chopped chives
cream	Paper frills
Juice of 1 lemon	

Trim the veal chops; season with salt and pepper. Sauté the chops slowly in a skillet with butter, then remove chops from pan and keep warm on a platter. Add crème fraîche and lemon juice to skillet and simmer sauce for 15 to 20 minutes; strain through a sieve into a saucepan and keep warm.

Preheat oven to 450 degrees. Arrange the apple quarters in a lightly buttered shallow Pyrex baking dish. Dot the apples with butter, sprinkle with confectioner's sugar, and bake in hot oven for 8 to 10 minutes (or place under the broiler until browned). Arrange the chops on a long serving platter, bone-side up. Surround with the apples, spoon sauce over, and sprinkle with chives. Serve with paper frills on the bones.

Côte de Veau Choletais Sautée Cordon Bleu
(Veal Chops Sautéed Cordon Bleu)

This dish was always served on special order. Chops stuffed in this way have a remarkable flavor, since the cheese makes the meat juicier. Leaf spinach is a particularly good accompaniment for this specialty.

6 veal chops, about 8 ounces each	⅓ cup Madeira wine
Salt and freshly ground pepper	¼ cup Cognac
6 thin slices boiled ham	6 large fresh mushrooms, minced
12 slices Gruyère cheese	2 pounds fresh leaf spinach, trimmed
⅔ cup butter	Pinch of grated nutmeg
⅓ cup Muscadet wine	Paper frills

Cut through the chops horizontally to make 2 equal flaps held together by the bone. (This is called the "wallet opening.") Season veal with salt and pepper; place a slice of ham between 2 slices of cheese and insert between the flaps of each chop. Press closed and skewer or fasten with toothpicks. Sauté chops slowly until golden in a heavy-bottomed skillet in half of the butter. If chops are thick, you can complete the cooking in an open moderate oven (325 degrees) for 5 to 6 minutes. Keep warm on a platter.

Add Muscadet, Madeira, and Cognac to pan; bring to a boil, scraping up brown particles. Strain sauce through a sieve into a saucepan and keep warm. Sauté the mushrooms in half of the remaining butter. Poach spinach in ½ cup lightly salted water for about 5 minutes. Drain well, squeezing out all the water. Sauté lightly in remaining butter; add salt and nutmeg.

Spread the spinach on a long platter. Arrange the veal chops on the spinach, coat with the pan drippings, and top with mushrooms. Place a paper frill on the bone end of each chop.

Côte de Veau de l'Allier Sautée Prince Orloff
(Sautéed Veal Chops Prince Orloff)

This dish is a challenging one, both as to preparation and cooking times. One evening we served 680 portions, and the success of the dinner set a record for our sauciers. I should like particularly to praise chef-sauciers Primaut and Fernon, and their teams, although their feat was actually beyond praise. Each portion was cooked in response to a specific order. Not a single chop was left in the kitchen, and every passenger who ordered the dish was served.

Craig Claiborne, food editor of the New York Times, *wrote after traveling with us on one cruise that the* France *was the best restaurant in the world. I was very grateful, and I doubt that even the* France *deserved such high praise. But I do admit that it was certainly the only restaurant in the world serving so refined a cuisine for so many guests.*

6 veal chops, about 8 ounces each	12 asparagus tips, cooked
Salt	6 tablespoons Sauce Mornay
Freshly ground white pepper	1 cup Madeira wine
2 shallots, chopped	¼ cup Sauce Demi-Glace
2 cups butter	6 artichoke hearts, halved and
2 pounds fresh mushrooms,	cooked
chopped	2 pounds potatoes, prepared as
¼ cup chopped truffles	Noisette Potatoes
6 tablespoons Sauce Hollandaise	Paper frills

Prepare veal chops for stuffing as for Veal Chops Sautéed Cordon Bleu. Season the cavities with salt and pepper.

Sauté shallots in ¼ cup of the butter, without allowing to brown. Add mushrooms, salt, and pepper and mix well; cook over low heat until the liquid from the mushrooms has evaporated. Add truffles and stir. Using a spoon or a pastry bag, stuff each of the chops. Sew or skewer openings.

Heat remaining butter until brown and sauté the chops. If they are thick, you can complete the cooking by putting the skillet in a hot oven (400 degrees) for 5 to 6 minutes.

Preheat oven to 450 degrees, if not already hot. When the chops are thoroughly cooked and nicely browned, arrange them on a heatproof platter. Put 1 tablespoon Sauce Hollandaise on each. Add asparagus tips and top with Sauce Mornay. Place under the broiler or in very hot oven for 3 to 4 minutes, or until golden. Meanwhile, discard half the fat from the skillet. Add Madeira and Sauce Demi-Glace, bring to a boil, scraping all particles, then sieve into a saucepan.

Add artichoke hearts and Noisette Potatoes to platter, with chops. Place a paper frill on end bone and top chops with sauce.

Gourmandines de Veau Laitier au Gratin "France"
(Veal Scallops au Gratin à la *France*)

This dish was created aboard the France. *A wealthy and faithful American woman, who was accommodated with her two daughters and three dogs in three luxury cabins, asked us to prepare veal scallops au gratin during a Caribbean cruise. We were embarrassed because veal is not a meat which lends itself to gratinéeing. To prevent the scallops from becoming dry, we hit upon the idea of stuffing them with mushrooms and wrapping them in a crêpe. The dish was delicious, but its appearance was disastrous! The woman, nevertheless, was delighted, and she ordered it on another Caribbean cruise (she went on four a year). On that occasion, we were inspired to use small scallops wrapped in miniature crêpes, to combine the mushrooms with diced chicken, and to bind the stuffing by gratinéeing it with an intensely flavored Sauce Suprême. Thus this delicious dish also became pleasing to the eye. The American came back to congratulate me. "Chef," she said, "the veal scallops were a real* gourmandise." *Without knowing it, she had helped to baptize the dish, which we called Gourmandines de Veau Laitier au Gratin "France." The Gourmandines became one of our greatest successes, on a par with our most renowned specialties.*

18 veal scallops, 3 ounces
    each, from milk-fed veal
    Salt
    Freshly ground white pepper
½ cup (8 tablespoons) butter,
    heated until foamy
2½ cups thick Sauce Suprême
    (1 cup reserved for stuffing)
1¼ cups grated Swiss cheese
¼ cup (4 tablespoons) butter

Crêpes:
4 eggs, separated
    Salt
1½ cups milk
1½ cups all-purpose flour

Stuffing:
1 broiling chicken, about
    2½ pounds
    Salt
2 carrots, chopped
2 leeks (green part only),
    chopped
1 stalk celery, chopped
1 onion, studded with 4 whole
    cloves
    Bouquet garni (fresh parsley,
    celery leaves, thyme)
10 large, fresh mushrooms, diced
½ cup (8 tablespoons) butter,
    heated until brown
    Juice of ½ lemon

Prepare stuffing. Cook chicken in water to cover with salt, carrots, leaks, celery, onion, and bouquet garni for 40 to 45 minutes or until tender. Skin and bone chicken, then finely dice meat. Sauté mushrooms lightly (about 5 minutes), without browning, in butter seasoned with salt and lemon juice. Mix chicken and mushrooms in a bowl and stir in 1 cup of the Sauce Suprême. Set aside.

    Pound veal scallops until paper-thin. Season with salt and pepper, then sear for a moment on each side in a skillet with butter (they should still be rare when taken from the pan).

    Prepare a batter for crêpes. Beat the egg yolks with salt, milk, and flour until smooth. Let the batter rest for a while, then make 18 7-inch crêpes in a lightly greased crêpes Suzette pan. Set crêpes out on a marble slab or mixing board and put a veal scallop on each. Using a metal spatula, spread each veal scallop with some of the stuffing, then roll the crêpes into cylinders.

    Preheat the oven to 400 degrees. Generously butter a large Pyrex gratin dish. Spread dish with half the remaining Sauce Suprême and sprinkle with half the cheese. Put the rolled crêpes into the pan and spoon remaining Sauce Suprême over. Sprinkle with remaining cheese and dot with butter. Bake in hot oven for 15 to 20 minutes or until piping hot. Serve immediately.

Escalope de Veau Laitier Sautée Verdunoise
(Sautéed Scallops of Veal Verdunoise)

6 veal scallops, about 8 ounces
  each
Salt
Freshly ground white pepper
Flour for dusting
2 eggs, beaten well
1 cup dry bread crumbs
⅔ cup clarified butter
2 cups Brown Veal Stock
1 tablespoon potato or cornstarch

3 pounds new potatoes, peeled
  and sliced thin
2 tablespoons olive oil
2 hard-cooked eggs, separated
6 pitted green olives
6 anchovy filets, packed in oil
Sprigs of fresh parsley
2 tablespoons chopped fresh parsley
1 lemon, peeled and cut into
  6 slices

Flatten the scallops with a mallet or the flat part of a cleaver or large butcher's knife. Season with salt and pepper, coat with flour, shaking each to eliminate excess flour. Dip scallops into egg, then into bread crumbs, pressing on each side with the heel of the hand to ensure even breading. Sauté to a golden brown in half the clarified butter. Remove scallops and keep warm; reserve pan drippings.

Mix stock and starch, and stir in a saucepan over low heat until thickened. Sauté potatoes in remaining butter mixed with oil, cooking them to a dark brown.

While meat or potatoes are cooking, prepare garnishes. Mince the whites of the eggs, then force the yolks through a sieve. Wrap each olive in an anchovy filet, then garnish with a leaf of parsley. Decorate the lemon slices by covering 2 with chopped egg white, 2 with some of the chopped parsley, and 2 with the sieved egg yolk. Place an olive with its anchovy filet in the center of each lemon slice.

Spoon sauce on platter and top with scallops arranged in an arc. Heap the potatoes in the curve. Place a lemon slice in the center of each scallop and sprinkle the potatoes with remaining chopped parsley. Drizzle pan drippings over meat and serve.

Escalope de Veau Laitier Grillée Napoléon
(Grilled Veal Scallops Napoleon)

6 veal scallops, about 6 ounces
  each
1 eggplant, peeled
Flour for dusting
Olive oil
Salt
3 medium tomatoes, cut in half
  lengthwise

6 fresh mushrooms, peeled
1 cup butter
Juice of ½ lemon
2 sprigs fresh parsley, chopped
1 bunch watercress, washed and
  trimmed

Flatten the scallops as in the recipe for Sautéed Scallops of Veal Verdonaise. Prepare coals, if grilling. Round off the edges of eggplant with a knife, then cut into 6 rather thick slices. Dust with flour, then fry in hot oil, ¼ inch deep, until brown. Drain on absorbent paper and salt lightly; keep warm.

Preheat oven to 400 degrees or heat broiler. Arrange tomato halves in a Pyrex dish, brush each with oil, and salt lightly. Bake in hot oven or broil, for 5 to 6 minutes. Keep warm.

Cook mushrooms in ¼ cup of butter; salt to taste.

Using a wooden spoon, soften remaining butter, then blend in a little salt, the lemon juice, and parsley, mixing well.

Brush the scallops with oil generously, sprinkle with salt, and grill for 5 minutes on each side over a hot charcoal fire, shifting the position to give them a criss-cross marking from the grill. (These can also be done in a broiler.)

Put the scallops on a long serving platter. In the center of each place a slice of fried eggplant, topped with a tomato half and a mushroom cap garnished with a tablespoon of the seasoned butter. Put a bouquet of watercress at each end of the platter and serve.

Blanquette de Veau à l'Ancienne
(Veal Stew with Mushrooms and Onions)

3 pounds boneless veal, cut into 1½-inch cubes	12 small onions, peeled
½ teaspoon sea salt	12 small, fresh mushrooms, trimmed
1 teaspoon white peppercorns	Salt
1 carrot, chopped	Juice of ½ lemon
1 onion, chopped	1 cup crème fraîche or heavy cream
2 stalks celery, chopped	4 egg yolks
Bouquet garni (fresh parsley, rosemary, thyme, bay leaf)	2 tablespoons water
½ cup + 2 tablespoons butter	Pinch of cayenne
½ cup flour	1 tablespoon chopped fresh parsley
	Rice Pilaf

Soak veal in ice water for several hours, then drain and place in a saucepan. Cover with water, season with sea salt, peppercorns, carrot, onion, celery, and bouquet garni. Bring to a boil, skimming foam carefully as needed, and simmer over gentle heat for 1 hour. When the veal is tender, transfer to a well-buttered saucepan. Strain the cooking juices and keep hot.

Melt ½ cup butter in a saucepan, then stir in flour. Mix with a whisk, then cook roux for a matter of seconds without browning over low heat. Stir in cooking juices a little at a time, mixing briskly with a whisk.

Cook onions in lightly salted boiling water for 15 minutes or until tender, then drain. Braise mushrooms in a little water, with remaining butter, 2 pinches of salt, and lemon juice to keep them from darkening. Add the onions and mushrooms to the veal, then strain the sauce onto the meat. Add the crème fraîche and simmer for 15 minutes over low heat.

Beat egg yolks with water, then beat in some of the hot sauce. Add egg-yolk mixture to saucepan, adjust seasoning, and add cayenne. Sprinkle with chopped parsley and serve the stew in a tureen with Rice Pilaf.

Jarret de Veau Laitier à l'Italienne
(Ossobuco)

6 slices veal shank with marrow
bone (as for ossobuco), each
slice about 2 inches thick
Salt
Freshly ground white pepper
Flour for dusting
½ cup (8 tablespoons) butter,
heated until brown

16 small onions, peeled
Clarified Brown Veal Stock
4 ripe tomatoes, peeled, seeded,
and diced
1 tablespoon tomato paste
4 slivers lemon peel (zest only)
Pinch of cayenne
Risotto, Milan Style

Preheat oven to 400 degrees.

Season the veal with salt and pepper, then dust lightly with flour. In an ovenproof skillet, brown shanks in butter, together with the onions. Add stock to cover, then pour in tomatoes and tomato paste. Add lemon peel, adjust seasoning with cayenne and bring to a boil. Cover the veal with a sheet of well-buttered parchment paper or foil and bake in hot oven for about 1 hour or until tender. Serve with Risotto, Milan Style.

LAMB

Selle d'Agneau Bajocasse Rôtie "France"
(Roast Saddle of Lamb à la *France*)

1 saddle of spring lamb
Salt
Freshly ground white pepper
8 large, fresh mushrooms,
trimmed and chopped
Juice of ½ lemon
⅓ cup crème fraîche or heavy
cream

½ cup dry white wine
½ cup Port wine
1½ cups Sauce Hollandaise
Glazed Mixed Vegetables
½ cup (8 tablespoons) butter,
heated until brown

Preheat oven to 350 degrees.

Trim the saddle of lamb, cutting off the layer of fat and membranes and sinews. Bone the saddle completely, then rub the inside with salt and pepper. Set aside.

Mix mushrooms with lemon juice and simmer in a saucepan until dry. Simmer crème fraîche until reduced by half, then stir in mushrooms. Season with salt and spread mixture inside lamb. Roll the lamb and truss securely with string.

Put lamb in a heatproof roasting pan, season with salt and pepper, and roast in moderate oven, turning and basting frequently, for 1 to 1½ hours (or until meat thermometer registers 150 degrees) for medium or 2½ hours for well done (180 degrees). When roasted to taste, remove from pan and let rest for 20 minutes on a platter. Discard the fat from the roasting pan and add both wines. Bring to a boil on top of stove, scraping up particles. Strain into a saucepan and keep warm.

Cover the lamb with Sauce Hollandaise and place under the broiler until golden brown. Surround meat with vegetables, pour butter over the vegetables, and serve sauce alongside.

Carré d'Agneau des Causses Rôti Bazadaise
(Roast Rack of Lamb Bazadaise)

This is another dish which I have never seen on any restaurant menu. This popular dish was, indeed, created aboard the France *and we often roasted two hundred racks of lamb for a single sitting. The parsley and shallot sauce gives a delicious taste to the meat, and the decoration makes it one of the most attractive of meat dishes.*

2 racks of spring lamb, 6 ribs each
Salt
4 shallots, minced
1 clove garlic, minced
½ cup peanut oil
1½ cups dry bread crumbs
2 tablespoons finely chopped fresh parsley
2 mill-turns freshly ground white pepper
1 cup dry white wine
1 large can (14 ounces) cèpes, drained and quartered
¼ cup (4 tablespoons) butter
2 pounds new potatoes
½ cup (8 tablespoons) butter, heated until brown
Paper frills

Preheat oven to desired temperature.

Trim 2 racks of lamb, leaving bone ends very long and cutting off some of the excess fat. Season with salt and put in a heatproof roasting pan and roast from 18 to 20 minutes in a hot oven (450 degrees), turning and basting frequently for rare, or American style (350 degrees) for 1½ hours (until meat thermometer registers medium—150 degrees). Keep warm.

Turn up oven to 450 degrees or heat broiler. Prepare a parsley and shallot sauce by sautéeing shallots and garlic in peanut oil. Let cool, then stir in bread crumbs, parsley, 1 teaspoon salt, and white pepper. Mix well, since the sauce should be well oiled; add a little oil if needed. Using the hand, spread the mixture over the meat side of the lamb, quite thickly, patting firmly to make an even layer. Brown the parsleyed side under the broiler or in very hot oven for 5 to 6 minutes. Set the 2 racks at one end of a long serving platter, parsleyed side up, with the ribs interlocked. Keep warm.

Pour the fat from the roasting pan and add the wine. Place pan on top of stove, and bring to a boil, scraping up all particles. Strain the sauce into a saucepan and keep warm.

Sauté cèpes in butter; sauté new potatoes in browned butter. Alternate clusters of mushrooms and potatoes around roast. Put a paper frill on each of the bones and serve sauce drizzled over slices of lamb.

Carré d'Agneau des Causses Rôti Sarladaise
(Roast Rack of Lamb with Truffled Potatoes)

2 racks of lamb, 6 ribs each
Salt and freshly ground pepper
Truffled Potatoes

Season, roast, and prepare sauce as in Roast Rack of Lamb Bazadaise. Set the lamb on a bed of Truffled Potatoes.

Agnelet Pascal Rôti St.-Laud
(Roast Spring Lamb St. Laud)

1 leg of lamb, about 4 pounds	¼ cup peanut oil
Salt	½ cup (8 tablespoons) butter
Freshly ground white pepper	2 pounds new potatoes, cooked
2 cloves garlic, cut into slivers	and peeled
¾ cup dry white wine	1 tablespoon chopped fresh parsley
2 cups Clarified Veal Stock	2 teaspoons finely chopped fresh
1 cup chopped tomato pulp	tarragon
6 artichokes, quartered	1 bouquet watercress, washed
Juice of 1 lemon	and trimmed

Preheat oven to 350 degrees. Rub the lamb with salt and pepper; insert garlic slivers into small cuts all over the leg. Roast in a heatproof pan in a moderate oven for 1½ to 2 hours, or until meat thermometer registers medium (150 degrees) for pink lamb. Place on platter and keep warm.

Discard fat from roasting pan, and add wine, stock, and tomato pulp; boil, scraping up all particles, for 5 minutes. Strain into a saucepan, pressing out all liquid, and keep warm.

Combine artichokes, lemon juice, salt, and peanut oil, in a saucepan. Braise for 15 minutes. Heat butter and sauté potatoes until golden. Add parsley and tarragon. Place vegetables around lamb on platter and garnish with watercress. Slice lamb and serve topped with sauce.

Gigot de Pré Salé Rôti à la Solognote
(Roast Leg of Lamb Solognote)

1 leg of lamb, about 4 to 5 pounds	1 bouquet watercress, washed and trimmed
Salt	Paper frill
Freshly ground white pepper	*Marinade:*
1 slice firm bread, sliced lengthwise	1 cup red wine vinegar
¼ cup (4 tablespoons) clarified butter	1 cup water
	1 medium onion, chopped
1½ pounds fresh green beans, trimmed and cut into 1-inch pieces	1 medium carrot, chopped
	1 stalk celery, chopped
	Few sprigs of fresh parsley, chopped
⅓ cup (5 tablespoons) butter	1 bay leaf
3 tablespoons capers	1 teaspoon leaf thyme

Trim the leg of lamb of excess fat and remove the pelvic bone. Tie lamb in several places to keep meat an even thickness throughout. Put the lamb in a small roasting pan, add marinade, and allow to sit for 3 hours, turning lamb several times.

Preheat oven to 350 degrees. Dry meat with kitchen towel, season with salt and pepper, and roast on a rack in a heatproof roasting pan in a medium oven for 1½ to 2 hours, or until meat thermometer registers medium (150 degrees). Turn the leg and baste frequently during roasting.

Meanwhile, transfer the marinade to a saucepan and boil until reduced by half. Strain, pressing the vegetables and herbs well to extract their juices.

When done, put the lamb on a long serving platter and keep warm. Pour off fat from roasting pan and add reduced marinade. Place pan on top of stove, bring to a boil, and scrape up brown particles. Strain this liquid into a saucepan and keep warm.

Brush bread slice with clarified butter and place under the broiler; toast until brown on both sides. Cook green beans in salted water, then drain, coat with butter, and sprinkle with capers. Place toast on serving platter and put lamb on top. Place the green beans around the roast and decorate bone end with paper frill. Garnish with watercress and serve the sauce in a sauceboat.

Gigot Pré Salé Rôti Savoyarde
(Roast Leg of Lamb Savoyarde)

1 leg of lamb, about 4½ pounds
2 cloves garlic, cut into slivers
Salt and freshly ground pepper

¼ cup (4 tablespoons) butter, softened
Gratinéed Potatoes Savoyarde

Prepare and roast leg of lamb as in Roast Spring Lamb St. Laud. Sprinkle lamb with salt and pepper and spread with butter. Roast, then serve with Gratinéed Potatoes Savoyarde.

Cotelettes d'Agneau Sautées St.-Antonin
(Breaded and Sautéed Lamb Chops)

12 rib lamb chops
4 shallots, minced
2 cloves garlic, minced
1 cup olive oil
3 cups soft fine bread crumbs, made from firm white bread
2 tablespoons chopped fresh parsley
Salt

Freshly ground white pepper
3 pounds new potatoes, peeled and sliced ⅛-inch thick
½ cup (8 tablespoons) butter, heated until brown
6 ripe tomatoes, cut in half
¼ cup (4 tablespoons) butter
12 paper frills

Trim excess fat from chops. Sauté shallots and garlic in 2 tablespoons of the olive oil. Mix shallots, ½ cup of the oil, and the bread crumbs. Add 2 teaspoons of the parsley, ½ teaspoon salt, and ¼ teaspoon pepper. Mix well, then use the mixture to bread the lamb chops, pressing down with the hand to ensure uniform breading.

Wash the potato slices to remove starch; dry and sauté in browned butter. Season with salt and pepper.

Put tomatoes, cut-side up, in a Pyrex dish, season with salt, and brush with 2 tablespoons of the oil. Place briefly under the broiler or in a hot oven (450 degrees) for 5 to 6 minutes.

Sear the chops in a skillet, then sauté slowly in remaining oil and butter according to your taste. Make a bed of potatoes on a long serving platter and arrange the lamb chops on it. Put the tomatoes around them and spoon the pan juices over the chops. Sprinkle remaining chopped parsley over the tomatoes and put a paper frill on each chop.

Kebab d'Agneau Grillé Persane
(Shish Kebab Persian Style)

1 leg of lamb, boned and
cut into 1½-inch cubes
(about 3 pounds)
3 large onions, quartered
3 large sweet peppers, cut into
1½-inch squares
⅓ cup olive oil
Pearl Barley

Marinade:
1 cup olive oil
⅓ cup dry white wine
Juice of 1 lemon
1 sprig fresh thyme, leaves only
1 teaspoon leaf marjoram
1 teaspoon cumin
Salt
Freshly ground white pepper

Sauce:
1 medium onion, minced
2 large, ripe tomatoes, peeled,
seeded, and chopped
1 tablespoon vegetable oil
⅓ cup dry white wine
¼ cup red wine vinegar
¼ teaspoon crushed peppercorns
2 cups Brown Veal Stock
Beurre Manié
2 drops Tabasco sauce

Prepare a marinade by combining oil, wine, lemon juice, thyme, marjoram, cumin, salt, and pepper. Beat with a whisk and marinate the lamb for 2 hours. Drain and pat meat dry.

While meat is marinating, prepare sauce. Sauté onion and tomatoes in oil in a large skillet. Add wine, vinegar, and peppercorns and simmer until thickened, about 15 to 20 minutes. Combine stock with Beurre Manié and simmer until thickened; add to tomato mixture. Season sauce with salt and Tabasco sauce, then simmer over gentle heat for about 15 minutes.

Prepare coals for grilling. Sauté onions and peppers in olive oil only until wilted. Dry the vegetables, then alternate cubes of lamb, onions, and peppers on skewers and grill over gray coals for about 10 minutes for rare meat, longer for medium or well done. (This can also be done in a broiler for the same length of time.) Turn kebabs several times to brown on all sides.

Spread Pearl Barley on a serving platter and top with kebabs. Spoon sauce over kebabs.

Sosati de Mouton du Transvaal au Maïs Égrené
(Lamb Kebabs with Creamed Corn)

1 leg of lamb or mutton, about
    4 to 5 pounds
    Salt
10 ears corn on the cob
¾ cup milk
1 pound smoked bacon, in 1
    piece
¼ cup (4 tablespoons) butter
1 cup crème fraîche or heavy
    cream
    Freshly ground pepper

Marinade:
2 cups vinegar
3 pinches leaf marjoram
1 teaspoon leaf thyme
1 small hot red pepper, finely
    chopped

Sauce:
1 onion, chopped
1 carrot, chopped
1 stalk celery, chopped
2 quarts water
    Salt
    Bouquet garni (celery leaves,
    parsley, thyme, tarragon)
4 large, ripe tomatoes, peeled,
    seeded, and chopped
2 tablespoons tomato paste
    Few drops of Tabasco sauce

Bone the lamb or mutton completely; reserve bones for sauce. Cut the meat into 1½-inch cubes, then sprinkle with salt. Prepare marinade and marinate lamb in the refrigerator for 2 days, turning often. Drain and dry meat.

Prepare the sauce by preheating the oven to 425 degrees. Cut the lamb bones into small pieces and brown with onion, carrot, and celery in hot oven for 1 hour. When nicely browned, transfer bones and vegetables to a saucepan and add water, salt, bouquet garni, and tomatoes. Bring to a boil; simmer, skimming foam as needed, until reduced by half. Strain and discard solids. Add tomato paste and Tabasco sauce. Simmer for 10 to 15 minutes further, until the sauce thickens slightly. Set aside.

Prepare coals for grilling and preheat oven to 450 degrees. Cook the corn in water to cover and with the milk for 8 to 10 minutes. Drain, let cool, and slice off the kernels. Set aside.

Cut thick slices from bacon slab and place them under the broiler or in hot oven for 5 to 6 minutes or until half cooked. Cut into 1½-inch cubes.

Alternate meat with bacon on skewers and grill 6 inches above gray coals to taste—rare, medium, or well done. (This can also be done in a broiler.)

Sauté the corn kernels briefly in butter. Meanwhile, simmer crème fraîche until reduced to ½ cup. Stir cream into corn and season lightly with salt and pepper.

Arrange the kebabs on a bed of creamed corn. Serve sauce separately in a sauceboat.

Note: If desired, add a little braised, diced sweet red or green pepper to the corn.

Étuvée d'Agneau au Currie Birmane
(Burmese Curried Lamb)

1 breast of lamb, about 4 pounds)	1 tablespoon tomato paste
Salt	Bouquet garni (fresh parsley, celery, thyme, rosemary)
2 tablespoons curry powder	1 coconut, shelled, peeled, and grated
¼ cup peanut oil	
1 medium onion, minced	2 bananas, sliced
2 tablespoons all-purpose flour	½ cup crème fraîche or heavy cream
1 quart clarified Brown Veal Stock or Chicken Consommé	1 large tomato, peeled, seeded, and chopped
	Rice Pilaf with Raisins

Preheat oven to 350 degrees. Cut the entire breast of lamb into 2-inch pieces. Season with salt and curry powder. Sear the lamb cubes in an ovenproof casserole in oil, then add onion to the pan and sauté until golden. Sift flour over the meat, mixing with a spatula. Add stock to cover, along with tomato paste, bouquet garni, coconut meat, and sliced bananas. Bring to a boil, cover, and continue cooking in a moderate oven for 40 to 45 minutes or until lamb is tender, skimming off fat.

Remove the lamb with a slotted spoon and put in another pan; set aside. Add ¼ cup of the fat skimmed from the surface of the cooking juices. Skim remaining fat and discard. Boil pan juices for 15 minutes, then strain (press out all liquid) and add to lamb. Add crème fraîche and tomato and simmer over low heat for a few minutes. Season to taste with salt and pepper.

Place the lamb in a tureen or large bowl. The sauce should be sharply flavored and pink in color. Serve with Rice Pilaf with Raisins.

Étuvée d'Agneau à l'Irlandaise
(Irish Stew)

1 shoulder of lamb, boned and cut into 1½-inch cubes	2 leeks (white part only), chopped
Salt	3 stalks celery, chopped
Pinch of cayenne	2 onions, chopped
3 medium potatoes, peeled and chopped	2 pounds small potatoes, peeled
	1 cup Sauce Crème à l'Anglaise
	1 tablespoon chopped fresh parsley

Put lamb in a kettle, add water to cover, and season with 1 teaspoon salt and cayenne. Add potatoes, leeks, celery, and onions. Bring to the boil, skimming foam as needed. Reduce heat, cover, and simmer for about 45 to 50 minutes or until lamb is tender. Remove lamb with a slotted spoon and put into a large heatproof casserole and keep warm. Press the vegetables and cooking juices through a sieve or food mill onto the lamb. (This can also be done in a blender or food processor.) The sauce should be naturally bound by the vegetables, especially with the potatoes. Simmer over gentle heat for several minutes.

Trim small potatoes into the size and shape of large olives. Cook these in a saucepan with boiling salted water until tender. Drain and add to stew or serve separately. Top both stew and potatoes with Sauce Crème à l'Anglaise and sprinkle with parsley.

Couscous Marocain
(Moroccan Couscous)

1 cup uncooked chick peas
Salt
1 broiler or frying chicken, about
  2½ pounds, cut up
½ shoulder of lamb, about
  2 pounds, boned and cut into
  1½-inch cubes
1 teaspoon paprika
  Dash of cayenne
1 dried hot pepper, crushed
⅓ cup olive oil or rendered
  chicken fat
3 large tomatoes, peeled and
  cut into wedges
  Bouquet garni (fresh parsley,
  thyme, rosemary)
  Pinch of cumin
  Pinch of ground cinnamon
4 carrots, quartered

4 artichoke hearts, quartered
2 turnips, peeled and quartered
2 sweet peppers, seeded and
  quartered
1 stalk celery, chopped
1 small cauliflower, broken
  into flowerets
1 stalk fennel, chopped
3 zucchini, quartered
2 small eggplants, quartered
4 cups durum wheat semolina
  (couscous or wheat pilaf)
2 tablespoons butter
1 cup golden raisins (optional)

Sauce:
1 tablespoon tomato purée
  Few drops of Tabasco Sauce

Soak chick peas for 12 hours before cooking. In a separate saucepan, cook chick peas in boiling salted water. Do not skim the pan while the chick peas are cooking. Simmer for 1½ to 2 hours or until tender. Drain and keep warm.

Season the chicken and lamb with salt, paprika, cayenne, and hot pepper. Sauté the meat and chicken in olive oil, barely browning it, then transfer to a couscous pot. Add tomatoes, bouquet garni, cumin, cinnamon, carrots, artichokes, turnips, peppers, celery, cauliflower, and fennel. Add water to just cover. Bring to a boil, then after 20 minutes, add zucchini and eggplant. Cook for about 30 minutes, according to the tenderness of the lamb.

As meat begins to simmer, prepare the couscous. Place semolina into a bowl. Add cold water in small quantities, kneading with the hand until the granules are well separated. Cover the sieve of the top part of a couscous pot with cheesecloth and put in the semolina, which will be cooked by the steam rising from the simmering meat. Place sieve over simmering stew and cover; it will take about 15 minutes for the semolina to cook.

Toss the semolina with a fork to separate the grains. Mix with butter and salt lightly. At this point, add raisins if you wish, but this is optional.

While couscous is steaming, prepare sauce. Put 1 cup of the cooking juices from the meat into a saucepan. Stir in tomato purée and Tabasco. Simmer until reduced by half.

Heap the semolina around the edge of a long serving platter. Pour the meat mixture into the center of the platter and sprinkle with chick peas. Serve the sauce in a sauceboat or spoon sauce over servings of couscous.

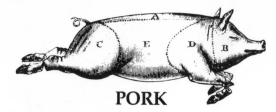

PORK

Jambon d'York Braisé Nesselrode
(Braised York Ham Nesselrode)

1 **York ham or precooked smoked ham, about 6 to 8 pounds**	1 **slice toast**
½ **cup confectioner's sugar**	**Sprigs of watercress**
½ **cup Madeira wine**	**Paper frill**
2 **cups Sauce Demi-Glace**	**Chestnut Mousseline**

Soak the ham in cold water for 12 hours. Place ham in a kettle, covering with lightly salted cold water and bring to a boil; simmer (the water should "shiver," not boil) for 1½ hours, or about 15 minutes per pound. Let cool, then cut the fat off evenly to preserve the shape of the ham.

Preheat oven to 400 degrees. Put the ham in a heatproof baking dish, sprinkle generously with confectioner's sugar on fat side only, and, at the side of the ham, pour in wine and Demi-Glace. Glaze the ham in a hot oven for about 20 minutes, basting frequently. Reserve pan juices.

Place the ham on a long serving platter, with the bone end resting on a square of toasted bread. Spoon reserved pan juices over ham and surround the ham with watercress. Put a large paper frill on the bone end. Serve the Chestnut Mousseline in a vegetable dish.

Jambon d'York Braisé Bayonnaise
(Braised York Ham with Pilaf)

1 **York ham, cooked as in Braised York Ham Nesselrode**	6 **Spanish chorizo sausages, chopped**
1 **red pepper, diced**	½ **cup olive oil**
1 **green pepper, diced**	2 **strands saffron**
3 **thick slices prosciutto, chopped**	**Rice Pilaf, made double quantity**

Cook ham as in Braised York Ham Nesselrode. Sauté peppers, prosciutto, and sausages in olive oil about 10 minutes. Drain, and add with saffron to Rice Pilaf at same time as consommé; continue to cook as per instructions, then press into baba molds. Place the ham on a long serving platter, spoon over reserved juices, and surround with unmolded pilaf mounds. **Serves 10.**

Jambon de Paris Grillé Hawaien
(Grilled Ham with Maple Syrup)

6 **thick ham steaks**	24 **whole cloves**
½ **cup corn oil**	6 **thick slices pineapple**
1 **teaspoon salt**	2 **cups maple syrup**
2 **tablespoons dry mustard**	

Prepare grill or heat broiler. Oil and season steaks, and grill over charcoal about 5 minutes per side, turning once to make a pattern. This may also be done under the broiler.

Preheat oven to 400 degrees. Remove steaks from grill, brush with mustard, and insert 4 cloves into each slice. Place onto an oiled baking dish, and cover each steak with a slice of pineapple. Pour over maple syrup, then glaze in a very hot oven about 8 minutes, or under broiler, basting frequently with syrup.

Medaillon de Porc Sauté à la Danoise
(Pork Medallions with Apples and Prunes)

1 pound dried and pitted prunes	1 loin of pork, approximately 4
½ cup sugar	pounds
2 thick slices lemon	½ cup oil
½ tablespoon ground cinnamon	Salt and pepper
4 green apples, peeled and	1 cup dry white wine
quartered	Watercress
1 cup butter, melted	

Soak prunes in water to cover for 2 hours. Drain, place in a casserole with fresh water to cover, add sugar, lemon, and cinnamon and poach about 20 minutes. Drain.

Preheat oven to 350 degrees. Place apples in baking dish, cover with half the butter and bake about 35 minutes.

Cut loin on the bias into 6 medallions, and flatten slightly with a cleaver or the bottom of a skillet, and sauté in oil approximately 5 minutes per side. Brown remaining butter and sauté prunes 5 minutes. Place medallions on a platter and surround with prunes and baked apples. Deglaze pan with white wine and pour over. Place watercress on ends of platter and serve.

Carré de Porc Braisé Bavaroise
(Pork Roast with Cabbage)

1 pork roast, first cut,	1 tablespoon lard
approximately 7 pounds	2 medium onions, minced
1 tablespoon coarse salt	2 cloves garlic, minced
Freshly ground pepper	2 cups Classic Beef Consommé
1 teaspoon thyme	Salt
3 medium red cabbages,	6 green apples, peeled and quartered
shredded	3 pounds new potatoes, peeled and
1 cup red wine vinegar	steamed

Rub roast with salt, season with pepper and thyme, and set aside for 12 hours. Marinate cabbage in vinegar and ½ teaspoon salt for 12 hours, then drain and squeeze dry. Cook for 5 minutes in boiling water and drain once more.

Preheat oven to 400 degrees. Place roast in roasting pan and cook in hot oven for 30 minutes. In a casserole, melt lard then sauté onions until clear and add garlic. Sauté briefly, then add cabbage, apples, and consommé and season with salt and pepper. After roast has cooked 30 minutes, pour over cabbage, cover, and continue to roast for about 1½ hours or until the center of the roast has lost its pinkness. Place cabbage on a platter, top with slices of roast, and surround with steamed potatoes.

Paupiettes de Jambon d'York Dorés Viroflay
(York Ham Rolls Viroflay)

1 **stewing chicken, about 4 pounds, cooked until tender**	2¼ **cups crème fraîche or heavy cream**
2 **pounds mushrooms, trimmed and diced**	**Pinch of grated nutmeg**
½ **cup (8 tablespoons) butter**	12 **thin slices York ham**
Salt	4 **pounds fresh spinach, trimmed and washed**
2 **tablespoons lemon juice**	1 **cup grated Gruyère cheese**

Skin and bone the cooked chicken; dice the meat.

Preheat oven to 450 degrees or heat broiler. Sauté the mushrooms in half the butter, salting lightly and drizzling with lemon juice to keep them from discoloring. Boil 1½ cups crème fraîche until reduced by half, then mix in the chicken and mushrooms. Season with nutmeg. Put 2 tablespoons of this stuffing on each of the ham slices and roll into cylinders.

Sauté the spinach in remaining butter, then spread spinach in a gratin dish. Top with ham rolls, then cover with remaining crème fraîche and sprinkle with cheese. Place under a broiler or in hot oven for 5 to 6 minutes or until browned. Serve immediately.

OTHER MEATS

Coeur d'Artichaut Dinandais au Gratin Friande
(Artichoke Hearts Stuffed with Sweetbreads and Truffles)

1 **pair veal sweetbreads (2 pair if small)**	2 **tablespoons chopped truffles**
6 **large, fresh mushrooms, trimmed and diced**	**Pinch of cayenne**
¼ **cup water**	6 **Braised Artichoke Hearts**
Salt	½ **cup grated Gruyère cheese**
1½ **lemons**	1 **bunch curly parsley, separated into sprigs**
2 **tablespoons butter**	
1¼ **cups crème fraîche or heavy cream**	

Prepare and cook sweetbreads as in Veal Sweetbreads Panetiére; let cool and cut into small cubes.

Preheat oven to 450 degrees or heat broiler. Place mushrooms in a saucepan and add ¼ cup water along with ½ teaspoon salt and juice of ½ lemon. Add butter, bring to a boil, and cook for 10 minutes or until liquid is absorbed.

Boil crème fraîche in a saucepan until thickened. Add the sweetbreads, mushrooms, truffles, salt to taste, and cayenne. Mix well with a wooden spoon and keep warm.

Spoon sweetbread-mushroom mixture over and into artichoke hearts. Sprinkle with cheese and brown under the broiler or in hot oven for 5 to 6 minutes.

Serve stuffed artichokes on a napkin or doily, garnished with sprigs of parsley.

Foie de Veau Laitier Sauté aux Beignets Lyonnais
(Sautéed Calf's Liver with Onion Rings)

6 slices calf's liver	**Deep-Fried Onion Rings**
Salt	1 bouquet watercress, washed and
Freshly ground white pepper	trimmed
2 tablespoons butter	**Fried Potatoes Sablées**

Season the liver slices with salt and pepper; sauté in a skillet in hot butter until done to taste (rare, medium, well done).

Arrange the liver on a long serving platter and place a cluster of onion rings on each slice. Place a bouquet of watercress at each end of the platter. Serve with Fried Potatoes Sablées.

Noix de Ris de Veau Panetière
(Veal Sweetbreads Panetière)

3 pair veal sweetbreads	6 large, crisp, round
⅔ cup butter	French bread rolls
1 onion, chopped	¼ cup rendered goose fat, melted
1 carrot, chopped	12 large, fresh mushrooms, trimmed,
1 stalk celery, chopped	washed, and minced
Few sprigs of fresh parsley,	1½ cups Sauce Béarnaise, mixed with
chopped	⅓ cup crème fraîche or heavy
Salt	cream
Freshly ground black pepper	

Soak the sweetbreads for 3 hours in several changes of cold water. Bring 3 quarts of well-salted water to the boil in a kettle, then blanch the sweetbreads for 5 minutes. Drain, let cool, then trim and remove the sinews.

Preheat oven to 350 degrees. Melt half the butter in a saucepan and add onion, carrot, celery, and some parsley. Place sweetbreads on top of vegetables and season with salt and pepper; cover and braise in moderate oven for about 30 minutes, basting often.

Thinly slice the tops off rolls and remove the insides. Using a pastry brush, coat the insides of the rolls with goose fat. Place on baking sheet, and set aside. Brown the mushrooms in remaining butter and salt lightly.

Remove the sweetbreads from the oven. Turn up temperature to 400 degrees and bake rolls in a hot oven until brown, about 8 to 10 minutes.

Strain the braising juices into the pan with the mushrooms. Simmer until liquid is absorbed.

Remove rolls from oven and turn up heat to 450 degrees. Spoon mushrooms and vegetables into loaves. Cut sweetbreads on the bias into large bite-sized pieces. Put sweetbreads atop the mushroom-stuffed rolls and top each with Béarnaise-cream mixture. Glaze the stuffed rolls under the broiler or in hot oven for 5 to 6 minutes.

Arrange rolls on a long serving platter covered with a napkin. Sprinkle remaining parsley around the rolls.

Gigue de Chevreuil Grand Veneur
(Haunch of Venison, Hunter's Style)

1 haunch of venison Salt Freshly ground white pepper 8 ounces fresh or salted pork fat, thinly sliced ⅓ cup crème fraîche or heavy cream 6 tablespoons currant jelly 2 cups Sauce Poivrade 6 slices firm white bread Chestnut Mousseline	*Marinade:* 2 medium onions, chopped 1 carrot, chopped 1 stalk celery, chopped 1 clove garlic, chopped 4 cups dry red wine Few sprigs of fresh parsley 1 sprig fresh thyme 1 bay leaf 1 teaspoon salt 1 teaspoon whole peppercorns

Trim the haunch and reserve trimmings. Simmer marinade for 40 minutes; let cool before putting in the venison to marinate. After 12 hours, remove meat and dry.

Preheat oven to 400 degrees. Place venison in a heatproof roasting pan, season with salt and pepper, and cover and tie with fat slices. Roast in a hot oven for 30 minutes per pound, turning and basting frequently.

Remove roast from oven and let cool for 20 minutes. Drain the fat from the pan, place pan on top of stove, and add crème fraîche, 1 tablespoon of the currant jelly, and Sauce Poivrade. Cook, scraping up all particles, until a sturdy sauce forms.

Cut heart-shaped croûtons from bread and toast on both sides. Spread with remaining currant jelly. Place the roast on a long serving platter and cover with the sauce. Place toasts around the roast and serve with Chestnut Mousseline. **Serves 10.**

Rognon de Veau Laitier Grillé
(Grilled Veal Kidneys)

6 veal kidneys Oil Salt 3 shallots, minced 2 tablespoons butter	2 large, ripe tomatoes, peeled, seeded, and diced 12 egg yolks Straw Potatoes 2 bouquets watercress, washed and trimmed

Prepare coals for grilling or heat broiler. Peel the membranes from the kidneys, leaving a little fat; cut them in half lengthwise. Spear them on skewers and brush lightly on all sides with oil. Season lightly with salt and grill over a charcoal fire, turning often (10 minutes for rare kidneys, 15 minutes for medium). These can also be done for the same length of time in a broiler.

Sauté shallots in butter for 5 minutes. Add tomatoes, season with salt and pepper, and simmer until all the juice from the tomatoes has evaporated, about 15 to 20 minutes. Fry egg yolks in oil ½-inch deep until firm, about 3 to 4 minutes.

Arrange the kidneys on a long serving platter. On each kidney half place 1 tablespoon tomato-and-shallot sauce and top with a fried egg yolk. Circle the kidneys with Straw Potatoes and decorate with bouquets of watercress.

PÂTÉS AND TERRINES

Terrine de Poularde Angevine
(Chicken and Pork Pâté with Truffles)

4 **medium truffles**	2 **teaspoons salt**
⅓ **cup Madeira wine**	¼ **teaspoon freshly ground white**
Few drops of Cognac	**pepper**
1 **roasting chicken, about 3**	3 **eggs, well beaten**
pounds	12 **ounces larding pork fat, cut into**
2½ **pounds boneless pork (half**	**thin slices**
fat, half lean)	¼ **cup rendered pork fat**

Marinate the truffles for 2 hours in Madeira and Cognac. Drain.

Skin and bone the chicken, removing breast halves whole. Cut each breast in half again lengthwise. Grind the pork and remaining chicken meat, using a medium grinding plate or a food processor. Put the ground meat in a bowl and season with salt and pepper. Add eggs and mix with the hand.

Line a 2-quart terrine with thin sheets of some of the fat. Cut 6 strips from the larding pork fat and reserve. Fill the terrine one-third high with the ground meats, pressing down lightly with your hand moistened with water. On top of this place 2 strips of chicken breast and 2 strips of pork fat. Fill the terrine to one-half with more of the ground-meat mixture. Place truffles in the center of the terrine, lengthwise, and cover with more ground-meat mixture to the two-thirds level. Repeat with remaining 2 strips of chicken and 2 of pork fat. Fill the terrine to the top with more ground meat and cover with a layer of remaining larding pork fat.

Preheat oven to 375 degrees. Put a sheet of aluminum foil over the terrine, cover and set in a flat pan containing water. Bake in a moderate oven for about 2 hours, then test with a trussing needle inserted into the middle of the terrine. When the juices run clear, the terrine is done.

Remove the aluminum foil and set a flat piece of wood on the surface weighted down with a 2-pound can. Let the pâté cool thoroughly. Remove the weight and the piece of wood, then wipe the inside edges of the terrine.

Heat rendered fat in a saucepan, then spoon over the surface of the pâté to harden. Refrigerate for 1 hour before serving.

Terrine de Caneton Duclairoise
(Duck and Pork Terrine with Truffles)

1 duck, 4 pounds	Freshly ground white pepper
1 cup dry white wine	3 eggs, well beaten
⅔ cup Cognac	3 tablespoons chopped truffles
2 pounds boneless pork (half lean, half fat)	2 larding leaves, about 4 ounces of pork fat
Salt	

Clean and sear the duck. Make an incision with a boning knife along the entire length of the duck's back and carefully remove the skin in 1 piece. Bone the duck completely, then cut the breast filets into 3 equal parts lengthwise. Set aside. Put the remainder of the duck meat to marinate in wine and Cognac for 2 hours; drain and reserve marinade.

Grind together the marinated duck meat and the pork, using a medium grinding plate or food processor. Add ½ cup of the marinating liquid to mixture, season with salt and pepper, and blend in eggs. Add 1 tablespoon of the truffles to the meat and spread remaining truffles on each of the larding leaves; roll them up.

Line the bottom and sides of a 1-quart terrine with the skin of the duck. Fill the terrine to the half-way mark with the meat, pressing with wet hands to eliminate air bubbles at the terrine walls. Lay the duck filets and 2 truffled larding leaves lengthwise on top of the meat. Fill the terrine with the rest of the meat and cover with the duck skin.

Preheat oven to 350 degrees. Cover terrine with aluminum foil, then put on the cover of the terrine itself. Bake and finish as in Chicken and Pork Pâté with Truffles.

Terrine de Foies des Volailles Truffée
(Truffled Poultry Liver Terrine)

2½ pounds lean boneless pork, diced	3 eggs, well beaten
¼ cup finely chopped truffles	Salt
2 cups dry white wine	Freshly ground white pepper
⅓ cup Madeira wine	12 ounces larding leaves of pork fat
1½ pounds livers from chicken, duck, or turkey	

Marinate pork and truffles in white wine and Madeira for 12 hours; drain and reserve marinade.

Grind together the pork and livers, using a very fine grinding plate or a food processor. Add eggs, salt, pepper, and truffles. Add ½ cup of the marinating liquid and mix all ingredients thoroughly with the hands.

Preheat oven to 350 degrees. Line the walls of a 2-quart terrine with some of the larding leaves. Fill to the brim with the stuffing and cover with larding leaf. Put a sheet of aluminum foil over the meat and position the terrine cover. Bake and finish as in Chicken and Pork Pâté with Truffles.

Terrine de Lièvre à la Diane
(Hare Terrine à la Diane)

1½ **pounds boneless hare or rabbit**	¼ **teaspoon freshly ground white**
⅓ **cup dark rum**	**pepper**
⅓ **cup Cognac**	3 **egg yolks**
2 **pounds boneless fat pork**	4 **shallots, minced**
8 **ounces boneless veal**	8 **ounces larding leaves of pork fat**
2 **teaspoons salt**	**Sprigs of fresh parsley**

On the evening before you plan to prepare the terrine, trim and remove sinews from hare or rabbit and cut into small cubes. Marinate overnight in rum and Cognac. Drain and reserve meat and marinade.

The next day, using a medium plate, grind fat pork and veal. Season with salt and pepper, then add egg yolks, shallots, hare, and marinade. Mix all ingredients well, using your hands.

Preheat oven to 350 degrees. Line a 2-quart terrine with larding leaves and add the pâté mixture, pressing with your hand to eliminate air bubbles. Moisten your hand and smooth out the surface. Cover with a larding leaf, tucking in the ends. Place a sheet of aluminum foil on top, cover the terrine, and finish as in Chicken and Pork Pâté with Truffles.

To serve, spoon fat off the surface, melt over low heat, then strain back onto the pâté. Chill until ready to serve. Serve the terrine on a long serving platter covered with a napkin and garnish with sprigs of parsley.

Terrine Marbrée
(Marbled Pork and Tongue Terrine)

¼ **cup chopped truffles**	2 **teaspoons salt**
⅓ **cup Madeira wine**	¼ **teaspoon freshly ground white**
2½ **pounds boneless pork (half fat,**	**pepper**
half lean)	3 **slices smoked beef tongue**
12 **ounces larding pork fat, thinly**	
sliced	

Marinate truffles in Madeira for 2 hours; drain and reserve marinade.

Grind the pork using a medium grinding plate or a food processor. Finely dice 2 tablespoons of the pork fat. Put the ground meat, fat, and truffles in a bowl; season with salt and pepper; and mix well with your hands.

Preheat oven to 350 degrees. Line bottom and sides of a 1½-quart terrine with layers of larding fat. Fill the terrine to one-third with the ground-meat mixture, pressing down with your moistened hands to eliminate any air bubbles.

Cut 6 strips of pork fat and 2 strips of smoked beef tongue. Lay the strips on the surface of ground meat, alternating 2 strips fat, 1 strip tongue, 2 of fat, 1 of tongue, 2 of fat. Add another third of the ground-meat mixture and repeat the operation. Add the final third and cover with a layer of larding fat. Place a sheet of aluminum foil on top of this and cover the terrine. Bake and finish as for Chicken and Pork Pâté with Truffles.

Terrine de Lapereau aux Pistaches
(Rabbit Terrine with Pistachios)

1 rabbit hindquarters, including filets
1 pound larding leaves of pork fat
⅔ cup dry white wine
⅓ cup Madeira wine
Few drops of Cognac

4 ounces pistachio nuts
2½ pounds boneless pork, preferably half lean, half fat
2 teaspoons salt
¼ teaspoon freshly ground white pepper
3 eggs, well beaten

Bone the rabbit. Cut the filets into 4 lengthwise strips, and wrap each in a thin larding leaf. Dice the remaining rabbit; marinate in mixture of white wine, Madeira, and Cognac. Cut a larding leaf into 9 equal strips the size of the strips of rabbit filet.

Blanch the pistachio nuts in boiling water. Peel and chop coarsely. Roll nuts in 2 thin larding leaves.

Using a medium plate or food processor, grind the pork. Season with salt and pepper, then add the eggs and mix well with the hands.

Preheat oven to 350 degrees. Line a 2-quart terrine with larding leaves, fill to one-third with the pork mixture, and press the meat down with moistened hands to eliminate all air pockets. Put 3 strips of larding leaf lengthwise over the pork, alternating with 2 strips of rabbit (about 1 inch apart), and in the center place a rolled lard leaf containing the pistachios. Repeat the operation, filling to two-thirds and adding strips as before. Fill to the top with the remaining mixture and cover with a layer of larding fat. Put a sheet of aluminum foil over the terrine and then cover. Bake and finish as for Chicken and Pork Pâté with Truffles.

Pâté de Foies de Lapin en Crépinettes
(Rabbit Liver and Pork Crépinettes)

12 rabbit livers
¾ cup dry white wine
⅔ cup Cognac
10 ounces boneless pork brisket

Salt
Freshly ground white pepper
12 ounces thinly sliced boneless fresh ham

Cut the livers into large cubes, being sure they are firm. Marinate in wine and Cognac for 6 hours. Drain and reserve marinade. Grind together livers and pork, using a medium plate, or use a food processor, and put the ground meats into a bowl. Season well with salt and pepper; mix well with the hands.

Pound ham until very thin, then cut into 6-inch squares. Place the squares on a marble slab or a cutting board and put equal portions of ground meats on each. Wrap the stuffing in the squares, folding the corners into the center and keeping a square form. Place them in overlapping rows in a terrine.

Preheat oven to 350 degrees. Place terrine in pan of water and bring to a boil. Bake in a moderate oven for about 1 hour, then test with a trussing needle to see if the juices run clear. Remove from oven, let cook, and refrigerate for about 1 hour before serving. The crépinettes should be served on a long platter covered with a napkin.

Vegetables

9

Artichauts
(Artichokes, General Preparation)

For whole artichokes, pull off the stems, then trim the tips of the leaves with a scissors. Wash carefully in several changes of water, then cook for about 30 minutes in water that has been lightly salted and has the juice of 1 lemon. The bottom of the artichoke should be able to be easily pierced. Drain, cool, then transfer to a round serving platter covered with a folded napkin. Serve with Hollandaise, Béchamel, or Mousseline sauces, or simply melted butter; if served cold, they can be accompanied by a Sauce Vinaigrette.

For preparing artichoke hearts, remove the outer leaves and trim the bottom. Cut in half and remove the choke. Cook as for whole artichokes—about 30 minutes.

For artichoke bottoms, cook artichokes as above, then remove leaves and choke. Trim the solid bottom piece into a small, saucerlike piece. Should you wish to cook only the artichoke bottoms, pull off stems of the artichokes and trim the leaves with a scissors. Cut off leaves at the level of the hearts, then round off the bottoms of the artichokes and remove the leaves entirely. Using a spoon, scoop out the chokes, then rub the bottoms with half a lemon. Plunge the bottoms into cold water to cover with juice of 1 lemon added, then transfer artichokes and soaking water to a saucepan. Bring to a boil and cook for about 20 minutes or until easily pierced. Drain the artichoke bottoms on a kitchen towel.

Artichauts Farcis à la Barigoule
(Stuffed Artichokes)

6 artichokes
4 shallots, minced
¼ cup (4 tablespoons) butter
1 clove garlic, minced
12 ounces sausage meat
10 fresh mushrooms, chopped
1 tablespoon tomato paste
½ teaspoon salt
Pinch of freshly ground pepper
½ cup dry white wine
1 tablespoon finely chopped fresh parsley

6 thin slices larding pork fat, cut into diamond shapes
1 large onion, chopped
1 carrot, chopped
¼ cup lard
1 bay leaf
Few sprigs of fresh parsley
1 sprig fresh thyme
2 cups Brown Veal Stock, mixed with 2 tablespoons potato starch

Cook artichokes as directed for whole artichokes. Using a teaspoon, open artichokes, remove the choke, wash the insides with cold running water. Set aside and prepare stuffing.

Sauté shallots in half the butter for 5 minutes. Add garlic, sausage meat, mushrooms, and tomato paste and season with salt and pepper. Mix all ingredients with a wooden spatula and cook over low heat until sausage is cooked. Add wine and stir stuffing from time to time. When cooking is completed, stir in parsley and let cool.

Skim excess fat off stuffing, then fill the centers of the artichokes with stuffing and place a square of larding fat over each, tying to ensure that the fat does not slip off.

In a Dutch oven, cook onion and carrot, without browning, in lard. Add parsley sprigs, bay leaf, and thyme. Pour in stock mixture and stir until thickened. Place artichokes in sauce and cover. Bring to a boil on top of the stove and simmer, covered, for 30 minutes.

Arrange artichokes on a round serving platter and remove trussing strings. Reduce the braising juices by half, skim excess fat, and strain sauce. Whisking steadily, beat in remaining butter, a small piece at a time. Spoon sauce over the artichokes and serve.

Fonds d'Artichauts Braisés
(Braised Artichoke Hearts)

  6 artichokes
  3 lemons, cut in half, plus juice
    of ½ lemon
  2 tablespoons oil

  1 teaspoon salt
  ½ cup (8 tablespoons) clarified butter

Break off the artichoke stems (do not cut them). Using a kitchen knife, remove the outer leaves, rounding off the hearts, then trim the leaves at the top of the hearts. Using a paring knife, peel the hearts as you would an apple, that is, with a continuous peel, until you have the heart. Rub each with half a lemon.

Put the artichokes in a saucepan and cover with water. Add oil, salt, and lemon juice; bring to a boil, reduce heat, and simmer for about 30 minutes (depending on how tender artichokes are). With a ladle or spoon, skim off the foam that forms on the surface.

Drain artichokes and, using your finger, open the centers and remove the chokes. Place the artichoke hearts in a skillet and brush with remaining clarified butter. Cover and braise for a few minutes.

Fonds d'Artichauts à la Valaisane
(Soufflé-Stuffed Artichoke Bottoms)

 12 artichoke bottoms
  2 tablespoons clarified butter,
    melted
  ½ batch Parmesan Cheese Soufflé
    batter, mixed with 6 ounces
    diced boiled ham

  2 ounces Gruyère cheese, sliced thin
    and cut into ovals
  Few sprigs of fresh parsley

Prepare cooked artichoke bottoms as directed in general preparations. Preheat oven to 425 degrees.

Arrange bottoms on a lightly buttered dish and brush the inside of the hearts with butter. Using a pastry bag with a round tip, fill the bottoms with soufflé mixture. Place cheese ovals like petals on top of the soufflé.

Bake in a hot oven until the soufflé rises, about 15 to 20 minutes. Transfer to a round serving platter covered with a napkin. Surround with sprigs of parsley and, like any soufflé, serve immediately.

Asperges de Malmaison Tièdes Sauce Sanguine
(Asparagus with Sauce Sanguine)

Asparagus are one of the most versatile of vegetables, and we served them all year on the France. In the Springtime, passengers could choose between the delicate, succulent European white asparagus and the green variety which we purchased in great quantities in the United States. Indeed, the American variety were available throughout the year as they had several growing seasons in California. M. Bory, a frequent passenger of ours and the owner of Fauchon, Paris' finest delicacy store, made a speciality of importing American asparagus into France, and exporting canned French asparagus to the United States!

Asparagus are served warm or cold, and should be placed on a platter covered with a white napkin for drainage. There are many delicious accompaniments whose recipes are included in the Sauce section of this book. Among my favorites are:

For warm asparagus: Hollandaise, Maltaise, Mikado, Mousseuse, and Mousseline.

For cold asparagus: Chantilly, Gribiche, Ravigote, Remoulade, and Vinaigrette.

2½ pounds fresh asparagus	**½ cup crème fraîche or heavy cream,**
1 teaspoon coarse salt	**whipped**
Sauce Hollandaise	**Sprigs of fresh parsley**
1 teaspoon grated orange rind	

Cut the ends of asparagus at point where they break off easily. Peel stalks, wash thoroughly, and tie in bundles with string. Cook for about 15 to 20 minutes in boiling, salted water. Exact cooking time will depend on how tender the asparagus are and your preference. Remove asparagus from water, place on platter, and remove string. Garnish with parsley at each end of platter. Fold orange rind and crème fraîche into Sauce Hollandaise and serve separately in a sauceboat.

Poire d'Avocat Garnie Baltimore
(Avocado with Crab)

3 avocados, halved lengthwise	**Sauce Vinaigrette**
and seeded	**1 shallot, minced**
Juice of 1 lemon	**3 sprigs fresh parsley, chopped**
Lettuce leaves	
2 cans (7 ounces) crabmeat,	
drained	

Brush cut surfaces of avocados with lemon juice, and arrange them on a lettuce-lined platter. Remove all traces of cartilage from the crabmeat, then shred. Mix dressing with shallot and parsley until thickened. Stir in crabmeat and spoon mixture into avocados; serve.

Poire d'Avocat Garnie au Roquefort
(Avocado with Roquefort Dressing)

8 ounces Roquefort cheese
Sauce Vinaigrette
Lettuce leaves

3 avocados, halved lengthwise and
seeded
2 tablespoons chopped chives

Press cheese through a fine sieve into a bowl; blend into dressing.

Cover a large, round platter with lettuce leaves and arrange the avocados in the form of a star. Fill the cavities of the avocados with the dressing. Sprinkle with chives and serve.

Poire d'Avocat Garnie Yacamole
(Guacamole)

3 avocados
2 tablespoons white vinegar
1 teaspoon salt
Pinch of cayenne
¾ cup peanut oil
1 sweet red pepper, minced

1 shallot, minced
3 sprigs fresh parsley, chopped
1 tomato, peeled, seeded, and
chopped
Lettuce leaves

Halve and remove seeds from avocados. Remove pulp with a spoon and force through a sieve into a mixing bowl, reserving the seeds and shells. Beat in the vinegar, a few drops at a time. Add salt and cayenne, then, as in preparing a mayonnaise, slowly beat in peanut oil. When the sauce has attained the smoothness and consistency of a light mayonnaise, gently stir in red pepper, shallot, parsley, and tomato.

Stuff the reserved avocado shells with the guacamole and set the seeds on top (the seeds will keep the guacamole from darkening; remove before serving). Line a round platter with lettuce leaves and place avocados on top. Serve with raw vegetables or crisp crackers for dipping.

Haricots Verts Frais Sautés au Beurre Noisette
(Green Beans Sautéed in Browned Butter)

3 pounds young green beans,
trimmed and left whole
½ cup (8 tablespoons) butter

1 teaspoon coarse salt

Cook beans, uncovered, in salted water at a rolling boil for 10 to 15 minutes or until tender but still firm. Drain.

Heat butter until brown and sauté beans for 1 to 2 minutes. Season to taste with salt before serving.

Haricots Verts Frais Sautés Amandine
(Young Green Beans Sautéed with Almonds)

2 pounds very young green   ¼ cup (4 tablespoons) butter
beans, trimmed and left whole   ½ cup slivered almonds

Cook the beans in salted water to cover until done, about 10 minutes. Heat butter and sauté almonds until pale gold. Add beans and sauté for another 1 to 2 minutes. Serve.

Choux de Bruxelles Rissolés Polonaise
(Polish-Style Brussels Sprouts)

3 pounds Brussels sprouts   1 tablespoon finely chopped fresh
6 tablespoons lard   parsley
Salt   1 cup fine, dry bread crumbs
2 hard-cooked eggs, chopped   2 mill-turns freshly ground white
    pepper

Trim Brussels sprouts. Wash very carefully in several changes of water and cook for 15 to 20 minutes in salted water. Be sure they are thoroughly cooked, then drain. Sauté sprouts in lard in a skillet until they are well coated with the fat. Correct seasoning with salt.

       Mix eggs with parsley, bread crumbs, salt, and pepper. Sprinkle this mixture onto the sprouts and sauté further for 1 to 2 minutes. Serve in a vegetable dish.

       Note: The lard can be replaced by butter, but it is preferable to use a good pork fat.

Carottes à la Crème
(Creamed Carrots)

3 pounds carrots, peeled   ½ teaspoon confectioner's sugar
6 tablespoons butter   1½ cups crème fraîche, approximately
½ teaspoon salt   Pinch of grated nutmeg

Using a paring knife, carve carrots into rounded pieces about the size and shape of large olives. Put carrots in a saucepan and add water to cover. Add butter, salt, and confectioner's sugar. Bring to a boil and cook until the water has evaporated.

       When the carrots have taken on a good color and glisten from the sugar and butter, add crème fraîche to half the depth of the carrots. Bring to a boil and boil over high heat for a few minutes, then lower heat and simmer for 10 minutes, stirring occasionally. Correct the seasoning with nutmeg and serve in a vegetable dish.

Choux-Fleurs
(Cauliflower, General Preparation)

Remove outer leaves and cut flowerets at the base to separate. Place in a saucepan and cook, covered, in lightly salted boiling water for 15 to 20 minutes. Drain and serve on a round serving platter covered with a folded napkin. Accompany with melted butter, Sauce Hollandaise, or Sauce Mousseline.

Choux-Fleurs à la Milanaise
(Cauliflower, Milan Style)

1 cauliflower	¼ cup grated Parmesan cheese
2 tablespoons butter	

Cook cauliflowerets as directed in general preparations. Drain and sauté in butter.
    Sprinkle half the cheese on the inside of a serving dish and add the sautéed cauliflower, then sprinkle with more Parmesan. Place under broiler and broil for 4 to 5 minutes or until golden.

Variation

Choux-Fleurs à la Polonaise

Cook and sauté the cauliflower as in Cauliflower Milan Style. Transfer to a heatproof vegetable dish, leaving the butter in the skillet.
    Finely chop 1 hard-cooked egg and mix it with ½ cup soft bread crumbs and 1 teaspoon finely chopped fresh parsley. Stir this mixture into the butter, then pour over the cauliflower. Put the vegetable dish under broiler and brown for 3 to 4 minutes.

Choux-Fleurs Dinandais Dorés au Gruyère
(Cauliflower au Gratin)

1 cauliflower	2 cups crème fraîche or heavy cream
¼ cup (4 tablespoons) butter	¾ cup grated Gruyère cheese
Salt	

Choose a very white, well-rounded cauliflower. Trim and separate the flowerets with a paring knife, then wash thoroughly and poach for about 15 minutes in lightly salted boiling water. Drain and braise 5 minutes in half the butter. Salt lightly.
    Preheat oven to 450 degrees. Boil crème fraîche until reduced to 1 cup. Line the inside of a 1-quart Pyrex dish with half of the crème fraîche, then sprinkle on half of the cheese. Replace the flowerets in the shape of the cauliflower, cover with remaining crème fraîche and sprinkle remaining cheese. Dot with remaining butter and brown in hot oven or under the broiler. Serve immediately.

Coeur de Céleri Mijoté à la Moëlle
(Celery Hearts with Beef Marrow)

6 celery hearts	Several sprigs of fresh parsley,
2 ounces pork fat, diced	minced
1 carrot, minced	Salt
1 onion, minced	1½ cups Sauce Madère
	8 ounces beef marrow

Remove any leaves from the celery, together with the extremity of the stalks. Break apart, peel the stalks, and cut into 6-inch lengths. Wash carefully and boil in lightly salted water for 10 minutes.

Preheat oven to 425 degrees. Fry fat until golden brown in a heatproof baking pan. Add carrot, onion, and parsley and sauté 5 minutes. Drain off fat and add celery and water to just cover; salt lightly. Cover with a sheet of parchment paper or foil, then put on pan cover. Braise in a hot oven for about 30 minutes, depending on the size of the celery stalks.

While vegetables are cooking, poach beef marrow in lightly salted water. Cut into slices and keep warm.

Drain and arrange vegetables on a round platter. Top with sauce and marrow slices.

Coeur de Céleri Braisé Bolognese
(Braised Celery Hearts Bolognese)

6 celery hearts	Few sprigs of fresh chervil
¼ pound pork fat, diced	¼ cup water
1 onion, chopped	2 cups Sauce Bolognese
1 carrot, chopped	

Cut celery hearts into half lengthwise. Fry pork fat in a skillet until crisp. Add celery, onion, carrot, and 1 sprig of chervil. Add water, cover, and braise 15 to 20 minutes or until tender. Add sauce and simmer additional 5 minutes.

Place the celery on a round platter, coat with the sauce, and sprinkle with chervil.

Branche de Céleri Garnie au Bleu d'Auvergne
(Celery Stuffed with Auvergne Cheese)

12 tender stalks celery	1 cup butter, softened
12 ounces bleu d'Auvergne or	Few pinches of paprika
other blue-veined cheese	Few sprigs of fresh parsley

Remove the larger leaves from celery, leaving only the tender tip leaves. Peel the celery with a vegetable peeler, cut lengthwise, and wash carefully in several changes of water.

Press cheese through a fine sieve and mix with butter, beating vigorously with a wooden spatula. Using a pastry bag fitted with a fluted tip, fill bag with cheese mixture, then pipe out filling into celery. Sprinkle with paprika. Arrange the stuffed celery in a star design on a large round serving platter covered with a paper doily, alternating the celery with parsley.

Marrons Braisés
(Braised Chestnuts)

4 **pounds chestnuts**	**Bouquet garni (bay leaf, thyme,**
⅔ **cup butter**	**celery leaves, sage)**
1 **cup Classic Beef Consommé or**	**Salt and pepper**
water	

Cut an *x* in the flat side of the chestnuts. Put into boiling water to remove skins, then take out a few at a time and peel. Be certain to remove all inner skin.

Melt butter in a skillet and cook chestnuts without browning. Add the consommé or water and bouquet garni. Salt and pepper lightly, cover, and cook over low heat for 30 minutes. The chestnuts will absorb the consommé and become mealy.

Serve as an accompaniment to poultry or game.

Mousseline de Marrons
(Chestnut Mousseline)

4½ **pounds fresh chestnuts**	**Bouquet garni (1 sprig thyme, bay**
2 **cups milk**	**leaf, celery leaves, 1 sprig parsley)**
2 **quarts water**	¼ **cup (4 tablespoons) butter**
1 **teaspoon salt**	2 **cups crème fraîche or heavy cream**

Boil chestnuts 5 minutes, peel, and carefully remove all brown membrane.

Bring milk and water to a boil. Add salt, chestnuts, and bouquet garni and simmer 30 minutes. When the chestnuts are fully cooked, drain well and press through a fine sieve or purée in a food processor. Add butter to the chestnut purée, mixing well with a wooden spatula or spoon.

Bring crème fraîche to a boil, then add to chestnut butter, a little at a time while stirring constantly. Correct seasoning with salt and serve in a vegetable dish.

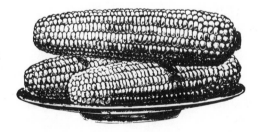

Maïs
(Corn on the Cob, General Preparation)

12 **ears corn**	**Melted butter or crème fraîche**
½ **cup milk**	

Shuck the corn and cut off the ends. Bring a large pot to a boil and add milk. Cook corn for about 10 minutes. Push corn pins into the ends of the ears and serve the corn on a long serving platter covered with a napkin folded into a rectangle. Accompany with melted butter or slightly reduced crème fraîche.

Maïs Égrené à la Hongroise
(Hungarian Creamed Corn)

12 ears corn	Salt and freshly ground pepper
Butter	Paprika
1 cup crème fraîche, approximately	

Cook the corn as directed in general preparation. Drain the ears and let cool. Using a sharp knife, remove kernels from cobs, then sauté in a saucepan with 2 tablespoons butter for each cup of kernels. Add crème fraîche to cover, season to taste with salt and pepper, and simmer for 10 minutes. Serve in a vegetable dish with a little paprika sprinkled on top.

Beignets de Maïs
(Corn Fritters)

12 ears corn	Salt
Fritter Batter	1 tablespoon chopped fresh parsley
Oil for deep-frying, heated to 360°	Sauce Tomate

Cook the corn as directed in general preparation, then cut kernels from cob.

Prepare Fritter Batter, then mix equal parts of kernels and batter. Deep-fry by heaping tablespoons until brown, 7 to 8 minutes. Turn fritters with a slotted spoon to brown on all sides. Drain the fritters on absorbent paper and serve, lightly salted, on a round platter covered with a napkin. Garnish with parsley and serve with Sauce Tomate.

Croquettes de Maïs
(Corn Croquettes)

12 ears corn	Salt
½ cup milk	Pinch of cayenne
3 tablespoons butter	Pinch of grated nutmeg
1½ cups Sauce Béchamel	Oil for deep-frying, heated to 360°
3 egg yolks, beaten	

Cook the corn as directed in general preparation. Drain and let cool.

Using a paring knife, cut the kernels from the cobs and place into a saucepan. Add butter and braise for 5 minutes.

Stir egg yolks into Sauce Béchamel. Season with salt, cayenne, and nutmeg, then stir in corn. Place in an oiled 13 x 9 x 2-inch pan and chill until firm. Cut corn mixture into ¼-cup portions. Roll each portion into a 1½-inch cylinder and chill again.

Deep-fry croquettes in oil for about 5 minutes. When nicely browned, drain on absorbent paper and salt lightly.

Concombres Étuvés à la Crème
(Creamed Cucumbers)

3 pounds small cucumbers
¼ cup (4 tablespoons) butter
1 teaspoon salt

1¼ cups crème fraîche or heavy cream
1 teaspoon finely chopped fresh parsley

Using a kitchen knife, trim the cucumbers into the shape and size of a pigeon's egg, without seeding.

Put the cucumbers into a saucepan and add butter, salt, and water to just cover. Bring to a boil and cook until all the liquid has evaporated. Add crème fraîche, bring to a boil, and simmer until the cream is thick and cucumbers are well coated.

Transfer the cucumbers to a vegetable dish, sprinkle with parsley, and serve.

Aubergine Frite Nîmoise
(Fried Eggplant with Tomato)

1 onion, chopped
1 clove garlic, chopped
2 tablespoons olive oil
3 tomatoes, peeled, seeded, and chopped
2 green peppers, diced

1 teaspoon salt
Tabasco Sauce
2 medium eggplants
Flour for coating
Oil for deep-frying, heated to 360°

Sauté onion and garlic in olive oil until golden. Add the tomato pulp and green peppers, season with salt and Tabasco, bring to a boil, and simmer over low heat for 30 minutes.

Peel eggplants, then cut into ¾-inch slices. Dip the slices into flour, then deep-fry in oil about 7 to 8 minutes or until they are fully cooked and nicely browned. Drain on absorbent paper and sprinkle with salt.

Arrange tomato mixture on a round platter and top with eggplant.

Aubergine Farcie Biscassienne
(Eggplant Stuffed with Lamb)

3 medium eggplants
2 medium onions, chopped
½ cup olive oil
12 ounces ground lamb
1 teaspoon salt

Pinch of cayenne
Pinch of cumin
1 cup dry bread crumbs
2 cups Sauce Tomate

Halve eggplants lengthwise. Prepare shells and bake as for Stuffed Baked Eggplant. Remove pulp and cut into small cubes; reserve shells intact.

Preheat oven to 400 degrees. Sauté onions in 2 tablespoons of olive oil until golden. Sauté eggplant cubes in remaining oil until soft and mushy. Mix onions, eggplant, lamb, salt, cayenne, and cumin, then use mixture to stuff eggplant shells. Top with bread crumbs and bake in hot oven for about 30 minutes.

When the eggplants are nicely browned, transfer to a round serving platter and spoon Sauce Tomate around them before serving.

Aubergine Farcie Languedocienne
(Stuffed Baked Eggplant)

3 long, slender eggplants
Salt
1 cup olive oil
2 shallots, minced
1 clove garlic, minced

Pinch of cayenne
3 sprigs fresh parsley, chopped
1 cup dry bread crumbs
4 cups Sauce Tomate

Preheat oven to 350 degrees. Halve eggplants, lengthwise. Using a paring knife, remove the pulp, leaving a ½-inch-thick shell. Mark the inner surface of the shells in a criss-cross design with the point of a knife and sprinkle with salt. Put the eggplant halves in a Pyrex baking dish and moisten with ½ cup of oil. Bake in a moderate oven for about 15 minutes or until the eggplant yields under the pressure of your finger.

Remove pulp and dice; reserve shells intact. Brown shallots in remaining olive oil, then add garlic and diced eggplant pulp. Season to taste with salt and cayenne. Cook over low heat until golden brown.

Turn oven temperature up to 450 degrees. Using a wooden spatula, mix parsley into eggplant mixture. Season to taste with salt, then spoon the mixture into the eggplant shells. Sprinkle with bread crumbs and place under the broiler or in very hot oven for 5 to 6 minutes or until golden brown.

Spoon sauce onto a round serving platter and arrange the stuffed eggplants onto it.

Endives Flamandes au Gratin Monselet
(Endive au Gratin Monselet)

12 Belgian endive
¼ cup (4 tablespoons) butter
Salt and freshly ground pepper

Juice of 1 lemon
1 cup Sauce Mornay
3 slices boiled ham, minced

Preheat oven to 450 degrees. Cut endive in half lengthwise. Drop into boiling water for 1 to 2 minutes, then drain. Heat butter in a skillet and braise endive for 5 minutes. Season with salt and pepper.

Add lemon juice to Sauce Mornay, then use half of the sauce to cover the bottom of a gratin dish. Place the endive in the dish and sprinkle with boiled ham. Cover the remaining sauce, then glaze in a very hot oven or under the broiler for a few minutes.

Endives Lilloises Meunière
(Endive Meunière)

6 Belgian endive (12 if they are small)
1 teaspoon salt
Juice of 1 lemon
¼ cup (4 tablespoons) butter

Flour for coating
Freshly ground white pepper
1 teaspoon chopped fresh parsley

Wash endive and cut in half lengthwise. Put in a saucepan and add salt, lemon juice, and half the butter. Add water to ⅓ the height of the endive, cover with buttered parchment paper or foil, add pan lid, and bring to a boil over high heat; lower heat and simmer 15 to 20 minutes or until tender.

Drain, dry, and roll endive in flour. Heat remaining butter in a skillet until brown, then cook endive, seasoning lightly with salt and pepper, for 5 minutes. Serve on a round platter, sprinkling with parsley before serving.

Coeurs de Laitue Braisés à l'Écarlate
(Braised Lettuce Hearts)

12 heads Bibb lettuce	Bouquet garni (bay leaf, parsley,
¼ cup lard	thyme)
¼ cup chopped ham fat	2 cups Sauce Madère
1 onion, chopped	6 slices French sandwich loaf or firm
1 carrot, chopped	white bread
1 stalk celery, chopped	6 slices cooked, smoked beef tongue

Trim lettuce, being careful to keep a short length of stalk. Wash carefully in several changes of water, then boil for 5 minutes in lightly salted water. Drain, let cool, then press out the water with your hands.

Heat lard and ham fat in a Dutch oven until golden. Add onion, carrot, and celery and sauté 5 minutes. Arrange the heads of lettuce on this bed and add bouquet garni. Add lightly salted water to barely cover, cover with parchment paper or foil, and bring to the boil over high heat. Lower heat and simmer 10 minutes. Cool.

Drain lettuce and reserve cooking liquid; reshape the lettuce hearts by gently folding the ends of the leaves, then replace in Dutch oven. Boil cooking liquid until only 2 cups remain.

Cut heart-shaped pieces from bread and toast until brown on both sides. Cover lettuce with Sauce Madère and simmer, basting frequently.

Place croûtons on platter, and put lettuce on toast; cover with tongue. Spoon the sauce over tongue.

Champignons de Couche Sautés Girondine
(Sautéed Mushrooms with Ham and Tomato)

2 pounds fresh mushrooms	½ cup diced boiled ham
3 tablespoons butter	1 large tomato, peeled, seeded, and
1 tablespoon olive oil	chopped
2 shallots, chopped	1 teaspoon chopped fresh parsley

Trim the mushrooms and gently break off the caps. Wash caps and stems thoroughly. Cut the caps and stems into quarters. Heat butter and olive oil in a skillet and sauté mushrooms until golden. Add the shallots and cook until wilted. Add ham and tomato and sauté additional 5 minutes.

Place mushrooms in a vegetable dish and sprinkle with parsley.

Cèpes à la Bordelaise

2 cans (14 ounces) cèpes, drained,
  or 2 cups dried mushrooms
  soaked in water for 1 hour
1 tablespoon oil
½ cup (8 tablespoons) butter

2 shallots, minced
2 mill-turns freshly ground black
  pepper
2 teaspoons chopped fresh parsley

Cut cèpes into quarters. Sauté in very hot oil and 2 tablespoons of the butter until the mushrooms have lost their liquid and are crisp (and therefore more flavorsome); drain.

Heat remaining butter until golden and sauté cèpes again. Add shallots and sauté additional 5 minutes. Do not salt, since canned mushrooms are already salted, but season with pepper.

Pour into serving dish and sprinkle with parsley.

Oignons Frits
(Deep-Fried Onion Rings)

3 onions, peeled, sliced, and
  rings separated
Fritter Batter

Oil for deep-frying, heated to 360°

Prepare the batter as in recipe for Fritter Batter. Dip each onion ring into the batter and fry until brown. Drain on absorbent paper and salt lightly. Serve hot.

Pissaladière
(Onion Tart with Anchovies and Ripe Olives)

1 pound Brioche Dough
3 large onions, minced
¾ cup olive oil
  Salt
  Pinch of cayenne

24 anchovy filets, packed in oil
  Few pitted ripe olives, quartered
6 small tomatoes, cut into quarters
  Few sprigs of fresh parsley

Preheat oven to 375 degrees. Roll out a sheet of dough, either 14 inches round or in a 10 x 14-inch rectangle. Place on cookie sheet and turn up a border about ¾ inch high.

Sauté onions in ½ cup of olive oil over low heat, stirring frequently with a spatula to avoid browning. Salt lightly and add cayenne. When the onions have given up all their juice and are very wilted, cool. Pour onions onto the bread dough, spreading into an even layer. Smooth the surface of the onions with a metal spatula.

Lightly dry the anchovies on paper towels and arrange them on top of the onions to make a lattice. Place 2 olive quarters in each square of the lattice. Arrange tomatoes around the edges of the *pissaladière*. Brush with remaining olive oil using a pastry brush. Bake in a moderate oven for about 20 minutes or until golden brown.

Serve on a platter covered with a doily, drizzling on a little oil at the last minute. Garnish with leaves of parsley.

Persil Frit
(Deep-Fried Parsley)

1 bunch fresh parsley, preferably curly parsley	Oil for deep-frying, heated to 360°

Trim the parsley and drop into hot oil. Stir frequently with a slotted spoon to keep the sprigs well separated, then remove and drain on absorbent paper. Cook parsley only for a few moments. Use as a garnish.

Petits-Pois Fins Étuvés aux Laitues
(Peas Braised with Lettuce)

2½ pounds fresh peas	1 teaspoon salt
3 hearts lettuce	1 teaspoon confectioner's sugar

Shell peas; wash and drain. Place lettuce in a saucepan. Add peas, salt, sugar, and water to cover. Cover tightly and cook over low heat for 10 to 15 minutes or until peas are tender.

Variation

Fresh Peas Cooked with Minced Lettuce

Prepare peas as above but sauté peas in ¼ cup (4 tablespoons) butter for 1 minute, then chop lettuce and add along with remaining ingredients.

Petits-Pois d'Eyssines à la Française
(Peas à la Française)

8 small white onions, peeled	1 sprig fresh savory
4 pounds very fresh young peas, shelled	2 teaspoons sugar
½ cup (8 tablespoons) butter	Salt
1 head Boston lettuce, chopped but with heart intact	Beurre Manié

Poach the onions in salted water for 20 minutes; drain. Sauté peas in a heavy-bottomed saucepan with half of the butter. Add onions, lettuce, and savory. Add lightly salted water to cover and sugar. Bring to a boil and simmer over low heat for about 15 minutes (do not cover the saucepan).

Remove peas and onions with a slotted spoon. Thicken the broth with Beurre Manié. Season to taste with salt and pour broth over peas.

Petits-Pois du Val de Loire Paysanne
(Fresh Peas Country Style)

3 pounds fresh peas	Few lettuce leaves, shredded
9 tablespoons butter	1 teaspoon salt
2 medium carrots, cut into julienne	1 teaspoon confectioner's sugar
2 white turnips, cut into julienne	2 tablespoons flour
12 boiling onions, peeled	

Shell peas. Braise in a saucepan with 7 tablespoons of butter for 2 minutes. Add carrots, turnips, onions, and lettuce and sauté the mixture for 5 minutes. Add water barely to cover, season with salt and sugar, bring to a boil, and cook, uncovered, for about 10 minutes.

Mix remaining butter with flour, and when peas are tender, stir mixture into peas until thickened.

Variation

Use 3 lettuce hearts cut in half instead of shredded lettuce. Add a sprig of savory to above recipe.

Salsifis de Lunéville en Beignets Orly
(Salsify Fritters)

2 bunches salsify	Oil for deep-frying, heated to 360°
2 tablespoons vinegar	2 cups Sauce Tomate
1 quart water	*Batter:*
Salt	½ cup flour
2 tablespoons flour	½ teaspoon salt
Juice of 1 lemon	1 tablespoon oil
½ cup olive oil	½ cup water
2 tablespoons minced fresh parsley	1 egg white, stiffly beaten

Peel the salsify with a vegetable peeler. Wash in water with vinegar added, then cut into sticks 4 inches long.

Place water, salt, flour, and all but 1 teaspoon of the lemon juice in a saucepan. Heat and stir until boiling. Add salsify and cook in the boiling liquid for about 20 minutes. Drain and then marinate for an hour in a deep dish with olive oil, remaining lemon juice, and parsley.

In a bowl, mix flour, salt, oil, and water for batter. Fold in egg white. Dip the salsify sticks one by one into batter, then deep-fry in oil for 5 to 6 minutes. Remove these fritters with a slotted spoon when they are nicely browned and drain on absorbent paper.

Arrange the salsify fritters on a round serving platter covered with a paper doily and serve with a sauceboat of Sauce Tomate.

Épinards
(Spinach, General Preparation)

Trim the spinach, removing stems and wilted leaves, and wash in several changes of water. Place spinach in a large saucepan with the water that clings to the leaves. Add ½ teaspoon salt for each pound of spinach. Cover and cook 5 minutes. Place into a sieve and press all the cooking liquid out with a spoon. Spinach can be served hot either in leaf form or puréed.

Velouté à la Normande
(Creamed Spinach)

4½ pounds fresh spinach
½ cup (8 tablespoons) butter
1 teaspoon salt

Pinch of grated nutmeg
½ cup Sauce Béchamel
⅔ cup crème fraîche or heavy cream

Cook spinach as in General Preparation. Melt butter in a saucepan. When the butter foams, add the spinach and season with salt, nutmeg, and Sauce Béchamel. Heat the spinach while stirring constantly with a spatula. Boil crème fraîche until thick. Transfer spinach to a serving dish, smooth the surface with a spatula, and spoon crème fraîche over.

Tomates à l'Ancienne
(Old-Style Stuffed Tomatoes)

6 large, ripe tomatoes
1 large onion or 6 shallots, minced
4 tablespoons butter
1 clove garlic, minced
12 ounces lean ground pork
6 fresh mushrooms, stems chopped and caps diced

1 teaspoon salt
Pinch of freshly ground black pepper
2½ cups soft bread crumbs
1 tablespoon chopped fresh parsley
1 cup Brown Veal Stock
1 tablespoon potato flour
1 teaspoon tomato purée

Preheat oven to 400 degrees. Cut the tops off the tomatoes. Scoop out pulp, leaving shells. Discard seeds and chop pulp of 1 tomato; discard remaining pulp. Put the tomato shells upside down on a rack to drain.

Sauté onion in half the butter for 3 to 4 minutes without browning. Add garlic and pork, then set aside. Sauté mushrooms in remaining butter without browning. Add tomato pulp and simmer 5 minutes; cool slightly. Mix the mushrooms and tomato pulp into the pork mixture and season with salt and pepper.

Place stuffing mixture in a baking pan and bake the stuffing in hot oven on a rack for about 40 minutes, stirring from time to time. When the stuffing is cooked, stir in 2 cups of bread crumbs and the parsley, mixing well.

Heat oven again to 400 degrees. Season the inside of the tomato shells with salt and pepper, then stuff them with pork mixture. Put the stuffed tomatoes in a round dish, sprinkle on remaining bread crumbs, and bake in a hot oven for about 15 minutes. Set the stuffed tomatoes on a round serving platter and keep warm. In a saucepan mix stock with potato flour and tomato purée. Stir over medium heat until thickened, then spoon over tomatoes.

Tomates à la Bressane
(Tomatoes, Bresse Style)

6 ripe tomatoes
Salt and freshly ground black
pepper
⅔ cup oil
6 shallots, minced
1 clove garlic, minced

1 cup soft bread crumbs
1 tablespoon chopped fresh parsley
6 chicken or duck livers
1½ cups Sauce Tomate
1 teaspoon lemon juice

Preheat oven to 400 degrees. Cut the tomatoes in half crosswise; sprinkle with salt and pepper. Grease a dish with some of the oil, set the tomato halves cutside up on the dish, and brush the tops with oil. Bake the tomatoes in a hot oven for about 5 minutes.

In a skillet, sauté shallots and garlic without browning in 2 tablespoons of the oil. Let cool, then add bread crumbs and parsley. In another skillet sauté livers in remaining hot oil until brown and firm. Salt lightly, then drain excess fat.

Chop livers finely and add to crumbs. Mix all ingredients well and spoon in a mound onto the baked tomato halves. Bake for another 5 minutes in hot oven. Transfer the tomato halves to a round serving platter. Heat Sauce Tomate with lemon juice and spoon around tomatoes.

Tomate Farcie Aurore
(Tomatoes Stuffed with Pork)

6 large, ripe tomatoes
1 onion, minced
4 shallots, minced
1 tablespoon butter
1 clove garlic, chopped
12 ounces ground boneless pork
(half fat, half lean)
10 fresh mushroom stems,
chopped

Salt
Freshly ground white pepper
¾ cup dry bread crumbs
1 tablespoon chopped fresh parsley
1 cup Sauce Demi-Glace
1 teaspoon tomato purée
½ cup Madeira wine
3 hard-cooked egg yolks, pushed
through a sieve

Prepare tomatoes for stuffing as in Stuffed Tomatoes with Madiera Sauce.

In large saucepan, sauté onion and shallots in butter for 5 minutes. Then add garlic, pork, and mushrooms. Season well with salt and pepper, then mix well with a wooden spatula until the stuffing is smooth. Cover the saucepan and braise about 20 minutes or until pork is cooked. Stir in crumbs and parsley.

Preheat oven to 350 degrees. Using a tablespoon, stuff the tomatoes, first sprinkling cavities with salt and pepper. Smooth the surface with your hand, sprinkle with more bread crumbs, and bake in a moderate oven for 20 minutes.

Mix together and heat Demi-Glace, tomato purée, and wine for 5 minutes. When tomatoes are done, arrange on a round serving platter. Spoon sauce over tomatoes and sprinkle with egg yolks.

Tomate Farcie Navarraise
(Stuffed Tomatoes with Madiera Sauce)

6 large, firm tomatoes for stuffing, cut in half	2 cups chopped, cooked chicken
Salt	¼ cup chopped truffles
1 cup crème fraîche or heavy cream	Pinch of cayenne
	½ cup dry bread crumbs
	2 cups Sauce Madère

Scoop out the pulp from the tomatoes. Salt insides lightly and turn upside down to drain. Remove seeds from the loose pulp, then dice.

Simmer crème fraîche until thick. Add chicken and truffles. Season with salt and cayenne, then stir in tomato pulp. Mix well with a wooden spatula or spoon, then let cool.

Preheat oven to 350 degrees. Spoon the stuffing into the tomatoes. Sprinkle with bread crumbs and bake in moderate oven for 20 minutes or until piping hot.

When the tomatoes are nicely browned, arrange them on a round serving platter and top with Sauce Madère.

Tomate du Val de Loire Farcie Provençale
(Tomatoes Provençale)

6 large, ripe tomatoes, cut in half crosswise	Few sprigs of fresh parsley, chopped
2 tablespoons olive oil	Salt
3 shallots, minced	Freshly ground black pepper
1 clove garlic, minced	¼ cup (4 tablespoons) butter, melted
½ cup dry bread crumbs	

Preheat oven to 400 degrees. Place tomato halves on a well-oiled baking sheet; brush the tops with half the oil and bake in a hot oven for 15 minutes.

Increase oven temperature to 500 degrees or heat broiler. Sauté shallots and garlic in remaining oil, being careful not to let the garlic burn. Remove from heat and mix with bread crumbs, parsley, salt, and pepper. Spread a thick coating of the mixture on each tomato and brown under the broiler or in a very hot oven for about 5 minutes. Watch the tomatoes carefully as the stuffing will brown very quickly.

Arrange the tomatoes on a round platter and baste with melted butter.

Courgette Frite à l'Anglaise
(Fried Zucchini, English Style)

6 zucchini	Salt
1 cup flour	Few sprigs Deep-Fried Parsley
Oil for deep-frying, heated to 360°	

Slice zucchini into ¼-inch-thick slices. Coat the slices with flour, then deep-fry about 3 to 4 minutes or until golden.

Drain on absorbent paper, sprinkle with salt, and serve at once on a round platter covered with a napkin or doily. Garnish with parsley.

Ratatouille Niçoise

1 onion, minced	4 large tomatoes, peeled, seeded, and
1 clove garlic, chopped	chopped
½ cup olive oil	Salt
2 medium eggplants, diced	Pinch of cayenne
2 zucchini, diced	1 tablespoon chopped fresh parsley
2 sweet green peppers, diced	12 pitted ripe olives, halved (optional)

In a large skillet, sauté onion and garlic in olive oil for 5 minutes. Add eggplant and zucchini. Do not worry about the vegetables absorbing the oil as they brown; they will shortly release it again.

Add peppers and tomatoes to the eggplant and zucchini. Season to taste with salt and cayenne. Mix well, bring to a boil, and cook over low heat for 20 minutes.

Serve the ratatouille in a vegetable dish, sprinkled with parsley and, if you wish, garnished with olives.

Jardinière de Primeurs Étuvée au Beurre Fin
(Garden Vegetables Braised in Butter)

1 pound young carrots, peeled	1 cup shelled fresh peas
1 pound white turnips, peeled	¼ cup (4 tablespoons) butter
½ pound fresh green beans	1 teaspoon salt

Cut the carrots, turnips, and beans into 1-inch lengths (this method is known as *legumes taillés Porte-Maillot*). Cook all vegetables separately in lightly salted boiling water to cover, for 10 to 15 minutes or until done.

In a skillet or saucepan, sauté carrots, turnips, beans, and peas in butter for 5 minutes. Season with salt, then serve in a vegetable dish.

Legumes Glacés
(Glazed Mixed Vegetables)

1 pound carrots, peeled	2 cups butter
1 pound white turnips, peeled	1 pound thin green beans, trimmed
Salt	1 pound fresh peas, shelled
Sugar	6 small, ripe tomatoes

Trim the carrots and turnips into the shape of large olives. In 2 separate saucepans, place carrots and turnips. Add water to cover in each saucepan and add a pinch each of salt and sugar, and ½ cup each of the butter. Bring to a boil, simmer until all the water has evaporated, then shake the pans to distribute the butter over the vegetables.

In 2 separate saucepans, cook beans and peas in lightly salted boiling water. Drain each and add ¼ cup butter to each saucepan. Peel the tomatoes, put them into a skillet, and dot with remaining butter. Salt to taste and braise over gentle heat for 5 minutes. Serve in separate piles on a large serving platter.

Potatoes,
Rice,
and Pasta

10

Pommes de Terre Anna
(Potatoes Anna)

6 pounds large potatoes, peeled   1 teaspoon salt
1 cup clarified butter

Preheat oven to 400 degrees. With a potato corer, cut out lengthwise cylinders from potatoes. Slice the cylinders into rounds about ⅛-inch thick. Wash carefully to remove starch, then drain and dry on a kitchen towel. Sauté the potato slices in butter, without browning, for a few minutes. Season with salt.

Heavily butter 6 baba molds and fill to top with potato slices in successive layers, making sure that each layer is rounded out to fit the flutes in the entire mold by pressing lightly with the fingers. Put the molds in a baking pan and add hot frying oil heated to 360° to the outer pan to about half the height of the molds. Cover the saucepan and bake in a hot oven for about 20 minutes. Loosen edges of mold with knife and unmold onto a round serving platter and serve.

Pommes de Terre Boulangère
(Baked Potatoes and Onions)

4½ pounds medium potatoes,   ½ teaspoon salt
   peeled   Freshly ground black pepper
2 medium onions, minced   3 cups Classic Beef or Chicken
¼ cup (4 tablespoons) butter   Consommé, approximately

Preheat oven to 400 degrees. Cut potatoes into ⅛-inch-thick slices. Wash slices well and reserve. In a saucepan or skillet, sauté onions in butter, mix onions with the potato slices, and transfer to a well-buttered 1½-quart casserole. Season with salt and pepper. Add consommé until potatoes are just covered. Bake in hot oven for about 20 minutes or until liquid is absorbed.

Pommes de Terre à l'Allemande
(German Fried Potatoes)

10 medium potatoes   ¼ cup (4 tablespoons) butter

Cook potatoes in boiling salted water to cover until tender, about 15 to 20 minutes. Peel and cut into ½-inch-thick slices. Heat butter until brown and sauté potatoes until brown on one side, turn and brown other side.

Variations

Lyonnaise Potatoes

Prepare potatoes as in *German Fried Potatoes*, cutting the slices only ¼ inch thick. For every pound of potatoes, sauté 1 onion, finely chopped, in 2 tablespoons butter for 5 minutes. Add potatoes and continue cooking until potatoes are lightly browned.

Parslied Potatoes

Prepare potatoes as in *German Fried Potatoes*, cutting the slices only ¼ inch thick. Sprinkle with 2 tablespoons finely chopped parsley just before serving.

Hash-Brown Potatoes

Cook and peel potatoes, then dice. Brown in butter, using ¼ cup butter for each pound of potatoes.

Pommes de Terre Colombine
(Potatoes and Sweet Peppers)

4 pounds new potatoes	**2 green peppers, cut into julienne**
1 cup butter	**2 tablespoons oil**
Salt and freshly ground pepper	

Peel potaotes and round them off with a paring knife. Cut into ⅛-inch thick slices, then soak thoroughly in cold water to eliminate starch; drain and dry on a kitchen towel.

Fry potato slices lightly in browned butter until lightly browned. Season with salt and freshly ground pepper. Sauté peppers in oil, then add to the potatoes.

Pommes de Terre Macaise
(Baked Potatoes Macaise)

6 large Idaho potatoes	**1 cup butter, melted**
Salt	**1 tablespoon chopped fresh parsley**
Pinch of grated nutmeg	**1 tablespoon fine bread crumbs**

Preheat oven to 350 degrees. Bake the potatoes approximately 30 minutes, or until done. Scoop out the pulp with a spoon, then mash with a fork or potato ricer. Season to taste with salt and nutmeg. Mix potato with butter and parsley. Spoon into small baba molds, which have been heavily buttered and sprinkled with bread crumbs. Bake as for Potatoes Anna, loosen edges and unmold.

Pommes de Terre Soufflées
(Puffed Potatoes)

6 large Idaho potatoes	**Salt**
Oil for deep-frying, heated to 350°	**Freshly ground black pepper**

Peel, wash, and dry potatoes on a kitchen towel. Cut into paper-thin, even lengthwise slices and trim each into an oval. Immerse into oil for 3 minutes. Lower temperature to 250 degrees and fry 2 minutes, then raise temperature to 300 degrees for 2 minutes. Drain on absorbent paper.

Heat second batch of oil to 400 degrees. Add a few potatoes and they will puff up and bob to the surface. Fry 1 to 2 minutes or until brown. Drain on absorbent paper and sprinkle with salt and pepper. Serve immediately.

Pommes de Terre Sablées
(Fried Potatoes Sablées)

10 medium potatoes, cooked and peeled
½ cup (8 tablespoons) butter, heated until brown

Dry bread crumbs
Salt

Cut potatoes into ½-inch-thick slices. Fry in a skillet with butter. When they are a golden brown on both sides, toss with a mixture of bread crumbs and a little salt. Sauté briefly until golden and serve in a vegetable dish.

Pommes Frites Pont-Neuf
(French-Fried Potatoes Pont-Neuf)

6 large potatoes
Oil for deep-frying, heated to 370°

Salt

Peel potatoes, trim them to rectangular blocks, then cut into sticks ½ inch square on the cross section. Soak in cold water to remove starch, then dry thoroughly in a kitchen towel. Deep-fry in hot oil for 8 minutes, without browning.

Just before serving, put potatoes back into oil until they take on a good coloring. Drain and salt lightly.

Pommes de Terre Fondantes
(Château Potatoes)

6 medium potatoes, peeled   2 cups Classic Beef Consommé

Preheat oven to 400 degrees. Using a sharp paring knife, cut the potatoes into shapes the size of a small egg. Arrange them in a baking dish and add consommé to cover. Lay a sheet of buttered wax paper or foil on top and bake in a hot oven for about 45 minutes. The potatoes will absorb all the liquid and color very little.

Pommes de Terre Dauphine
(Dauphine Potatoes)

½ cup Chicken Consommé
¼ cup (4 tablespoons) butter
Salt
Dash of grated nutmeg
½ cup all-purpose flour

2 eggs
2 large Idaho potatoes, cooked, peeled, and mashed
Oil for deep-frying, heated to 360°

Heat consommé and butter in large saucepan until boiling. Stir in ½ teaspoon salt, nutmeg, and flour until a ball of dough is formed. Cool.

Beat eggs into flour mixture, one at a time, then add potatoes. Drop mixture by teaspoons into hot oil and fry until golden, about 5 to 6 minutes. Sprinkle with salt and serve at once.

Pommes Noisette
(Noisette Potatoes)

6 large potatoes, peeled   Salt
½ cup (8 tablespoons) clarified
   butter

Using a melon baller, cut balls from potatoes. Boil 10 minutes. Drain, then sauté in butter until brown. Serve sprinkled with salt.

Pommes de Terre Lorette
(Lorette Potatoes)

3 pounds potatoes, peeled   Salt
   Cream Puff Pastry
   Oil for deep-frying, heated to 360°

Preheat oven to 400 degrees. Boil the potatoes in salted water, drain, dry in hot oven, and force through a fine sieve or potato ricer.

   Mix the Cream Puff Pastry with potatoes. Using a tablespoon, drop little balls 1 inch in diameter into the oil. Turn the potato balls as needed with a slotted spoon to ensure even frying. When done, remove them and drain well on absorbent paper. Salt and serve.

Pommes de Terre Sardalaise
(Truffled Potatoes)

2½ pounds medium potatoes   ½ cup dry white wine
 1 medium onion, minced   2 cups Classic Beef Consommé or
 ½ cup (8 tablespoons) butter   water
 ¼ cup sliced truffles   2 mill-turns freshly ground white
 1 teaspoon salt   pepper

Preheat oven to 400 degrees. Peel and slice the potatoes paper thin, then wash again to remove starch. Put them into a roasting pan in which a roast has been prepared. Sauté onion in butter, then add onion and drippings to the sliced potatoes.

   Chop some of the truffles until you have 2 tablespoons. Slice remaining truffles. Mix chopped truffles and salt into potatoes.

   Tuck slices of truffle under the potato slices on top to conceal them partially. Add wine and enough consommé or water barely to cover; season with pepper and cover with a sheet of aluminum foil. Bake in a hot oven for about 30 minutes.

Alternative Method:
   Sauté the potato slices in ½ cup (8 tablespoons) clarified butter until they are nicely browned, salting lightly during cooking. Add sliced truffles and cook for 5 minutes.

Pommes de Terre Savoyarde
(Savoy Gratinéed Potatoes)

½ clove garlic
2 pounds potatoes, peeled
1 teaspoon salt

2 mill-turns freshly ground pepper
1½ cups milk
½ cup grated Swiss cheese

Preheat oven to 350 degrees.

Rub a heatproof baking dish with garlic and butter generously. Slice potatoes thin, wash to remove excess starch, and arrange in baking dish; sprinkle with salt and pepper. Add milk to cover, bring to a boil on top of stove, and simmer for 15 minutes. Sprinkle with cheese and bake in a moderate oven for 30 minutes, until brown.

Pommes Croquettes
(Potato Croquettes)

1¼ pounds potatoes, peeled and
   diced
¼ cup (4 tablespoons) butter,
   melted
4 egg whites
Salt

Flour for dusting
2 eggs, beaten
1 cup dry bread crumbs
Oil for deep-frying, heated to 375°

Cook the potatoes in lightly salted water. Drain and cook over low heat, shaking pan so all liquid is evaporated.

Push potatoes through a sieve or food mill into a bowl. Beat in butter and egg whites. Season to taste with salt. Spread the mixture out to a thickness of 1 inch on a floured board and let it cool.

Divide potato mixture into sections of about ¼ cup each. Roll each of the sections into log-shaped croquettes. Dip into flour, then into egg, then into bread crumbs. Dip each croquette again into flour, egg, and crumbs and deep-fry, using a fry-basket, for 5 to 6 minutes. Drain well on absorbent paper and salt lightly.

Pommes Paille
(Straw or String Potatoes)

6 large Idaho potatoes
Oil for deep-frying, heated to 370°

Salt

Peel and wash potatoes; cut into very thin slices lengthwise. Cut the slices into ⅛-inch strings, then soak in cold water to remove the starch. Drain and dry on a kitchen towel.

Put the potatoes into a frying basket and deep-fry, stirring constantly with a slotted spoon to ensure even browning and to keep the strings from sticking together. When the potatoes are nicely browned, drain on absorbent paper and season evenly with salt. Serve immediately.

Note: The slicer which French cooks call a *mandoline*, with blades set into a hardwood board, can be used for making very thin potato slices.

Risotto alla Milanese
(Rice, Milan Style)

½ cup (8 tablespoons) butter
1 large onion, minced
2 cups uncooked Italian or long-
  grain rice

½ cup dry white wine
5 cups Chicken Consommé
1 teaspoon saffron
1 cup grated Parmesan cheese

Heat butter in a large saucepan. Sauté onion until pale yellow. Add rice and sauté for 3 minutes. Add wine and stir over medium heat until liquid is absorbed. Add 2 cups of the consommé and cook, stirring occasionally, until liquid is absorbed. Add 2 cups of the consommé and cook again, stirring occasionally, until liquid is absorbed.

Mix remaining consommé and saffron; add to rice and simmer until liquid is absorbed and rice is tender. Stir in cheese and serve at once with additional cheese, if desired.

Riz Pilaw
(Rice Pilaf)

⅓ cup (6 tablespoons) butter
2 cups uncooked long-grain rice
4 cups Classic Beef Consommé

1 teaspoon salt
Bouquet garni (bay leaf, celery
leaves, parsley sprigs, thyme
sprigs)

Preheat oven to 400 degrees; heat butter in heatproof baking dish and sauté rice until pale yellow. Add consommé, salt, and bouquet garni. Cover and bring to a boil. Bake in a hot oven for 17 to 20 minutes or until liquid is absorbed. Remove bouquet garni and fluff rice with a fork.

Variations:

Raisin Pilaf

Soak 1 cup raisins in ½ cup Madeira wine. Drain, then add to hot rice.

Saffron Pilaf

Add 1 teaspoon saffron threads to rice when it is sautéed; cook as above.

Rice St. Denis

This is simply a pilaf with the addition of 6 fresh mushrooms, minced and sautéed with onion. Add 1 cup Sauce Tomate, ½ teaspoon Glace de Viande, and ⅓ cup grated Gruyère to rice, then add consommé and cook as above. Season to taste.

Spanish Rice

Prepare a pilaf, but before rice is cooked add a pinch of saffron, 2 diced chorizo sausages, the chopped pulp of 1 large tomato, and 2 diced sweet peppers. Add consommé and cook as above. Season to taste.

Pilaw de Riz Sauvage
(Wild Rice Pilaf)

Wild rice grows naturally in marshes and is expensive since it must be gathered by hand. The grains are long and thin, grayish in color. Wild rice is recommended as an accompaniment for game.

1 onion, minced	Chicken Consommé
¼ cup (4 tablespoons) butter	Salt
8 ounces wild rice, rinsed	½ cup crème fraîche or heavy cream

Preheat oven to 400 degrees. Sauté onion in butter in a large saucepan. Add the rice, cover to twice its depth with the consommé, and bring to a boil. Cover, bake in a hot oven for 35 to 40 minutes or until rice is tender.

Drain the rice, season with salt, and pour out onto a buttered platter, using a fork to separate the grains. Spoon crème fraîche over top.

Croquettes de Riz
(Rice Croquettes)

¾ cup uncooked Italian rice	¼ cup (4 tablespoons) butter, cut into
Salt	small pieces
1 quart milk	½ cup fine dry bread crumbs
5 egg yolks plus 2 whole eggs, well beaten	Oil for deep-frying, heated to 360°

Rinse rice, then cover with lightly salted water to twice its depth. Cook 5 minutes, then drain, pouring cold water over rice to stop cooking; drain again.

Bring lightly salted milk to the boil, add the rice, and simmer until milk is completely absorbed. Carefully blend in the egg yolks and butter and mix well. Spread the rice mixture in a well-buttered pan to a depth of 4 inches and let cool for several hours.

Take a large tablespoon of the rice mixture and roll out into corklike shapes on a marble slab or floured countertop. Dip in beaten egg, then in bread crumbs. Place the croquettes in a frying basket and lower into oil. Fry until golden, about 6 to 7 minutes. Drain on absorbent paper and serve.

Gnocchi à la Parisienne
(Gnocchi, French Style)

1½ cups Cream Puff Pastry	2 cups crème fraîche
Salt	Grated nutmeg
1½ cups grated Gruyère cheese	

Blend a pinch of salt and ½ cup cheese with the pastry, then, using a pastry bag with ½-inch round tip, squeeze out pieces of gnocchi about 1 inch long. Drop them 1 at a time into boiling salted water. When the gnocchi rise to the surface, remove with a slotted spoon and drain on paper towels.

Preheat oven to 400 degrees. Put the cooked gnocchi into saucepan with crème fraîche and simmer until the sauce has thickened. Season to taste with salt and nutmeg, then pour gnocchi and sauce into a well-buttered 1½-quart gratin dish. Sprinkle with remaining cheese and bake in hot oven for 15 to 20 minutes. The gnocchi will rise slightly, like a soufflé. Serve immediately.

Gnocchi à la Romaine
(Gnocchi, Roman Style)

1 cup cream of wheat	5 egg yolks, beaten
4 cups milk, heated to boiling	Clarified butter
Salt	1 cup finely grated Gruyère cheese
Grated nutmeg	

Cook cream of wheat in milk until thickened. Season to taste with salt and nutmeg, and, when the semolina is thick, blend in the egg yolks, stirring with a wooden spatula. Pour the mixture onto a well-buttered pan in a layer about 1 inch deep. Let cool, then refrigerate for 3 hours.

Preheat oven to 450 degrees or heat broiler. Turn out semolina onto a cutting board or marble slab and, using a biscuit cutter, cut out gnocchi in 2-inch rounds. Dip the gnocchi in clarified butter, then roll in grated cheese. Arrange gnocchi in overlapping layers in a well-buttered gratin dish. Place under the broiler or in hot oven for 5 to 6 minutes, or until lightly browned on top. Serve immediately.

Orge Perlé
(Pearl Barley)

8 ounces pearl barley	Salt
1 medium onion, minced	Pinch of cayenne
2 tablespoons butter	Bouquet garni (celery leaves,
Water or Classic Beef	thyme, oregano)
Consommé	⅓ cup crème fraîche or heavy cream

Preheat oven to 400 degrees. Put barley, onion, and butter into a heatproof casserole and sauté 5 minutes. Add water or beef stock to 3 times the depth of the barley. Season with a little salt and cayenne; add the bouquet garni. Bring to a boil, cover, and bake in a hot oven for 25 minutes.

When barley is done, stir in crème fraîche, mixing lightly with a fork to separate the grains.

Nouilles Fraîches
(Fresh Noodles)

Although pasta is an Italian speciality, it has been a tradition on transatlantic liners to include a farinaceous dish on the menu. Aboard the France, pasta was extremely popular and we produced it fresh in large quantities and in an endless variety of shapes and forms. Many pasta sauces are included in the Sauce section of this book. Among those I would recommend are the following: Bolognese, Caruso, Genovese, Italienne, Livournaise, Tomato, Toocane, Tyrolienne, Venicienne, and Zingara.

4½ cups sifted all-purpose flour	3 tablespoons warm water
2 teaspoons salt	3 whole eggs and 6 yolks

Arrange flour in a circle on a marble slap or chopping block, and make a hole in center. Dissolve salt in warm water and add along with the eggs and yolks. (For heartier pasta, you may just use yolks and forget the whites.) Mix and knead thoroughly to ensure that flour is well integrated and the mixture is smooth. When pasta is very firm, wrap in a wet cloth to prevent drying and set aside for about an hour or until it loses its elasticity. Divide the dough into pieces the size of an egg and roll out each piece into the shape of a large, very thin pancake. Spread dough out on baking sheets covered with sheets of paper and dry about 1 hour before cutting into desired shapes. To cook, plunge noodles into 1 quart salted, boiling water for 8 to 10 minutes. Drain, and serve with your favorite sauce.

Salads

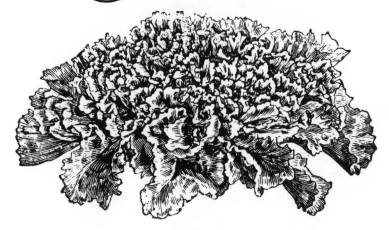

11

Coeurs des Laitues à la Russe
(Lettuce Hearts Russian Style)

3 heads Bibb lettuce
3 beets, cooked, peeled, and
  sliced
3 hard-cooked eggs, sliced

Creamy Mayonnaise (see Lettuce,
  Endive, Celery, and Beet Salad)
2 tablespoons black caviar
2 tablespoons chopped fresh chives

Trim, wash, and dry the lettuce, then cut each head in half. Arrange halves in a star pattern on a large, round platter. Top with beets and hard-cooked eggs. Chill.

Mix Creamy Mayonnaise with caviar. Spoon over salad just before serving and garnish with chives.

Salade Archiduc
(Endive and Beet Salad)

1 pound Belgian endive
1 beet, cooked, peeled, and diced

2 stalks celery, diced
Sauce Vinaigrette

Cut, wash, and dry endive. Put into a salad bowl and garnish with beet and celery. Chill.

Spoon Vinaigrette over salad just before serving.

Salade des Augustins
(Lettuce and Green Bean Salad)

1 head romaine lettuce
2 tomatoes, quartered
3 hard-cooked eggs, cut into
  wedges
½ cup cooked peas

6 ounces cooked green beans, cut
  into 1-inch pieces
Creamy Mayonnaise (see Lettuce,
  Endive, Celery, and Beet Salad)
2 teaspoons Sauce Crème à l'Anglaise

Trim, wash, and dry lettuce. Tear each leaf into thirds and place in a salad bowl. Top with tomatoes and egg wedges arranged in a star pattern with peas at the center. Put the green beans around them.

Prepare Creamy Mayonnaise as in recipe; stir in Sauce Crème à l'Anglaise. Just before serving, pour over salad and toss well.

Salade de Batavia Moscovite
(Moscow Salad)

1 head leaf lettuce	1 cup sour cream
1 navel orange, peeled and sliced	½ teaspoon salt
1 cucumber, unpeeled, sliced	Pinch of cayenne

Trim, wash, and dry lettuce. Tear off pieces into a salad bowl. Garnish with orange and cucumber slices. Chill.

Mix sour cream with salt and cayenne. Spoon over salad just before serving.

Salade Béatrice
(Beatrice Salad)

2 hearts chicory	12 tips cooked asparagus
2 cups julienne strips cooked chicken	Creamy Mayonnaise (see Lettuce, Endive, Celery, and Beet Salad)
2 medium truffles, cut into julienne	2 teaspoons Dijon-style mustard
2 potatoes, cooked, peeled, and cut into julienne	

Trim, carefully wash and dry the chicory hearts, and separate into leaves. Put in a salad bowl and top with chicken, truffles, and potatoes. Place a bouquet of asparagus in the middle. Chill.

Mix Creamy Mayonnaise with mustard. Spoon dressing over salad just before serving.

Salade Beaucaire
(Celeriac and Endive Salad with Apples, Ham, and Potato)

4 Belgian endive	4 small potatoes, cooked, peeled, and sliced
¼ celeriac, peeled and shredded	Creamy Mayonnaise (see Lettuce, Endive, Celery, and Beet Salad)
4 slices boiled ham, cut into julienne	
2 apples, peeled and cut into julienne	

Separate the endive leaves. Wash, dry thoroughly, and cut each leaf into thirds crosswise. Place in salad bowl and sprinkle celeriac, ham, and apple over the endive.

Arrange potato slices around the edge of the bowl, with the slices overlapping. Chill.

Spoon Creamy Mayonnaise over salad just before serving.

Salade Bouginaise
(Bouginaise Salad)

6 small hearts of red leaf lettuce or Bibb lettuce	1½ teaspoons salt
3 navel oranges	3 ripe plum tomatoes, sliced
7 small limes	¼ teaspoon freshly ground white pepper
¼ cup uncooked long-grain rice	1 teaspoon dry mustard
¾ cup water	¾ cup peanut oil

Trim, wash, and dry the lettuce hearts and arrange them in a star pattern on a round platter.

Peel and quarter the oranges, making sure to remove the white membrane. Peel 3 of the limes and cut them into thin rounds.

Boil the rice in water with ½ teaspoon salt for 17 minutes; drain and wash in several changes of cold water, then drain again.

Place rice and orange, tomato, and lime slices on lettuce. Chill.

Mix remaining salt, pepper, and mustard with the juice of 4 remaining limes, stirring well with a whisk. Add the oil drop by drop, still whisking vigorously. Spoon dressing over salad just before serving.

Salade Lorenzo
(Lorenzo Salad)

1 heart lettuce	2 medium pears, cored and quartered
1 head chicory	2 stalks celery, cut into julienne
1 head escarole	Creamy Mayonnaise (see Lettuce Endive, Celery, and Beet Salad)
2 small beets, cooked, peeled, and sliced	
2 hard-cooked eggs, sliced	

Trim, wash, and dry the leaves from lettuce heart, chicory, and escarole. Tear into bite-sized pieces and put into a salad bowl. Add beet and egg slices and pear sections, alternating the beets, egg, and pear. Top the salad with celery. Chill.

Just before serving, pour Creamy Mayonnaise over salad and toss well.

Salade Madécasse
(Mixed Salad with Pink Dressing)

1 head chicory	10 green olives, halved
1 head leaf lettuce	3 stalks celery, cut into julienne
4 beets, cooked, peeled, and sliced (save 2 tablespoons cooking liquid)	2 hard-cooked eggs, chopped
	Sauce Vinaigrette

Trim, wash, and dry the chicory and lettuce. Mix leaves in a salad bowl and garnish the edge of the bowl with overlapping beet slices and green olives. Top with celery and egg. Chill.

Mix Vinaigrette with reserved beet juice. Spoon over salad just before serving.

Salade Mercédès
(Chicory, Celery, and Beet Salad)

1 head chicory
2 hard-cooked eggs, quartered
2 plum tomatoes, quartered
2 stalks celery, cut into julienne

1 beet, cooked, peeled, and cut into julienne
Sauce Vinaigrette

Trim chicory, then wash thoroughly and dry. Tear off bite-sized pieces into a salad bowl and top with alternating quarters of eggs and tomatoes. Place celery and beet in the center. Chill.

Just before serving, pour dressing over salad and toss to coat well.

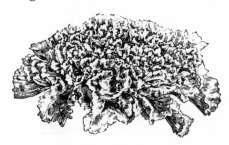

Salade Ninon
(Mixed Salad with Almonds)

1 head leaf lettuce
5 plum tomatoes, quartered
1 navel orange, peeled and sliced
2 hard-cooked egg yolks, pushed through a sieve

2 sprigs fresh parsley, minced
½ cup slivered almonds
Sauce Vinaigrette
Juice of 1 lemon
1 tablespoon Sauce Anglaise

Trim and separate the lettuce leaves, reserving a small heart. Wash thoroughly and dry. Tear into bite-sized pieces and put in a salad bowl. Garnish the edge of the bowl with tomatoes. Arrange orange slices in a rosette in the middle of the salad and place the lettuce heart in the center. Sprinkle yolks, parsley, and almonds onto the salad.

Mix Vinaigrette, lemon juice, and Sauce Anglaise. Spoon dressing over salad just before serving.

Salade de Pissenlits aux Rillons
(Dandelion and Bacon Salad)

1 pound dandelion greens
3 slices bacon, diced
1 clove garlic, minced
4 mill-turns freshly ground white pepper

2 tablespoons red wine vinegar
1 teaspoon Dijon-style mustard

Trim the dandelion greens; cut lengthwise. Wash in several changes of water and dry well.

Fry bacon bits until crisp, then put the bacon and drippings into a salad bowl. Add garlic, pepper, vinegar, and mustard. (No salt is needed, since it is supplied by the bacon.) Mix well, then add the dandelion greens, mix again, and serve immediately before the bacon fat sets.

This salad can also be made with spinach leaves or arugula.

Salade Santiago
(Santiago Salad)

1 head leaf lettuce
1 navel orange, peeled
2 sweet red peppers, slivered
3 slices boiled ham,
  cut into julienne

¾ cup crème fraîche or heavy cream
½ teaspoon salt
  Pinch of cayenne
  Juice of 2 limes

Trim and separate lettuce leaves. Wash thoroughly and dry. Tear into bite-sized pieces and place into a salad bowl. Cut orange rind into julienne strips; dice pulp. Top lettuce with orange peel and pulp, red pepper, and ham. Chill.

Mix crème fraîche with salt, cayenne, and lime juice. Spoon over salad just before serving.

Salade Turquoise
(Chicory Mixed Salad)

1 head chicory
3 tablespoons chopped tomato
  pulp or 2 tomatoes, peeled,
  seeded, and chopped
2 stalks celery, cut into julienne

1 sweet green pepper, chopped
  Creamy Mayonnaise (see Lettuce,
  Endive, Celery, and Beet Salad)

Trim the green leaves from the chicory. Put chicory in a salad bowl and mix with tomato pulp, celery, and green pepper. Chill.

Spoon Creamy Mayonnaise over salad just before serving.

Salade Caprice
(Mixed Salad Caprice)

1 small head escarole
1 heart lettuce
1 small head chicory
2 slices boiled ham, cut into
  julienne

3 thin slices smoked beef
  tongue, cut into julienne
1 cup julienne strips cooked chicken
1 small bunch watercress, trimmed
  Sauce Vinaigrette

Trim, wash, and dry escarole, lettuce, and chicory. Tear into bite-sized pieces and put into salad bowl. Garnish with ham, tongue, and chicken and place a bouquet of watercress in the center. Chill.

Spoon Vinaigrette over salad just before serving.

Salade Cauchoise
(Mixed Salad Cauchoise)

1 head leaf lettuce
  Few sprigs each fresh parsley
  and chervil, chopped
1 shallot, chopped
2 slices boiled ham, diced
1 apple, cored and diced

1 cup crème fraîche or heavy
  cream
  Juice of ½ lemon
  Salt
  Freshly ground white pepper

Trim and separate the leaves of the lettuce; wash and dry thoroughly, then put the leaves into a salad bowl. Sprinkle parsley, chervil, shallot, ham, and apple onto the lettuce. Chill.

Mix crème fraîche with lemon juice and season to taste with salt and pepper. Spoon dressing over salad just before serving.

Salade Châtelaine
(Mixed Salad with Truffles)

2 hard-cooked eggs, sliced	4 medium tomatoes, cut into
3 small potatoes, cooked,	wedges
peeled, and sliced	2 tablespoons chopped truffles
1 head chicory	Sauce Vinaigrette

Line the inside of a glass salad bowl with alternating slices of egg and potato. Wash the chicory carefully and discard all but the white leaves. Dry the chicory and place it in the salad bowl. Arrange small segments of tomato around the salad. Sprinkle with truffles. Chill.

Spoon Vinaigrette over salad just before serving.

Salade Chiffonade
(Chiffonade Salad)

1 head Boston lettuce	4 plum tomatoes, sliced
1 heart escarole	1 medium beet, cooked,
1 heart chicory	peeled, and cut into julienne
1 bunch watercress	2 stalks celery, cut into julienne
3 hard-cooked eggs, sliced	Sauce Vinaigrette

Trim, wash thoroughly, and dry the lettuce, escarole, chicory, and watercress. Place lettuce in a salad bowl with a bouquet of watercress in the middle. Around side, alternate slices of eggs and tomatoes, then top with beet and celery.

Just before serving, pour dressing over salad and toss to coat well.

Salade Figaro
(Lettuce, Endive, Celery, and Beet Salad)

1 head romaine lettuce	*Creamy Mayonnaise:*
2 Belgian endive	1 cup Mayonnaise
2 stalks celery	⅓ cup crème fraîche or heavy cream
2 small beets, cooked, peeled, and thinly sliced	
8 anchovy filets	
1 large, ripe tomato, peeled, seeded, and chopped	

Trim, wash, and dry greens and celery. Cut into julienne and put in a salad bowl; top with beet slices. Arrange anchovy filets in a lattice pattern on top of salad. Put a small amount of tomato in each square of the anchovy pattern.

Gradually beat crème fraîche into Mayonnaise, then pour dressing over salad and toss well just before serving.

Salade Gadski
(Gadski Salad)

3 small heads romaine lettuce	1 bunch small seedless grapes
2 avocados, peeled, seeded, and thinly sliced	1 truffle, diced
1 apple, cored and diced	1 green pepper, diced
	Sauce Vinaigrette

Trim the romaine and cut each head in half. Wash thoroughly and dry, then arrange the segments in a star pattern on a long serving platter. Arrange avocado slices on each lettuce half. Top with apple, grapes, truffle, and green pepper. Chill.

Spoon Vinaigrette over salad just before serving.

Salade Japonaise
(Japanese Salad)

1 pound Chinese cabbage	Creamy Mayonnaise (see Lettuce,
1 grapefruit, peeled and sliced	Endive, Celery, and Beet Salad)
2 slices pineapple, quartered	2 teaspoons chopped fresh parsley

Trim, wash thoroughly, and dry cabbage. Shred finely into a salad bowl and top with grapefruit slices arranged to form a rosette. Surround the rosette with pineapple quarters. Chill.

Mix Creamy Mayonnaise with parsley. Spoon dressing over salad just before serving.

Salade Lakmé
(Salad with Curried Vinaigrette)

1 head escarole	1 onion, chopped
1 green-and-red sweet pepper, diced	½ cup cooked rice
	Sauce Vinaigrette
1 medium tomato, diced	1 teaspoon curry powder

Trim, wash thoroughly, and dry escarole. Tear into bite-sized pieces and put into a salad bowl; top with pepper, tomato, onion, and rice. Chill.

Mix Vinaigrette with curry powder. Spoon dressing over salad just before serving.

Doughs and Desserts

12

BASIC DOUGHS

Pâte Feuilletée
(Puff Pastry Dough)

4 cups unsifted all-purpose flour	**1⅓ cups cold water**
½ teaspoon salt	**2 cups (1 pound) unsalted butter**

Place flour in a bowl and add salt. Stir in water and mix lightly with the hands to get a smooth, soft but not sticky dough. Shape into a ball, dust with flour, and let rest for 15 minutes. Meanwhile, knead the butter with hands sprinkled with cold water to soften it and make it pliable. Dry butter on paper towels.

Flour a cutting board or marble slab, put the dough on it, and shape it into a 10-inch square. Likewise, shape the butter into a 7-inch square on wax paper. Put the butter square diagonally on top of the pastry square, remove wax paper, and fold up the corners to meet in the center. Pinch edges to seal and let stand 5 minutes.

Roll the dough out gently to an oblong 7 x 18 inches, about ½ inch thick; keep an even thickness throughout. Fold dough into 3 layers as you would a letter and seal with the rolling pin. Turn dough so that the open edge of the fold looks like a book ready to be opened. Roll again to 7 x 18 inches. Fold into 3 layers once again and chill covered for 15 to 20 minutes.

Repeat the folding and rolling process 4 more times, letting the dough rest for 10 minutes after each new rolling. After rolling and folding is completed, wrap and chill dough overnight. Refrigerate up to 1 week or freeze for several months. To use, thaw in wrappings overnight. **Makes 2½ pounds dough**.

Variation

Half-Puff Pastry

Follow the preceding recipe, using only 10 ounces (1¼ cups) butter and rolling out the dough 2 fewer times (4 times instead of 6).

Pâte Brisée
(Tart Pastry)

2 cups unsifted all-purpose flour	⅔ cup unsalted butter, softened but
1 egg	not melted
½ teaspoon salt	3 tablespoons cold water

Place flour in a bowl. Make a hollow in the center and add remaining ingredients. Mix with a fork until a ball of dough forms, then knead a few times until you have a smooth ball. Wrap and chill 1 hour before rolling. **For 1 10-inch tart or 8 3-inch tarts.**

Pâte à Brioche
(Brioche Dough)

2 envelopes active dry yeast	8 to 10 cups unsifted all-purpose
1¾ cups lukewarm water	flour
3 tablespoons granulated sugar	1 pound unsalted butter
1 teaspoon salt	1 egg, well beaten with 2
7 eggs	tablespoons water (for glaze)

Mix yeast with ¼ cup water in a bowl until dissolved. Stir in sugar, salt, remaining water, and eggs. Blend in flour until a soft, sticky dough forms. Turn dough out onto a floured surface and knead 15 minutes or until smooth and elastic.

Knead the butter with hands sprinkled with cold water until soft and pliable. Dry butter on paper towels, then add butter to dough and knead the dough for about 15 minutes, or until it has become smooth and homogenous.

Put the ball of dough into a floured bowl, cover with a kitchen towel, and allow to rise in a warm place for 2 hours. After the dough has doubled in bulk, put on a floured surface and strike it several times with the rolling pin to flatten it.

Let dough rest for 10 minutes, then use as intended, either as part of another recipe or as brioche—1 large brioche or 36 small ones. To make the small brioche, cut the dough into 36 pieces, then cut ⅕ off each piece for the tops. Preheat oven to 400 degrees. Shape the larger dough pieces into smooth balls and place into greased brioche pans. Brush tops with beaten egg. Shape the smaller pieces into little balls. Make a depression in the centers of the larger balls and press the smaller balls into them. Brush again with egg mixture and let rise until doubled again in bulk. Brush again with egg and bake in hot oven for 15 minutes, or until richly browned. Serve warm. **Makes 36**.

Pâte à Choux
(Cream Puff Pastry)

1 cup water	1 cup unsifted all-purpose flour
½ teaspoon salt	4 eggs
½ cup butter or margarine	

Combine water, salt, and butter in a saucepan and bring to a boil. Stir with a wooden spatula while adding flour all at once and continue stirring until a ball of dough forms. Remove from heat and beat in eggs, 1 at a time, until all are incorporated smoothly. (You can also beat eggs into dough using a food processor.) Chill dough before using.

To make cream puffs or eclairs, preheat oven to 400 degrees. Shape as desired and bake in hot oven for 30 to 35 minutes for large puffs or eclairs, 20 minutes for tiny puffs. When done, slash the pastries at the side to allow steam to escape and place in a turned-off oven for 10 minutes to dry. **Makes about 1 pound.**

Pâte à Croissants
(Leavened Croissants)

1 envelope active dry yeast	2 cups lukewarm milk
¼ cup lukewarm water	8 cups unsifted all-purpose flour
1 teaspoon salt	1 cup unsalted butter, softened
3 tablespoons granulated sugar	1 egg, well beaten

Dissolve yeast in warm water. Add salt, sugar, and milk. Mix in flour until a sticky dough forms, then knead on a floured surface until smooth and elastic. Roll out the dough to a thickness of 1 inch. Dot two-thirds of the rolled dough with small pieces of the butter. Fold the rolled dough into thirds and let rest, covered, in refrigerator for 20 minutes. Flour again and roll out to same size. Fold into thirds, cover, and chill 20 minutes. Repeat 2 more times. Cover the dough with a kitchen towel and let rest in a cool place for 8 hours.

Flour a cutting board or marble slab, roll out the dough to a thickness of ⅛ inch, and cut it into strips 4 inches wide. Cut each strip in turn into large triangles. Flour the board well and roll each triangle toward the long point to make croissants, with the point of the triangle on top (bend the 2 ends slightly to give the dough the traditional crescent shape).

Put the croissants on a lightly greased baking sheet with sides (to prevent messy drips if butter leaks) and let rest for 2 hours in a warm place or until double in bulk.

Preheat oven to 425 degrees. Using a pastry brush, paint each croissant with beaten egg, then bake in a hot oven for 12 to 15 minutes, or until puffed and brown. **Makes 36.**

Pâte à Frire
(Fritter Batter)

2 cups unsifted all-purpose flour	1 envelope active dry yeast, dissolved
½ teaspoon salt	in ¼ cup lukewarm water
⅓ cup oil	2 cups lukewarm milk
4 egg yolks	4 egg whites, stiffly beaten

Combine all ingredients except egg whites, and beat until smooth. Let the dough rise for 2 hours in a warm place.

Fold the egg whites into the dough; batter is ready to be used as directed in main recipe. **Makes 1 quart**.

For fruit fritters, add 2 tablespoons sugar to the batter and marinate the slices of fruit in liqueur before using (use Calvados for apple fritters, Cognac for other fruit fritters).

This batter is also good for vegetables, chicken, ham, and shrimp.

Pâte à Genoise
(Genoise Sponge Layer)

7 eggs	1¾ cups sifted all-purpose flour
1 cup granulated sugar	½ cup (8 tablespoons) clarified butter,
1 teaspoon vanilla extract	melted

Preheat oven to 350 degrees. Butter and flour cake pans of desired size.

Put eggs and sugar in a bowl placed over a pan of hot water. Beat gently with an electric mixer for 15 minutes until the mixture takes on a whitish color and triples in volume.

Gently stir in vanilla and fold in flour and butter alternately. Pour batter into cake pans and bake in moderate oven for 15 to 20 minutes for 15 x 15-inch layer or 20 to 25 minutes for 9-inch layers. Cake should spring back when touched lightly.

Remove cake from pan when done and let cool on a rack before using. **Makes 2 9-inch layers or 1 15 x 15 x 1-inch cake.**

Pâte à Savoie
(Savoy Sponge Layer)

6 eggs	1 teaspoon vanilla extract
1 cup granulated sugar	2 cups sifted cake flour

Preheat oven to 350 degrees. Butter and flour a 2-quart ring mold. Put eggs, sugar, and vanilla into a mixing bowl set over a pan of simmering water. Beat with an electric mixer until eggs take on a whitish color and triple in volume. Gently fold in flour, then pour batter into pan and bake in moderate oven for 30 to 35 minutes, or until firm to the touch.

Remove from mold and let cool on a rack before using. **Makes 1 cake**.

Appareil à Meringues
(Meringue Shell)

6 egg whites   2 cups granulated sugar
½ teaspoon cream of tartar

Preheat oven to 275 degrees. Line a large baking sheet with foil or parchment paper. Beat egg whites with cream of tartar until very stiff. Beat in sugar, ¼ cup at a time, until whites are stiff and glossy. Mold the meringue with spoon or fill a pastry bag with a large fluted or smooth nozzle and trace a large shell or 12 small shells on the baking sheet. Bake in a slow oven, 1 hour for the large meringue shell and 30 minutes for the small. When done, turn off oven and allow to cool in oven. When cold, store in an airtight container until ready to use. **Makes 1 8-inch shell or 12 individual shells.**

CREAMS

Crème Anglaise
(Custard Cream)

6 egg yolks   2½ cups milk, heated until boiling
¾ cup granulated sugar   1 teaspoon vanilla extract

In a bowl, beat the egg yolks with the sugar until they are light and thickened. Gradually add the hot milk, blending well. Place bowl over water in saucepan and continue to beat, heating steadily until the liquid becomes thick and smooth. Immediately set into a bowl of ice water and cool, then chill. **Makes about 4 cups.**

Crème Chantilly
(Sweetened Whipped Cream)

1 quart crème fraîche or heavy   1 cup confectioner's sugar
  cream, chilled   1 teaspoon vanilla extract

Whip the crème fraîche until it thickens and doubles in volume. Fold in the confectioner's sugar and add the vanilla. **Makes about 4 cups.**

Crème Frangipane
(Frangipane Cream)

1 cup whole blanched almonds   4 cups milk
4 eggs   ½ cup butter, melted
1 cup confectioner's sugar   1 tablespoon vanilla extract
1 cup sifted all-purpose flour

Grind almonds to a powder in food processor or blender.

Put eggs, confectioner's sugar, and flour in a saucepan. Mix gently with a wooden spatula until the batter is smooth. In another saucepan bring milk to the boil, then pour the milk into the batter, whisking gently. Cook over low heat stirring with a wooden spatula, until the cream is very smooth and thick. Stir in melted butter, ground almonds, and vanilla. Mix vigorously. Cover and chill until ready to use. **Makes 6 cups**.

Crème Patissière
(Pastry Cream)

¾ cup all-purpose flour	6 eggs
1 cup granulated sugar	4 cups milk, heated to boiling
1 tablespoon butter, melted	2 teaspoons vanilla extract

In a mixing bowl, combine the flour with the sugar and butter and blend well. Gradually add the eggs, blending thoroughly after each. Slowly whisk in the hot milk and then add the vanilla. Place bowl in a saucepan with hot water and continue to cook, stirring constantly, until mixture thickens. Cool rapidly. **Makes about 4 cups**.

DESSERTS AND PASTRIES

Pudding à la Noix de Coco
(Coconut Pudding)

1 cup confectioner's sugar	10 egg yolks
½ cup (8 tablespoons) butter	15 egg whites, stiffly beaten
1 cup milk	1½ cups flaked coconut
½ cup all-purpose flour	2 cups Crème Anglaise

Preheat oven to 350 degrees. Butter a 2-quart soufflé dish and coat with sugar. Place confectioner's sugar and butter in a saucepan with milk and bring to a boil. Sift in flour and take off heat, stirring constantly with a wooden spatula to blend mixture. Whisk in egg yolks, one at a time, then fold in egg whites and coconut. Pour the mixture into soufflé dish and place the dish in another pan filled with water. Bake the pudding in moderate oven for 40 to 45 minutes or until firm. Remove from heat, cool, and unmold onto a serving platter. Cover with Crème Anglaise.

Oeufs à la Neige
(Snow Eggs)

10 egg whites
1½ cups confectioner's sugar
1 quart milk

2 cups Crème Anglaise, using milk
left from poaching egg whites

Beat egg whites until stiff. Gradually beat in confectioner's sugar, 1 tablespoon at a time. Heat milk in a skillet until simmering. Using a large spoon, shape the egg whites into oval mounds and drop into the milk. Turn the egg whites from time to time with a wooden spatula. When they are firm, remove with a slotted spoon and drain on a kitchen towel. Pile the snow eggs in a deep dish and cover with Crème Anglaise.

Crème Renversée au Caramel
(Caramel Custard)

1¼ cups granulated sugar
7 eggs

1 quart milk

Heat ½ cup sugar in a small skillet until golden brown and liquid. Pour into a 1½-quart charlotte mold and rotate to cover bottom and sides. Let caramel cool.

Preheat oven to 350 degrees. Beat eggs and remaining sugar in a bowl. Bring milk to a boil in a saucepan and gradually beat into the egg-sugar mixture, whisking continuously. When caramel is cooled, pour the egg mixture into the charlotte mold, filling almost to the brim. Place mold in a larger pan filled with water, so that water in pan comes 1 inch up the sides of the charlotte mold. Bake in moderate oven for about 1 hour or until firm.

Remove custard from oven and chill well in the refrigerator. Just before serving, loosen edges and unmold the caramel custard on a round serving platter. Caramel will be the topping for the custard.

Mousse au Chocolat
(Chocolate Mousse)

2 cups crème fraîche or heavy
cream
5 squares (5 ounces) semisweet
chocolate

¼ cup water
1¼ cups confectioner's sugar
1 tablespoon vanilla extract

In a bowl, whip crème fraîche until stiff. Chill.

Melt chocolate in a small saucepan, together with water. Stir in confectioner's sugar and mix well with a wooden spoon, adding a little more water if necessary to keep the mixture smooth and the consistency of a fudge sauce. Cover and cool to room temperature.

Stir vanilla into chocolate, then carefully fold in whipped cream. Pour the mousse into a glass compote dish and swirl top. Refrigerate for 1 hour before serving.

Variation

Mocha Mousse

Add 1 tablespoon instant coffee to the melted chocolate.

Bavaroise au Café
(Bavarian Coffee Cream)

3 envelopes unflavored gelatin	1 tablespoon instant coffee
3½ cups milk	1 cup crème fraîche or heavy cream,
10 egg yolks	whipped
2 cups confectioner's sugar	Clarified butter

In a saucepan, heat gelatin and milk until dissolved and boiling. In a bowl beat egg yolks together with confectioner's sugar. Add a ladle of hot milk to eggs to warm them, then add egg mixture to milk, whisking vigorously as you do so. Add the coffee and chill until syrupy.

Fold whipped cream into egg mixture and pour into a 1½-quart mold very lightly greased with clarified butter. Chill until firm. Unmold the Bavarian on a round serving platter covered with a napkin. Serve immediately, with additional sweetened whipped cream, if desired.

Riz à l'Impératrice
(Empress Rice)

½ cup uncooked long-grain rice	2 cups crème fraîche or heavy cream
3 cups milk, heated to boiling	½ cup chopped candied fruits
1 cup confectioner's sugar	⅔ cup kirsch
3 cups Crème Anglaise	½ cup red currant jelly
3 envelopes unflavored gelatin,	
mixed with ¼ cup cold water	

Carefully wash rice, place in saucepan, and add water to cover. Bring to a boil, let it boil for 2 minutes, drain, then add boiling milk and confectioner's sugar. Reduce heat, cover, and cook rice gently until done. Cool.

Heat Crème Anglaise and add gelatin mixture. Cool to room temperature, then chill 30 minutes. Whip the crème fraîche and fold into the Crème Anglaise, together with candied fruits and kirsch. Add the rice, mixing it thoroughly with the Crème Anglaise.

Heat jelly until boiling. Paint a 2½-quart charlotte mold with a thick layer of the jelly, then cool until set. Pour the rice mixture into the mold and refrigerate for several hours or until firm. Unmold just before serving (the mold should be dipped in warm water before removing the dessert). Garnish, if desired, with whipped cream and additional candied fruits.

Mont-Blanc aux Marrons
(Chestnut Mont Blanc)

½ recipe for Meringue Shell,
 unbaked
1½ pounds chestnuts
1½ cups granulated sugar
 2 teaspoons vanilla extract
 ¼ cup dark rum

1 Savoy Sponge Layer, baked in a 10-
 inch round cake pan
4 cups Crème Chantilly
12 marrons glacés
 Crystallized violets

Preheat oven to 275 degrees. Using a pastry bag with a large star tip, press out 12 3-inch-long strips of meringue. Bake in a slow oven for 40 to 45 minutes, or until hard to the touch.

Score the flat sides of chestnuts, cook briefly in boiling water, then remove shells and thin inner skins. Cover with water and cook at a simmer until very tender, about 1 hour. Drain and then press while warm through a sieve or food mill or purée in a food processor. Replace in saucepan, add sugar and vanilla, and cook over low heat until sugar is dissolved and mixture is very thick. Stir in rum.

Place Savoy Sponge on a platter and, using a pastry bag with a large fluted nozzle, garnish edge of cake with rosettes of chestnut purée, using about one-third of the purée. Change the nozzle for a ¼-inch round tip and cover the center of the cake with thin strands of remaining chestnut purée. Heap the meringues at the center, cover with two-thirds of the Crème Chantilly. Smooth the Chantilly with a metal spoon, then, using a pastry bag with a small fluted nozzle, dot the top with remaining Crème Chantilly. Arrange marrons glacés around the edge of the dish and top with crystallized violets.

Charlotte à la Russe
(Charlotte Russe)

10 to 20 ladyfingers, split open
 6 cups Crème Anglaise
 3 envelopes unflavored gelatin,
 mixed with ¼ cup cold water
 3 cups crème fraîche or heavy
 cream

1 cup kirsch
1 cup quartered candied cherries
2 tablespoons granulated sugar
1 teaspoon vanilla extract

Line a 2-quart lightly buttered charlotte mold with ladyfingers. Trim the edges slightly and cut the tops off level with mold.

Set aside ⅓ of the Crème Anglaise; cover and chill. Heat the remaining custard and stir in gelatin mixture. Refrigerate for 1 hour or until thickened.

Whip 2 cups of the crème fraîche, then blend with thickened Crème Anglaise and add ⅔ cup of the kirsch and the cherries. Pour the flavored custard filling into the charlotte mold, taking care to keep the ladyfinger lining in place. Refrigerate for several hours or until firm.

Whip remaining crème fraîche with sugar and vanilla. Unmold the charlotte onto a round serving platter and, using a pastry bag with a medium fluted nozzle, decorate the charlotte with remaining whipped crème fraîche. Serve charlotte with an accompanying dish of reserved Crème Anglaise flavored with remaining kirsch.

Charlotte Chantilly

15 to 25 ladyfingers, split open
4 cups Crème Chantilly

3 egg whites, stiffly beaten
Sweetened whipped cream

Line a 2-quart charlotte mold, sides and bottom, with ladyfingers, then trim to be even with edge of mold.

Gently fold beaten whites into Crème Chantilly, then pour into mold. Freeze until hard, then unmold the charlotte onto a round serving platter. Put additional whipped cream into a pastry bag with a medium fluted nozzle and decorate the top of the charlotte.

Omelette aux Fruits
(Fruit Omelet)

12 eggs
¼ cup confectioner's sugar
Pinch of salt
¼ cup (4 tablespoons) butter

2 cups diced fresh fruit or berries
⅓ cup dark rum
¼ cup granulated sugar
Confectioner's sugar

Break eggs into a bowl and beat with confectioner's sugar and salt. In a large skillet, heat butter until brown and add eggs, preparing a classic omelet. Mix fruit with rum and sugar, then spoon onto omelet. Roll the omelet in the pan and then transfer to a long serving platter. Sprinkle with confectioner's sugar and, using a red-hot wire or the edge of a heated knife, char the sugar lengthwise and crosswise to make a pattern of squares.

Soufflé Sucré
(Sweet Soufflé)

¼ cup all-purpose flour
¼ cup cornstarch
2 cups milk
10 egg yolks
⅔ cup granulated sugar

2 tablespoons vanilla extract
12 egg whites, stiffly beaten
¼ cup (4 tablespoons) butter, softened
Granulated sugar
Confectioner's sugar

Beat flour and cornstarch with milk in a saucepan. Whisk steadily over low heat while bringing to a boil. Beat in egg yolks, 1 at a time, then add sugar and vanilla. Cool.

Preheat oven to 375 degrees. Butter generously 2 1½-quart soufflé dishes, then sprinkle with sugar, shaking out excess. Fold one-quarter of the stiffly beaten egg whites into the cooled egg yolk mixture. Fold them in gently so as to preserve the stiffness of the whites, then fold in remaining egg whites.

Fill the soufflé dishes to three-fourths of their height and place on the middle rack of the oven. Bake for 20 minutes in a medium hot oven. Sprinkle on a little confectioner's sugar while the soufflés are in the oven, and continue to bake until a cake tester comes out clean, about 10 more minutes. Serve immediately.

Variations

Harlequin Soufflé

Divide Sweet Soufflé batter in half. Fold ⅓ cup sifted cocoa into half the batter just before egg whites are folded into sauce. Fill the soufflé dishes with alternating layers of chocolate-flavored soufflé batter and vanilla-flavored batter.

Embassy Soufflé

Stir ½ cup sweetened chestnut cream (available in cans) into the Sugar Soufflé mixture. Flavor with ⅓ cup kirsch just before egg whites are folded into the sauce. Serve with marrons glacés.

Violet Soufflé

Stir 1 teaspoon of violet extract and ½ cup crystallized violets into Sugar Soufflé just before folding in egg whites.

Praline Soufflé

Use firmly packed brown sugar instead of granulated sugar in Sugar Soufflé mixture. Stir in ½ cup powdered candied almonds just before folding in egg whites.

Fruit Soufflé

Stir ½ cup puréed raspberries or strawberries into Sugar Soufflé just before folding in egg whites.

Tarte aux Fruits
(Fruit Tart)

Pâte Brisée
2 cups Crème Patissière
3 cups prepared fruit (peeled and sliced peaches, apricot halves, seedless grapes, hulled strawberries, raspberries, blueberries)

½ cup apricot preserves
1 tablespoon water

Chill tart pastry for 1 hour, then turn the dough out onto a well-floured cutting board or marble slab. Roll out with a rolling pin to 13-inch round. Use the pastry to line the bottom and sides of a 10-inch tart pan. Prick the bottom with a fork, then chill the pastry for at least 30 minutes.

Preheat oven to 400 degrees. Coat a sheet of aluminum foil with butter and place, butter-side down, into the tart shell, fitting the foil to the shell. Fill with weights. Bake shell in hot oven for 12 to 15 minutes. Check midway through baking time and remove foil and weights. Prick bottom again if it bulges during baking.

Cool the tart shell, then fill with pastry cream and cover with desired fruit, arranging the fruit in a decorative pattern. Heat the apricot preserves with the water until liquid, then strain and use to glaze the tart.

Gâteau Saint-Honoré
(Cream Puff Cake)

Pâte Brisée
Pâte à Choux
Crème Patissière
1 envelope unflavored gelatin, mixed with 2 tablespoons cold water

8 egg whites
½ cup confectioner's sugar
1⅓ cups granulated sugar
⅓ cup water

Preheat oven to 400 degrees. Cut out a circle of Pâte Brisée about 9 inches in diameter and ¼ inch thick. Trim edges smoothly. Place this on a lightly buttered baking sheet. Pipe a crown of half the Pâte à Choux around the edge of the pastry, using a pastry bag with a large, smooth nozzle. With the point of a kitchen knife, cut slits in the Pâte Brisée.

On another lightly buttered baking sheet, using a pastry bag and a small, smooth nozzle, prepare about 20 little balls of Pâte à Choux about the size of walnuts. Bake both for about 20 minutes in hot oven and set aside to cool.

Set aside half the Crème Patissière and chill, covered. Stir gelatin mixture into second half of Crème Patissière. Cool to room temperature.

Beat egg whites until stiff, then beat in confectioner's sugar, 1 tablespoon at a time, until stiff and glossy. Fold egg whites into thickened Crème Patissière. Place baked tart pastry on a serving plate and fill with Crème Patissière mixture; chill until firm. When ready to serve, use a pastry bag with a small nozzle to fill the small cream puffs with chilled plain Crème Patissière.

Boil sugar and water until it reaches 310° on a candy therometer. Dip small cream puffs into caramel and stick in place on top of crown around edge of pastry. With a fork, drizzle remaining caramel in thin threads over top of entire cake. **Makes 1 large cake**.

Flan aux Cerises
(Cherry Flan)

Pâte Brisée
3 cups canned pitted dark sweet cherries, well drained
3 eggs

½ cup confectioner's sugar
½ cup all-purpose flour
⅓ cup (5 tablespoons) butter, melted
2 cups warm milk

Preheat oven to 350 degrees. Line the bottom and sides of a 10-inch tart pan with pastry. Cover the bottom of the mold with cherries.

Break eggs into a bowl and add confectioner's sugar and flour. Whisk until you have a very smooth batter. Add butter, still stirring with the whisk, and warm milk. Mix all ingredients well, then pour over the cherries. Bake the flan in a moderate oven for about 1 hour.

*Note: You can substitute pitted apricots or peaches or cored pears for the cherries. In each case the fruit should be cut into small pieces.

Savarin au Rhum
(Rum Baba)

Pâté à Brioche, made with ½ recipe
1 cup dried currants
1 cup sugar

1 cup water
½ cup dark rum

Knead currants into brioche dough before first rise. Let rise until doubled in bulk, about 2 hours.

Grease a 1½-quart ring mold or 12 baba molds and fill three-fourths full with dough. Let rise until doubled in bulk, about 1 hour.

Preheat oven to 350 degrees. Bake in moderate oven for about 30 to 35 minutes for the savarin, 20 minutes for individual babas.

Boil sugar and water for 5 minutes, then remove from heat, cool, and stir in rum. Place ring or babas into a shallow dish and prick the cakes with a fork. Spoon syrup over the cakes, allowing the syrup to be absorbed into cakes. Serve, if desired, with whipped cream. **Makes 1 9-inch ring or 12 small babas.**

Mille-Feuilles
(Napoleons)

Pâté Feuilletée
Crème Patissiere

½ cup finely chopped toasted almonds
Confectioner's sugar

Preheat oven to 400 degrees. Roll out Pâté Feuilletée into 2 oblongs 12 x 10 inches and ⅛ inch thick. Cut each oblong into strips, each about 2 inches wide and 10 inches long. Put the strips on a lightly buttered baking sheet, prick with a fork, and bake in a hot oven until crisp; remove from oven when the pastry has risen nicely.

Let pastry cool, then spread 10 of the strips with a thin layer of Crème Patissière, using a metal spatula to spread the cream. Pile up 5 of the strips in each stack, then top each with sixth plain strip. Cut each stack into 3 pieces. Spread edges of each pastry with remaining Crème Patissière. Sprinkle sides with almonds and dust confectioner's sugar on top of each. **Makes 6.**

Plum Pudding

8 ounces golden raisins
8 ounces Smyrna raisins
8 ounces Corinth raisins
20 pitted dried prunes, chopped
1 cup mixed candied fruits
1 pound beef kidney suet, finely chopped
Pinch of salt
Pinch of grated nutmeg

Pinch of ground ginger
1 pound dark brown sugar
½ cup Madeira wine
1⅓ cups dark rum
4 cups all-purpose flour
10 eggs
Confectioner's sugar
Dark rum

In a large bowl, mix all the ingredients except flour and eggs and marinate for 12 hours.

Preheat oven to 350 degrees. Add flour and eggs and mix well with a wooden spoon until a soft consistency is achieved. Pour into a well-buttered 10 x 3 x 3-inch loaf pan, and put the mold into a larger pan with water coming halfway up the sides of pan. Bring the water to a boil, then transfer to moderate oven and bake for 50 to 60 minutes or until firm to the touch. Unmold the plum pudding onto a long silver serving platter. Sprinkle with confectioner's sugar and pour on a good bit of dark rum and set aflame. **Makes 1 10 x 3 x 3-inch loaf.**

Gâteau au Miel Portugais
(Portuguese Honey Cake)

½ cup Malaga raisins
¼ cup Madeira wine
4 cups all-purpose flour
1 cup honey, heated until warm
3 cups confectioner's sugar
⅔ cup butter
⅔ cup lard, softened
4 eggs
Grated peel of 1 orange and 1 lemon
3½ cups chopped walnut meats

1 envelope active dry yeast
½ cup chopped blanched almonds
½ cup diced lemon pulp, without seeds
Pinch of ground cinnamon
1 Star anise, crushed
4 whole cloves, crushed
Pinch of freshly ground white pepper
¼ cup brandy

Marinate raisins in Madeira for 2 or 3 hours; drain and reserve wine.

Sift flour into a bowl. Add honey, sugar, butter, lard, and eggs. Knead the mixture with your hands until it is smooth. Add the marinated raisins, reserved Madeira, and remaining ingredients. Mix gently, lifting the ingredients with a wooden spatula. Let rest for 24 hours in a cool place, covered with a dampened kitchen towel.

Preheat oven to 350 degrees. Pour the mixture into a well-buttered and floured 2-quart mold, then bake in moderate oven for 40 to 50 minutes or until firm. **Makes 1 large cake.**

Sorbet aux Fruits
(Fruit Ice)

1½ cups water
1½ cups granulated sugar
3 cups fruit juice or purée orange, pineapple, or lemon juice or strained puréed strawberries or raspberries)

Juice of 2 oranges and 2 lemons (for lemon sherbet, omit oranges and use 4 lemons)

In a saucepan, combine water and sugar. Bring to a boil and boil 5 minutes. Cool. Stir in desired fruit. Pour into an ice cream freezer container and process according to manufacturer's instructions, stirring every 30 minutes, until firm. Cover and freeze until needed. **Makes 1½ quarts.**

Glace à la Vanille
(Vanilla Ice Cream)

1 vanilla bean	6 egg yolks
1 quart light cream	2 cups confectioner's sugar

Put vanilla bean in milk and bring to the boil. Using a wooden spatula, mix egg yolks and confectioner's sugar, stirring until the mixture is completely smooth. Pour boiling milk over the sugar–egg mixture and remove the vanilla bean. Put the mix in a double boiler and stir constantly over simmering water until the cream covers a spoon. Do no allow to boil. Let cool and freeze in an ice cream machine or crank freezer, according to manufacturer's instructions. **Makes 1¼ quarts**.

Variations

Coffee Ice Cream

Omit vanilla bean and add 2 tablespoons instant coffee to hot milk.

Chocolate Ice Cream

Omit vanilla bean and add 4 ounces (4 squares) unsweetened chocolate to milk. Heat until melted.

Pistachio Ice Cream

Fold in ½ cup each finely chopped blanched almonds and pistachios.

Almond and Fruit Ice Cream

Prepare Vanilla Ice Cream. Blanch 1 pound almonds, grind fine in food processor, and add to the ice cream mix, together with 1 cup fruit preserves (peach, apricot, cherry, pineapple, strawberry, raspberry, blueberry).

Chocolate Ice Cream Liègoise

1¼ quarts Chocolate Ice Cream	½ cup confectioner's sugar
5 ounces (5 squares) unsweetened chocolate	½ cup crème fraîche or heavy cream
2 cups milk, heated to boiling	

In a saucepan over very low heat, melt chocolate. Gradually whisk in milk and sugar. Bring to a boil, lower heat, and simmer 10 minutes or until thick. Cool and then chill.

Whip the crème fraîche. Spoon chocolate sauce into dessert goblets and top with chocolate ice cream. Place whipped cream into a pastry bag with a star tip and pipe rosettes on top.

Cassata à la Néapolitain
(Neapolitan Cassata)

1¼ quarts Vanilla Ice Cream   1 cup Crème Chantilly
1½ pints Chocolate Ice Cream

Line a 2-quart melon mold with cheesecloth and pour in a thick layer of Vanilla
Ice Cream. Freeze until hard. Fill center with Chocolate Ice Cream, cover, and
freeze until hard.

    When hard, dip mold into lukewarm water and then use cheesecloth
to pull ice cream out of mold. Place on a platter and remove cheesecloth. Garnish
with rosettes of Crème Chantilly.

Parfait Rothschild

 8 egg yolks   ½ cup fruit preserves
1¾ cups water   2 cups crème fraîche or heavy cream
1½ cups granulated sugar
 ⅓ cup kirsch

Using a whisk, mix egg yolks with ¼ cup cold water. Bring remaining water and
sugar to a boil and boil 5 minutes. Gradually beat hot syrup into egg yolks and
continue beating until the mixture cools completely. Stir in kirsch and fruit
preserves. Whip crème fraîche and fold into egg mixture. Pour into a cheese-
cloth-lined 2-quart mold, cover with foil, and freeze until hard. If desired,
mixture may be frozen in parfait glasses.

    Dip mold into lukewarm water for a few seconds and use cheesecloth
to pull out of mold. Remove cheesecloth and serve.

Omelette à la Norvégienne
(Baked Alaska)

1 Genoise Sponge Layer   6 egg whites
½ cup apricot preserves   ¾ cup confectioner's sugar
1 quart desired ice cream

Preheat oven to 450 degrees. On a heatproof platter, place cake layer and spread
with preserves. Spoon ice cream in a mound on top of cake. Replace in freezer.

    Beat egg whites until stiff in a bowl. Gradually beat in sugar, 1
tablespoon at a time, until whites are stiff and glossy. Cover ice cream with some
of the meringue. Using a metal spatula, smooth out meringue, giving it a round
shape. Decorate, using a pastry bag with a medium fluted nozzle, with rosettes
of remaining meringue. Put the Baked Alaska on rack of very hot oven and bake
until nicely browned, about 3 to 4 minutes.

Postscript

Some time ago, the *France*—under another name—left Le Havre for good. Could it have continued to sail under the French flag? That is not up to me to say, and far more competent people than myself were tormented over this problem without any happy result. It is nevertheless quite painful to concede that another country was better equipped to exploit this great ship.

In 1937, at the beginning of my long career, there were many old salts who felt that ships—like people—have a soul, and like people enjoy fluctuating fortunes, good and ill luck. This is certainly true, as certain vessels only know success while others are dismal failures from the start. In view of the *France's* brilliant career, she surely left for Bremerhaven with a light heart, sailing along a route she knew so well. People in Le Havre still remember the great ship's last appearance, the whole town acclaiming her from the docks. The next day, the local paper *Havre Libre* had a headline: FRANCE COMES HOME. This great Norman port, which had seen the great ship come and go so often, was heartbroken to see her slowly rot over a period of five years on what is justly called "the dock of the forgotten."

The *France* deserved more consideration. She was sold to an oil tycoon, who wished to make her into a museum full of masterpieces. But a boat is not made to be a prisoner to a dock. She must dominate the seas, so it was with some relief that I learned of the *France's* new destiny. Sold to a Norwegian shipowner, she is plying the tourist routes again, and I wish her, with all my heart, a long life and hope she never meets the sad fate of her predecessors: the *Lafayette* which burned in dry dock at Le Havre in 1938, the *Paris* that burned in Le Havre in 1939 as she was about to leave for New York, or the proud *Normandie* that perished in the same way, drowned by tons of water poured over her as she burned at New York's Pier 88. And there were others. The famous *Île-de-France*, known as the "Rue de la Paix of the Atlantic" had a brilliant and heroic war record, only to be sold to the Japanese in 1958 and burned to make a film. Then, there was the gracious *Antilles*, "the gazelle of the sea," which foundered on a coral reef near Mustique, burning up like a match box, the flames rapidly reaching the elegant dining room that was dominated by a lovely—and preordained—tapestry entitled *Firebird*.

Hopefully, when the *France* has finished her brilliant career and has reached a ripe old age, she will be discreetly scrapped as was her predecessor at Dunkerque. In the meanwhile, I wish good luck and fair winds to this great ambassador of my country, to this wonderful liner on which I spent twelve of the happiest and most fulfilled years of a maritime life.

Henri Le Huédé
Bourg de Batz, October 15, 1979

Index

African peanut (ground nut) soup, 69
Agnelet Pascal Rôti St.-Laud, 172
Aiguillette de Charolais à l'anglaise ou à la ficelle, 162
Aïoli sauce, 48
Albigeoise sauce, 49
Allemande sauce, 47
Almond(s)
    and fruit ice cream, 240
    young green beans sautéed with, 192
Alsatian onion soup with cheese, 66–67
Américaine sauce, 43
Anchovies
    and ripe olives, onion tart with, 200
    tuna, shrimp and, scrambled eggs with, 77
Andalouse(ian)
    cream of tomato soup, 64
    sauce, 49
Antiboise sauce, 50
Antilles okra soup, 68–69
Appareil à meringues, 230
Apple(s)
    celeriac and endive salad with ham, potato, and, 219
    fritters, roast duckling with, 96–97
    Normandy omelette, 79
    roasted stuffed quail with, 106
    sautéed veal chops normande, 165
Arlésienne sauce, 36
Artichauts farçis à la Barigoule, 188–189
Artichauts, see *Fonds d'artichauts*
Artichoke(s)
    general preparation, 188
    bottoms, soufflé-stuffed, 189
    hearts
        braised, 189
        filet mignon with sweet peppers, mushrooms, new potatoes, and, 160
        stuffed with sweetbreads and truffles, 180
    soufflé, 83
    soup with duck quenelles, cream of, 61–62
    stuffed, 188–189
Asperges de Malmaison tièdes sauce sanguine, 190
Asparagus
    sauces for, 190
    with sauce sanguine, 190
    soup with sorrel, cream of, 62

Aubergine
    farcie biscassienne, 197
    farcie languedocienne, 198
    frite nîmoise, 197
Augeoise
    sauce, 49
    shrimp cocktail with sauce, 144
Aurore sauce, 43
Avocado
    with crab, 190
    guacamole, 191
    with roquefort dressing, 191

Baba, rum, 238
Bacon
    chicken in red wine with mushrooms, onion, and, 90–91
    and dandelion salad, 221
Baked Alaska, 241
Ballottine de dindonneau truffée et braisée, aux marrons de l'Ardèche, 109–110
Bar argenté de golfe braisé ou rôti Jean-Bart, 129
Barley
    broth Miss Belsey, 56
    oxtail soup with, 57
    pearl, 215
Bass, *see* Sea bass
Bavarian coffee cream, 233
Bavaroise au café, 233
Bean(s)
    with almonds, young green, 192
    in browned butter, 191
    garden vegetables braised in butter, 206
    glazed mixed vegetables, 206
    green, 191–192
    salad, lettuce and green, 218
    soup, Portuguese, 68
Béarnaise
    grilled salmon steaks with sauce, 125
    sauce, 44
Beatrice salad, 219
Béchamel sauce, 34
Beef, 152–163
    boiled English style (on the string), 162
    Brazilian picadinho, 161
    consommé
        classic, 54
        clear double, 54
    kebab São Paulo with pilaf, 163
    marrow, celery hearts with, 194

peppered steak with armagnac, 160–161
roast:
  with artichoke hearts, sweet peppers, mushrooms, and new potatoes, 160
  Boston style, 156
  Bressane, 154–155
  Ducs de Bourbon, 155
  à l'Île de France, 153–154
  Kansas beef, Virginia style, 153
  loin roast Armenonville, 157
  Ohio boneless rib with glazed vegetables, 132–133
  and Yorkshire pudding, 156–157
sirloin grilled with shallot butter, 161
tournedos
  bergerette, 157
  Monselet, 159
  Rossini, 158
  Henri IV, 158
Beet(s)
  chicory and celery salad, 221
  and endive salad, 218
  lettuce, endive, celery, and, salad of, 223
Beignets de maïs, 196
Belgian endive, *see* Endive
Bercy sauce, 44
Beurre
  de fines herbes, 35
  manié, 35
Biarrotte sauce, 50
Bird's nest soup, 60
Bisque de homard Cleveland, 72
Blanquette de veau à l'Ancienne, 169
Blinis with caviar, 150
Bolognese sauce, 36
Bordelaise sauce, 36
Borscht lithuanien au fumet de caneton, 72
Bouginaise salad, 270
Bouillabaisse de vieux port, 70–71
Bourride provençale, 71
Brains and eggplant, fried eggs with, 77
Branche de céleri garnie au bleu d'Auvergne, 194
Brandade de morue Bénédictine, 134–135
Brazilian
  fish and shrimp soup, 148
  picadinho, 161
Bread sauce, roast Scottish grouse with, 104–105
Brignolaise sauce, 50
Brill, 121–123
  braised medallion of, stuffed with salmon mousse, 122
  gourmet's filet of, 123
  sautéed medallions Périnette, 122
  steamed steaks Véronique, 121
Brioche dough, 227
Brochettes de foies de volailles grillées, 93
Brown sauces, 36–43
Brown veal stock, 55
Brussels sprouts, Polish style, 192

Burmese curried lamb, 176
butter(s)
  clarified, 35
  compound, 35
  herbed, 36

Cabbage, pork roast with, 179
Cailles farcies
  braisées "France," 107
  de la Suisse, normande, 106
Cake
  cream puff, 237
  Portuguese honey, 239
Calf's liver, sautéed with onion rings, 181
Calvados, chicken fricassée with, 90
Cambridge sauce, 50
Caneton
  d'Aylesbury rôti aux oranges, 94–95
  braisé au Chambertin, 97
  Chalandais farci, rôti "France," 98–99
  duclairois en salmis à la rouennaise, 100
  de Long Island rôti à l'ananas frais, 95–96
  nantais braisé aux navets nouveaux, 99
  nantais rôti Dame Catherine, 98
  rouennais rôti aux beignets, augerons, 96–97
Caprice mixed salad, 222
Caramel custard, 232
Cardinal des mers au gratin Thermidor, 142
Carottes à la crème, 192
Carré d'agneau des Causses rôti bazadaise, 171
Carré d'agneau des Causses rôti sarladaise, 171
Carré de porc braisé bavaroise, 179
Carré de veau de l'Allier braisé armentierais, 163–164
Carrots
  creamed, 192
  garden vegetables braised in butter, 206
  glazed mixed vegetables, 206
  peas, cauliflower, and, boiled eggs with, 79–80
Caruso sauce, 37
Cassata à la néapolitaine, 241
Cauchoise mixed salad, 222–223
Cauliflower
  general preparation, 193
  au gratin, 193
  Milan style, 193
  peas, carrots, and, boiled eggs with, 79–80
Caviar d'Astrakhan aux blinis Gretshnevoi, 150
Caviar, blinis with, 150
Celeriac and endive salad with apples, ham, and potato, 219
Celery
  hearts
    with beef marrow, 194
    Bolognese, 194
  salad
    beet, chicory, and, 221
    beet, lettuce, endive, and, 223
  stuffed with Auvergne cheese, 194

Cèpes à la bordelaise, 200
Champagne, roast chicken with, 86–97
Champignons de couche sautés girondine, 199
Chanterelles, roast squab with, 101
Chantilly
    charlotte, 235
    sauce, 50
Charcutière sauce, 41
Charlotte
    chantilly, 235
    russe, 234
Chasseur sauce, 37
Château potatoes, 210
Chateaubriand sauce, 37
Cheese croquettes, savoy, 82–83
Cherry flan, 237
Chervil and croûtons, cream of lettuce soup
        with, 63
Chestnuts
    ballottine of turkey with, 109–110
    braised, 195
    Mont Blanc, 234
    mousseline, 195
Chevreuil sauce, 38
Chicken, 86–94
    consommé
        basic, 55
        chancelière, 59
        clear double, 55
        with crème royale, 59
        with quenelles, 61
        and shrimp, 58
    Crébillon, braised, 89
    fricassée with calvados, 91
    Kiev, 92
    liver(s)
        en brochette, 93
        spread, 94
    and mushrooms, stuffed eggs with, 80
    pâté
        and pork, with truffles, 183
        truffled poultry liver terrine, 184
    and potatoes, poached eggs with, 75
    in red wine with onions, bacon, and
        mushrooms, 90–91
    roast
        with champagne, 86–87
        English style, stuffed, 88
        stuffed with truffles, 87
        with Virginia smoked ham, stuffed,
            88–89
    soup
        mulligatawney, 66
        with sorrel, cream of, 66
        and tongue, cream of mushroom soup
            with, 62
        with vegetables, 58
        with vegetables and pastry sticks, 59
        See also consommés
    with tomato sauce, grilled, 92–93

Chicory
    mixed salad, 222
    salad of celery, beets, and, 221
Chiffonade salad, 223
Chilienne
    crab and shrimp cocktail with sauce, 146
    sauce, 49
Chocolate
    ice cream
        recipe for, 240
        liègeoise, 240
    mousse, 232
Choron sauce, 44
Choux de Bruxelles rissolés polonaise, 192
Choux-fleurs
    à la polonaise, 193
    dinandais dorés au Gruyère, 193
    à la milanaise, 193
Churrarco en brochette paulista, 163
Cingalaise sauce, 50
Clarified butter, 35
Classic beef consommé, 54
Clear double consommé
    beef, 54
    chicken, 55
Clear oxtail soup, 57
Cocktail de crabe sauce tango, 146
Coconut pudding, 231
Coeur d'artichaut dinandais au gratin friande,
        180
Coeur de céleri
    braisé Bolognese, 194
    à la moëlle, 193
Coeur de Charolais rôti Ducs de Bourbon, 155
Coeur de laitue
    braisés à l'écarlate, 199
    à la Russe, 218
Coffee ice cream, 240
Cold sauces, 48–52
Concombres étuvés à la crème, 197
Consommés (*consommé*), 54–61
    Belle Gabrielle, 58
    with chicken and shrimp, 58
    de Caret aux herbes, 56–57
    with cucumbers and rice, 58
    with garnishes, 56–61
    des gladiateurs, 57
    aux nids salanganes, 60
    oxtail clair, 57
    à la siamoise, 58
    de volaille
        Boieldieu, 61
        Chancelière, 59
        Murillo, 59
        des viveurs, 59
Contrefilet
    auvergnat rôti Armenonville, 157
    Limousin grillé au beurre d'échalottes, 161
    salessois rôti avec Yorkshire Pudding, 156–157
Coq au vin sauté à l'auxerroise, 90–91

Coquelet
  de Basse-Cour farci et rôti à l'anglaise, 88
  de Métairie grillé languedocienne, 92–93
Coquille St.-Jacques au gratin "France," 146–147
Corn
  on the cob, 195
  creamed, Hungarian, 196
  croquettes, 196
  fritters, 196
  lamb kebabs with creamed, 175
  soup, American cream of, 65
Côte de boeuf de l'Ohio rôti fleuriste, 152–153
Côte de veau
  Choletais sautée Cordon Bleu, 165–166
  de l'Allier sautée Prince Orloff, 166
  du Gatinais sautée normande, 165
Cotelettes d'agneau sautées St.-Antonin, 173–174
Coupes
  de camarons sauce mousquetaire, 144
  de crevettes sauce audoise, 144
  de fruits de mer sauce chilienne, 146
Courgette frite à l'anglaise, 205
Court bouillon, 34
Couscous marocain, 177
Crab, 145–146
  Antilles stuffed, 145
  avocado with, 190
  cocktail with sauce tango, 146
  and shrimp cocktail with sauce chilienne, 146
Crabes farcis à l'antillaise, 145
Crayfish
  and mussel garnish, braised stuffed red snapper with, 131–132
  sauce, poached salmon with, 124
Cream, whipped and sweetened, 230
Cream puff
  cake, 237
  pastry, 228
Creamed soups, 61–72
Creams, *see* Pastry creams
Crème
  anglaise, 230
  à l'anglaise sauce, 45
  Chantilly, 230
  fraîche, 35
  frangipane, 230–231
  de legumes glacée vichyssoise, 65
  de maïs Washington, 65
  patissière, 231
  renversée au caramel, 232
  royale, chicken consommé with, 59
  de volaille Germiny à l'oseille, 66
  de volaille Mulligatawney, 66
Crêpes (*crêpes*)
  de fruits de mer au gratin "France," 149
  seafood, au gratin à la *France,* 149
Crevettes sautées bordelaise, 144
Croissants, leavened, 228

Croquettes (*croquettes*)
  corn, 196
  de homard, 143
  lobster, 143
  de maïs, 196
  de pommes de terre, 212
  potato, 212
  rice, 214
  de riz, 214
Croquignolles Savoyardes, 82–83
Cucumbers
  creamed, 197
  and rice, consommé with, 58
Cuisses de grenouilles
  sautées provençales, 136
  sautées arlésiennes, 136
Curry
  sauce, 45
  vinaigrette, salad with, 224
Custard
  caramel, 231
  cream, 230

Dandelion and bacon salad, 221
Darne de saumon
  grillée, sauce béarnaise, 125
  rose grillée languedocienne, 126
Dauphine potatoes, 210
Daurade
  fraîche du Pacifique braisée Douamont, 131–132
  fraîche sénégalaise braisée à la goréenne, 130–131
  Lozia al Dao, 131
Délices de sole
  Douvres étuvés au whisky, 116
  étuvés Castiglione, 113
  étuvés Grandousier, 114
  honfleuraise étuvés normande, 115
  de la Manche "France," 114–115
Demi-glace, 33
Desserts, 231–241
Diable
  grilled squab with sauce, 103
  sauce, 38
Doughs, recipes for, 226–230
Duck, 94–100
  with apple fritters, 96–97
  braised in wine, 97
  consommé, Lithuanian Borscht with, 72
  à la *France* (roasted and stuffed), 98–99
  with new turnips, 99
  with orange, 94–95
  with pineapple, 95–96
  and pork terrine with truffles, 184
  with prunes, 98
  quenelles, cream of artichoke soup with, 61–62
  à la rouennaise, salmis of, 100

Egg(s), 73–84
  au gratin Antonin Carême, 82
  baked
    with morels, 75
    with smoked ham and mushrooms, 75
    with tomato and eggplant, 74
  boiled
    with cauliflower, peas, and carrots,
      79–80
    tarts with ham and mushrooms, 82
  en cocotte
    with beef tongue, 74
    chanoinesse, 74
  fried
    Ali-Bab, 76
    with brains and eggplant, 77
    with mixed vegetables, 76
  nissarde, 81
  omelet, *see* Omelet
  poached with potatoes and chicken, 75
  scrambled with shrimp, anchovies, and
    tuna, 77
  stuffed
    with chicken and mushrooms, 80
    Oudinot, 80–81
Eggplant
  and brains, fried eggs with, 77
  ratatouille niçoise, 206
  stuffed
    baked, 198
    with lamb, 197
  and tomato
    baked eggs with, 74
    fried, 197
Embassy soufflé, 236
Empress rice, 233
Endive
  au gratin Monselet, 198
  meunière, 198–199
  salad
    and beet, 218
    and celeriac, with apples, ham, and
      potato, 219
    celery, beet, lettuce, and, 223
Endives
  Flamandes au gratin Monselet, 198
  lilloises meunière, 198–199
Épinards, 203
Escalope de veau laitier
  grillée Napoléon, 168–169
  sautée verdunoise, 168
Essence de Poisson, 34
Étuvée d'agneau
  au currie Birmane, 176
  à l'irlandaise, 176

Farce à Gratin, 94
Filet de boeuf
  du Kansas rôti à la façon de Virginie, 153
  de la marche rôti bressane, 154–155

Filet de boeuf de Charolais
  rôti à la Boston, 156
  rôti "Île de France," 153–154
  sauté languedocienne, 160
Filets de sole de la Manche étuvés Coquelin,
  112–113
Fish, 11–135
  extract, 34
  glaze, 34
  and shrimp, Brazilian, 148
  soup, provençal, 71
  stock, 56
  velouté, 33
  See also individual fishes
Flan aux cerises, 237
Flan, cherry, 237
Foie de veau laitier sauté aux beignets lyonnais,
  181
Fonds d'artichauts
  braisés, 189
  à la valaisane, 189
Foyot sauce, 44
Frangipane cream, 230–231
French-fried potatoes, Pont-Neuf, 210
Fritter batter, 229
Frogs legs
  arlésienne, 136
  provençale, 136
Fruit
  and almond ice cream, 240
  ice, 239
  omelet, 235
  soufflés, 236
  tarts, 236–237

Gadski salad, 224
Garden vegetables braised in butter, 206
Gâteau
  au miel, portugais, 239
  Saint-Honoré, 237
Gavarnie
  poached turbot with sauce, 117
  sauce, 46
Gazpacho, 69
Gênoise
  sauce, 50
  sponge layer, 229
Genovese sauce, 38
German fried potatoes, 208
Gigot de pré salé
  rôti savoyarde, 173
  rôti à la solognote, 172–173
Gigot de chevreuil grand veneur, 182
Gingered broth, 60
Glace
  de poisson, 34
  de viande, 33
  à la vanille, 240

Glazed vegetables
  mixed, 206
  squab with, 102
Glazes, see Meat glaze, Fish glaze
Gnocchi (gnocchi)
  French style, 214–215
  à la parisienne, 214–215
  à la romaine, 215
  Roman style, 215
Goujonnettes de sole frites sauce Gribiche, 116
Gourmandines de veau laitier au gratin
  "France," 167
Green beans, see Beans
Gribiche
  fried sole with sauce, 116
  sauce, 52
Grimod sauce, 50
Ground nut soup, African, 69
Grouse (grouse)
  with bread sauce, roast Scottish, 104–105
  écossaise rôtie avec bread sauce, 104–105
Guacamole, 191
Guinea hen
  à la France, boneless breast of, 108–109
  with stuffed tomatoes, boneless breast of,
    107–108

Half-glaze, 33
Half-puff pastry, 226
Ham, see Pork
Hare terrine à la Diane, 185
Harlequin soufflé, 236
Haricots verts frais
  sautés amandine, 192
  sautés au beurre noisette, 191
Harvester's salt pork omelet, 79
Hash-brown potatoes, 209
Herbed butter, 35
Hollandaise sauce, 45
Homard
  de l'Atlantique grillé à la Léonard, 138–139
  aux douze aromates, 139
Honey cake, Portuguese, 239
Hussarde sauce, 38–39

Ice, fruit, 239
Ice cream
  almond and fruit ice, 240
  chocolate, 240
  coffee, 240
  liègeoise, chocolate, 240
  pistachio, 240
  vanilla, 240
Irish stew, 176
Irlandaise sauce, 45
Italian wine soup, 68
Italienne sauce, 39

Jambalaya de Damao, 148–149
Jambon

de Paris grillé Hawaïen, 178–179
d'York braisé Nesselrode, 178
d'York braisé bayonnaise, 178
Japanese salad, 224
Jardinière de primeurs étuvée au beurre fin, 206
Jarret de veau laitier à l'italienne, 170

Kebab d'agneau grillé persane, 174
Kebabs
  lamb, with creamed corn, 175
  Persian style shish, 174
Kidneys, grilled veal, 182

Lamb, 170–177
  Burmese curried, 176
  chops, breaded and sautéed, 173–174
  couscous, Moroccan, 177
  eggplant stuffed with, 197
  kebabs
    with creamed corn, 175
    Persian style shish, 174
  roast
    leg of, savoyarde, 173
    leg of, solognote, 172–173
    rack of, bazadaise, 171
    rack of, with truffled potatoes, 171
    saddle of, à la France, 170
    spring lamb, St. Laud, 172
  stew, Irish, 176
Langouste
  fraîche de Bonne Espérance rôtie aux épices,
    142
  rose de Hong Kong rôtie à la diable, 141
  de tropiques étuvée Newburg, 141
Lavallière sauce, 37
La Varenne sauce, 50
Legumes glacés, 206
Lentil soup, cream of, 63
Lettuce
  braised with peas, 201
  hearts
    braised, 199
    Russian style, 218
  peas cooked with minced, 201
  salad
    endive, celery, beet, and, 223
    and green bean, 218
  soup with croûtons and chervil, cream of,
    63
Lithuanian borscht with duckling
    consommé, 72
Livournaise sauce, 39
Lobster, 138–143
  à l'américaine, 140
  bisque with bourbon, 72
  with butter sauce, 140
  croquettes, 143
  à la diable, 141
  grilled, 138–139
  gratinéed à la Dunkirk, 143

Newburg, 141
roasted with herbs, 142
and shrimp jambalaya, 148–149
Thermidor, 142
with twelve herbs, 139
Longe de veau de l'Allier braisée Vallée de Bray,
164–165
Lorenzo salad, 220
Lorette potatoes, 211
Lotte de mer sautée girondine, 133
Loup de Calanque
braisé "France" ou à la facon du chef, 128–129
grillé aux herbes de Lavandou, 130
Lyonnaise potatoes, 208

au Madère sauce, 42
Madiera sauce, stuffed tomatoes with, 205
Magali sauce, 50
Maïs égrené à la hongroise, 196
Maître de chai sauce, 39
Maltaise sauce, 46
Marrons braisés, 195
Mayonnaises, 48–51
sauce, 49
See also individual sauces
Meat glaze, 33
Meats, 151–186
See also individual meats
Médaillon de barbue
étuvé véronique, 121
nordique étuvé havraise, 122
nordique sauté périnette, 122
Medaillon de porc sauté à la danoise, 179
Medaillon de saumon québecois farci sauté
Gastera, 127
Medaillon de turbot
boulonnaise braisé bonne hôtesse, 120
lorientais sauté Périnette, 119
Meringue shell, 230
Messine sauce, 46
Mikado sauce, 46
Mille-feuilles, 238
Mixed salad
with almonds, 221
with pink dressing, 220
See also individual salads and ingredients
Mocha mousse, 233
Monkfish, sautéed girondine, 133
Mont Blanc, chestnut, 234
Mont-Blanc aux marrons, 234
Mont Bry sauce, 50
Morels, baked eggs with, 75
Mornay sauce, 46
Moroccan couscous, 177
Moscow salad, 219
Mousquetaire
sauce, 51
Spanish prawns with sauce, 144
Mousse au chololat, 232
Mousseline
de marrons, 195

de saumon, 127
sauce, 46
poached turbot with, 117
Moutarde
poached turbot with, 117
sauce, 46
Mulligatawny soup, 66
Mushrooms
baked eggs with smoked ham and, 75
cèpes à la bordelaise, 200
chicken in red wine with onions, bacon,
and, 90–91
and chicken, stuffed eggs with, 80
and ham, boiled egg tarts with, 82
with ham and tomato, sautéed with, 199
and new potatoes, filet mignon with artichoke hearts, sweet peppers, and,
160
and pepper omelet, 78
soufflé, 84
soup, cream of, with tongue and chicken,
62
veal stew with onions and, 169
Mussel(s)
and crayfish garnish, braised stuffed red
snapper with, 131–132
braised stuffed turbot medallions, 120

Nantua sauce, 47
Napoleons, 238
Neapolitan cassata, 241
Niccolini parfumé au Chianti, 68
Noisette potatoes, 211
Noix de ris de veau panetière, 181
Noodles, fresh, 216
Normande sauce, 47
Normandy omelet, 79
Nouilles fraîches, 216

Occitane sauce, 51
Oeufs
brouillés Offenbach, 77
en cocotte
bridaine, 74
chanoinesse, 74
au gratin Antonin Carême, 82
farcis
Fadette, 80
nissarde, 81
Oudinot, 80–81
au plat Amélie, 75
frits
Ali-Bab, 76
Camus, 77
Hortillone, 76
mollets
aubergiste, 82
Grisélidis, 79–80

à la neige, 232
au plat
    Catherinette, 74
    Ermenonville, 75
    pochés Belle Otéro, 75
Oignons frits, 200
Okra soup, Antilles, 68–69
Olive(s)
    onion tart with anchovies and ripe, 200
    and shallot sauce, braised red snapper with, 131
Omelet
    fruit, 235
    harvester's salt pork, 79
    Normandy, 79
    pepper and mushroom, 78
    with smoked pork, potato, and cheese, 78
Omelette
    Brayaude, 78
    aux fruits, 235
    des moissonneurs, 79
    à la normande, 79
    à la norvégienne, 241
    piperade, 78
Onion(s)
    baked potatoes and, 208
    chicken in red wine with bacon, mushrooms, and, 90–91
    deep-fried rings, 200
    soup
        with cheese, Alsatian, 67
        with pasta, cream of, 67
    tart with anchovies and ripe olives, 200
    veal stew with mushrooms and, 169
Orange, roast duckling with, 94–95
Orge perlé, 215
Ossobuco, 170
Oxtail soup
    with barley, 57
    clear, 57
Oyster sauce, sole with, 115

Paloise sauce, 44
Parfait Rothschild, 241
Parmesan cheese soufflé, 83
Parsley, deep-fried, 201
Partridge salmis Sologne, 105
Pasta
    basic recipe for, 216
    cream of onion soup with, 67
    sauces, *see* sauce section
Pastry
    cream, 231
    creams, 230–231
    dough, *see* Doughs
Pâte
    à brioche, 227
    brissée, 227
    à choux, 228

à croissants, 228
    feuilletée, 226
    à frire, 229
    à gênoise, 229
    à Savoie, 229
Pâté and terrines, 183–186
    See also individual meats
Pâté de foies de lapin en crépinettes, 186
Paulette sauce, 48
Paupiettes de jambon d'York dorés Viroflay, 180
Peanut soup, African, 69
Pearl barley, 215
Pea(s)
    boiled eggs with carrots, cauliflower, and, 79–80
    braised with lettuce, 201
    cooked with minced lettuce, 201
    country style, 202
    à la française, 201
    garden vegetables braised in butter, 206
    glazed mixed vegetables, 206
    soup, cream of fresh, 64
Pepper(s)
    filet mignon with mushrooms, new potatoes, and sweet, 160
    and mushroom omelet, 78
    potatoes and sweet, 209
    ratatouille niçoise, 206
Périgueux sauce, 40
Persil frit, 201
Petit homard
    de l'Atlantique à la nage, 140
    du Maine à l'américaine, 140
Petit langouste rose du Cap au gratin dunkerquois, 143
Petite marmite du Vert-Galant, 58
Petits-pois
    d'Éyssines à la française, 201
    fins étuvés aux laitues, 201
    du val de Loire paysanne, 202
Picadinho à la brésilienne, 161
Picadinho, Brazilian, 161
Pigeon, *see* Squab
Pigeonneau
    biset grillé crapaudine, 103
    biset sauté minute, 104
    de nid, 101
    en compôte St.-Germain, 102
    rôti bucheronne, 101
    rôti sur canapé, 102-3
Pike quenelles à la *France*, 135
Pilaf, *see* Rice
Pilaw de riz sauvage, 214
Pineapple, roast Long Island Duckling with, 95–96
Piquante sauce, 40
Pissaladière, 200
Pistachio ice cream, 240
Pistou du pays provençal, 71
Plum pudding, 238–239

Poire d'avocat garnie
  Baltimore, 190
  au Roquefort, 191
  yacamole, 191
Poivrade sauce, 40
Pommes de Terre
  à l'allemande, 208
  Anna, 208
  boulangère, 208
  colombine, 209
  croquettes, 212
  dauphine, 210
  frites Pont-Neuf, 210
  fondantes, 210
  Lorette, 211
  macaise, 209
  noisette, 211
  paille, 212
  sablées, 210
  sardalaise, 211
  savoyarde, 212
  soufflées, 209
Pork, 178–180
  and duck terrine with truffles, 184
  and rabbit liver crépinettes, 186
  ham
    baked eggs with mushrooms and, 75
    boiled-egg tarts with mushrooms and,
      82
    roasted stuffed chicken with Virginia
      smoked, 88–89
    with maple syrup, grilled, 178–189
    nesselrode, braised York, 178
    with pilaf, braised York, 178
    salad celeriac and endive, with apples,
      potato, and, 219
    soufflé, 84
    and tomato, sautéed with mushrooms
      with, 199
    rolls viroflay, York, 180
  medallions with apples and prunes, 179
  pâté with truffles, chicken, and, 183
  roast with cabbage, 179
  smoked, omelet with potato, cheese, and,
    78
  tomatoes stuffed with, 204
  and tongue terrine, marbled, 185
au Porto sauce, 41
Portuguese
  bean soup, 68
  honey cake, 239
Pot roast, *see* Beef
Potage
  à l'arachide, 69
  de gombos à l'antillaise, 68–69
  Saoto Babati, 60
Potato(es), 208–212
  Anna, 208
  baked
    macaise, 209

  with onions, 208
  stuffed with codfish, 134–135
  château, 210
  croquettes, 212
  dauphine, 210
  filet mignon with artichoke hearts, sweet
    peppers, mushrooms, and new, 160
  French-fried, Pont-Neuf, 210
  fried sablées, 210
  savoy gratinéed, 212
  hash-brown, 209
  Lorette, 211
  lyonnaise, 208
  noisette, 211
  omelet of cheese, smoked pork, and, 78
  parslied, 209
  with peppers (sweet), 209
  poached eggs with chicken and, 75
  puffed, 209
  salad of celeriac and endive with
    apples, ham, and, 219
  straw or string, 212
  stuffed with codfish, baked, 134–135
  truffled, 211
Poularde
  Bressane poêlée au champagne, 86–87
  dorée à la Kiev, 92
  du louragois farci rôti périgourdine, 87
  nantaise farci poché crébillon, 89
Poulet en fricassée valée d'Auge, 91
Poultry, 85–110
  See also Chicken, Duck, Squab
Poussin de Métairie farci rôti Virginie, 88–89
Praline soufflé, 236
Prawns with sauce mousquetaire, Spanish,
  144
Provençal
  fish soup with sauce aïoli, 71
  vegetable soup with garlic, basil, and
    herbs, 71
Prunes, roasted duckling with, 98
Pudding
  coconut, 231
  plum, 238–239
Pudding à la noix de coco, 231
Puff pastry dough, 226

Quail, 106–107
  with apples, roasted stuffed, 106
  à la France, stuffed braised, 107
Quenelles *(quenelles)*
  de brochet de Loire "France," 135
  chicken consommé with, 69
  cream of artichoke soup with duck, 61–62
  pike, *à la France*, 135
Quiche *(quiche)*
  du pays lorrain, 84
  lorraine, 84

Rabbit
  liver and pork crépinettes, 186
  terrine with pistachios, 186
Raifort sauce, 47
Raisin pilaf, 213
Ratatouille niçoise, 206
Ravigot sauce, 52
Red snapper
  braised à la goréenne, 130–131
  filets with olive and shallot sauce, 131
  stuffed, with mussel and crayfish garnish,
    131–132
Réforme sauce, 42
Régence sauce, 41
Rémoulade sauce, 51, 52
Rice, 213–214
  croquettes, 214
  empress, 233
  Milan style, 213
  pilaf, basic, 213
    raisin, 213
    saffron, 213
  St. Denis, 213
  Spanish, 213
  See also Wild rice
Riche
  poached turbot with sauce, 117
  sauce, 45
Risotto alla milanese, 213
Riz
  à l'impératrice, 233
  pilaw, 213
Robert sauce, 41
Rognon de veau laitier grillé, 182
Roquefort dressing, avocado with, 191
Rothschild, parfait, 241
Rouelle de thonine au four à l'algérienne, 134
Rum baba, 238
Russe sauce, 51

Saffron pilaf, 213
Salade
  archiduc, 218
  des Augustins, 218
  de Batavia Moscovite, 219
  Béatrice, 219
  beaucaire, 219
  bouginaise, 220
  caprice, 222
  châtelaine, 223
  cauchoise, 222–223
  chiffonade, 223
  Figaro, 223
  Gadski, 224
  japonaise, 224
  Lakmé, 224
  Lorenzo, 220
  madécasse, 220
  Mercédès, 221

Ninon, 221
de pissenlits aux rillons, 221
Santiago, 222
turquoise, 222
Salads, 217–224
Salmis de perdreaux à la solognote, 105
Salmon, 124–127
  braised à la France, 125
  filets, braised turbot with, 118–119
  medallions
    breaded Lemaire, 126
    stuffed, 127
  mousse, braised medallion of brill stuffed
    with, 122
  mousseline, 127
  poached with crayfish sauce, 124
  steaks
    with sauce béarnaise, 125
    with herbed butter, 126
Salsifis de Lunéville en beignets Orly, 202
Salsify fritters, 202
Salt cod, baked potatoes stuffed with,
  134–135
Sambel, 145
Sambel de crevettes de Java, 145
Sanquine sauce, asparagus with, 190
Santiago salad, 222
Sauces, 31–52
  bases for 33–34
  brown, 36–43
  white, 43–48
Sauces
  aïoli, 48
  albigeoise, 49
  allemande, 47
  andalouse, 49
  antiboise, 50
  augeoise, 49
  Aurore, 43
  béchamel, 34
  Bercy, 44
  biarotte, 50
  bolognese, 36
  bordelaise, 36
  brignolaise, 50
  Caruso, 37
  chasseur, 37
  Chateaubriand, 37
  chevreuil, 38
  chilienne, 49
  Choron, 44
  currie, 45
  diable, 38
  Foyot, 44
  Gavarnie, 46
  gênoise, 50
  genovese, 38
  Gribiche, 52
  Grimod, 50
  hollandaise, 45

hussarde, 38–39
irlandaise, 45
italienne, 39
Lavallière, 37
La Varenne, 50
maître de Chai, 39
maltaise, 46
mayonnaises, 48–51
messine, 46
Mikado, 46
Mont Bry, 50
Mornay, 46
mousquetaire, 51
mousseline, 46
moutarde, 46
Nantua, 47
normande, 47
pâloise, 44
Périgueux, 40
piquante, 40
poivrade, 40
Raifort, 47
ravigotte, 52
réforme, 42
régence, 41
rémoulade, 51–52
riche, 45
Robert, 41
russe, 51
sanguine, 190
toscane, 42
vénitienne, 48
vert-pré, 51
verte, 51
Vincent, 51
vinaigrette, 53
zingara, 43
Saumon rose
   de gare braisé "France," 125
   de gare braisé castel de Nérac, 124
   de St.-Laurent sauté Lemaire, 126
Savarin au rhum, 238
Savoy
   cheese croquettes, 82–83
   gratinéed potatoes, 212
   sponge layer, 229
Scallops
   au gratin à la *France,* 146–147
   in wine sauce à la *France,* 147
Sea bass
   Gulf, braised or roasted, 129
   Mediterranean
      braised à la *France,* 128–129
      grilled with herb sauce, 130
Seafood crêpes à la *France,* 149
Selle d'agneau bajocasse rôtie "France," 170
Shallot
   butter, grilled sirloin with, 161
   and olive sauce, braised red snapper with,
      131

Shellfish, 137–150
   See also individual kinds
Shish kebabs, *see* Kebabs
Shrimp(s), 144–146
   bordelaise, sole with, 144
   and chicken, consommé with, 58
   cocktail with sauce audoise, 144
   and crab cocktail with sauce chilienne, 146
   and fish, Brazilian, 148
   and lobster jambalaya, 148–149
   prawns with sauce mousquetaire, 144
   sambal (simmered in coconut milk), 145
   sautéed, bordelaise, 144
   scrambled eggs with anchovies, tuna,
      and, 77
Sirloin Steak au poivre sauté à l'Armagnac,
   160–161
Snow eggs, 232
Sole *(sole),* 112–116
   coquelin, poached filets of Channel,
      112–113
   with sauce Gribiche, fried, 116
   Meunière de la Manche frite Saint-Honorat,
      112
   meunière Saint Honorat, 112
   with oyster sauce, 115
   stuffed, à la *France,* 114–115
   with shrimp bordelaise, 114
   with shrimp and mussel sauce, baked, 113
   with whiskey sauce, poached Dover, 116
Sorrel
   cream of asparagus soup with, 63
   cream of chicken soup with, 66
Sosati de mouton du Transvaal au maïs égrené,
   175
Soufflé *(soufflé)*
   artichoke, 83
   embassy, 236
   fruit, 236
   ham, 84
   harlequin, 236
   mushroom, 84
   au parmesan, 83
   Parmesan cheese, 83
   praline, 236
   spinach, 83
   -stuffed artichoke bottoms, 189
   sucré, 235
   sweet, 235
   violet, 236
Soupe
   de Feijãos, 68
   à l'oignon gratinée au Traminer, 66–67
Soups, 53–72
   thick, 61–72
   See also individual kinds
Sorbet aux fruits, 239
Spanish rice, 213
Spinach
   Aïda, turbot au gratin with, 121

creamed, 203
general preparation, 203
soufflé, 83
Squab, 101–104
with chanterelles, 101
with glazed vegetables, 102
with sauce diable, 103
sautéed, 104
on toast, 102–103
Steak, *see* Beef
Stew, *see* Beef, Lamb, etc.
Stocks, 54–56
Straw potatoes, 212
String potatoes, 212
Suédoise sauce, 51
Suprême de barbue à la façon des Gastilleurs, 123
Suprême de pintadeau
fermier doré Belle-Otéro, 107–108
doré "France," 108–109
Suprême sauce, 47
Suprême de turbot ostendais sauté Aïda, 121
Sweet soufflé, 235
Sweetbreads
panetière, 181
and truffles, artichoke hearts stuffed with, 180

Tango
crabmeat cocktail with sauce, 146
sauce, 51
Tarts
fruit, 236–237
pastry for, 227
Tartare sauce, 52
Tartes aux fruits, 236–237
Terrine
de caneton duclairoise, 184
de foies des volailles truffée, 184
de lapereau aux pistaches, 186
de lièvre à la Diane, 185
marbrée, 185
de poularde angevine, 183
Terrines and pâtés, 183–186
See also individual meats
Thourin Roumanille, 67
Tolosa sauce, 51
Tomate
à l'ancienne, 203
à la bressane, 204
farcie
Aurore, 204
navarraise, 205
du val de Loire farcie provençale, 205
Tomato(es)
Bresse style, 204
and eggplant
baked eggs with, 74
fried, with, 197
glazed mixed vegetables, 206
and ham, sautéed mushrooms with, 199

provençal, 205
ratatouille niçoise, 206
sauce
recipe for, 41
grilled chickens with, 92–93
soup, Andalusian cream of, 64
stuffed
with guinea hen, 107–108
with madiera sauce, 205
old-style, 203
with pork, 204
Tongue
cream of mushroom soup with chicken
and, 62
eggs in cocotte with beef, 74
and marbled pork terrine, 185
Toscane sauce, 42
Tournedos, *see* Beef
Tournedos de Charolais
grillé bergerette, 157
grillé Henri IV, 158
sauté Monselet, 159
sauté Rossini, 158
Truffles
artichoke hearts stuffed with sweetbreads
and, 180
chicken and pork pâté with, 183
duck and pork terrine, with, 184
mixed salad with, 223
potatoes
recipe for, 211
roast rack of lamb with, 171
poultry liver terrine with, 184
roast chicken stuffed with, 87
Truite de torrent
étuvée "France," 132
sautée à la façon du Heas, 133
Trout, 132–133
poached à la *France*, 132
sautéed, 133
Tuna
braised Mediterranean steaks, 134
scrambled eggs with anchovies, shrimp,
and, 77
Turban de coquilles St.-Jacques "France," 147
Turbot, 117–21 *(turbot)*
with gavarnie sauce, 117
au gratin with spinach Aïda, 121
gravelinois poché sauce moutarde, 117
medallions
braised stuffed, 120
sautéed, périnette, 119
with mousseline sauce, 117
with mustard sauce, 117
with *riche* sauce, 117
with salmon filets, 118–119
saumonné braisé à la Presidente, 118–119
Turkey ballottine with chestnuts, 109–110
Turnips
braised duckling with new, 99

garden vegetables braised in butter, 206
glazed mixed vegetables, 206
Turtle soup
à la *France*, cream of, 64–65
with herbs, 56–57
Tyrolienne sauce, 42

Valapa de poisson de Bahia, 148
Vanilla ice cream, 240
Veal, 163–170
braised rack of, 163–164
à la Bray valley, braised loin of, 164–165
chops
cordon bleu, sautéed, 165–166
normande, sautéed, 165
Prince Orloff, sautéed, 166
ossobuco, 170
and poultry stock, white, 55
scallops
au gratin à la *France*, 167
Napoleon, grilled, 168–169
verdunoise, sautéed, 168
stew with mushrooms and onions, 169
stock, brown, 55
velouté, 34
See also Sweetbreads, kidneys
Vegetables, 187–206
soup with garlic, basil, and herbs, provençal, 71
Velouté
fish, 33
ordinary, 33
veal, 34
Velouté
d'artichauts danoise, 61–62

d'asperges Comtesse, 62
de champignons Agnès Sorel, 62
de laitue Choisy, 63
de lentilles Premier Consul, 63
à la Normande, 203
ordinaire, 33
de petits-pois Fontanges, 64
de tomates andalouse, 64
de tortue "France," 64–65
Venison, Hunter's style, haunch of, 182
Vénitienne sauce, 48
Vert-pré, sauce, 51
Verte sauce, 51
Vichyssoise with vegetables, 65
Vin blanc sauce, 48
Vincent sauce, 51
Vinaigrette sauce, 53
Violet soufflé, 236

Whipped cream, sweetened, 230
Whiskey sauce, poached Dover sole with, 116
White sauces, 43–48
White veal and poultry stock, 55
Wild rice pilaf, 214
Wine soup, Italian, 68

Yorkshire
pudding, roast beef and, 156–157
sauce, 42–43

Zingara sauce, 43
Zucchini
English style, 205
ratatouille niçoise, 206